PRAISE FOR

BECOMING SELF-DIRECTED LEARNERS

"The Stories Renew our Faith in the Human Drive for Self-Fulfillment"

Becoming Self-Directed Learners is an amazing collection of testimonies, memoirs, and reflections from graduates of a school intent on fostering self-directed learning, providing a longitudinal study of the positive and long-lasting effects of instruction in which students must self-manage, self-monitor and self-modify. Graduates who have excelled and achieved prominence in a variety of fields—politics, the arts, science, and international relations—provide compelling evidence of the positive effects that self-directed learning has contributed to their success.

What these stories disclose is that humans learn best what they want to learn. They demonstrate that learning derived from a carefully structured program of self-directedness does not fade away after the test or even in several months. Rather, it lasts for a lifetime.

As you read the stories in this book, three recurring patterns emerge. It becomes evident that these Center students demonstrated they were self-directed:

- They have dreams, aspirations, desires, and ideals and, because they are effective, they translate those dreams into action. (Self-managing)

- They are keenly aware of themselves, their beliefs, internal states, emotions, their strengths and gaps. (Self-monitoring)

- They are open to and seek feedback in a never-ending desire for adaptation, change, learning, and growth. (Self-modifying)

These stories show how our perceptions of "being educated" need to shift from educational outcomes that are primarily an individual's collections of sub-skills to include successful participation in socially organized activities and the development of students' identities as conscious, flexible, efficacious, and interdependent meaning-makers.

We must also let go of having learners acquire *our* meanings and have faith in the processes of students' construction of their own and shared meanings through individual activity and social interaction. This will cause great discomfort because the individual and the group may *not* construct the meaning we want them to: a real challenge to the basic educational framework with which most schools are comfortable.

The stories in this book, however, renew our faith in the human drive for self-fulfillment. When we know what we consist of and what our ideal self could be, then we can achieve our greatest potential. The evidence of this on these pages is clear, strong and lasting.

> *Arthur L. Costa, Ed.D. is Professor Emeritus, California State University, Sacramento; Co-founder, The Institute for Habits of Mind, Past President of the Association for Supervision and Curriculum Development (ASCD), and author of many books that promote thinking and problem solving.*

"The Center's Contribution to Curriculum was Substantial"

Becoming Self-Directed Learners highlights a critical chapter of American educational history. Its emphasis on the individual experiences of participants in a great experiment is exemplary and necessary. Increasingly the most productive educational literature will be composed of systematic studies of individual learning experiences. After all is not each learning experience individual? As Jim Bellanca suggests in his introduction, apart from the individual student, the teacher, the learning goal, and the conditions of their encounter, there are *no* axiomatic "best practices."

You will not find anything dated in this chronicle from the last century. The problems, challenges, and struggles for solutions faced by the New Trier Center for Self-Directed Learning are real and credible in our contemporary educational environment. Indeed in many ways educational institutions are growing increasingly oppressive for all involved and so the need for alternatives becomes all the more compelling.

The New Trier Center's contribution to curriculum was substantial. Mainstream education has historically focused on attainment of concepts as a primary indicator of success in school. This is in large part because it is seemingly easier to construct tests to measure concept attainment. Because critical life skills and dispositions are typically not measured they are likely to be neglected in program evaluation. The New Trier Center was a leader, a forerunner, in going beyond simple concept attainment. Its primary learning goal was *self-directed learning*, a disposition of lasting significance and one of the most fundamental attributes of an educated person! Moreover, ongoing assessment of competence was a central feature of their program. Standards of assessment were themselves subject to ongoing review and refinement over time. This was true formative evaluation directed to building community as well as to supporting teaching and learning. New Trier was indeed a "lighthouse."

Readers of this book will be interested to know that self-directed learning is alive and advancing. Kenneth Danford's North Star program of self-directed learning for teens and its sister centers have been proceeding carefully to grasp the demands of contemporary social institutions and find ingenious ways to re-direct existing systems to serve the best interests of learners. More lighthouses are appearing.

What are the educational programs of our dreams? To bring them to life and sustain that life we must demonstrate their worthiness and importance. This chronicle of the struggle to develop self-directed learners in the 1970s, told "from the inside" through the experiences and reflections of participants, will be a profitable companion to anyone who would take on such a challenge in our contemporary educational climate.

Paul Zachos directs ACASE, a professional association of scientists and educators founded in 1991 and dedicated to develop the scientific capabilities of educators, secondary and college students, and the general public.

"This Collection Contains Much Wisdom"

Many of the pieces in this collection are riveting, some are rich in humor, a few are downright moving. Taken as a whole these student and faculty recollections provide a multi-dimensional, detailed record of a brilliantly crafted experiment in alternative education, wonderfully executed by a highly motivated faculty devoting an incredible amount of time and commitment. The faculty called themselves facilitators; they sought to be treated as co-learners rather than teachers. Students were central to decision making, which was by consensus not majority rule. They learned a lot about building consensus and a lot about community.

As a Center alumna summarized the Center's approach to self-directed learning: Decide what you want, figure out what you need to learn to get there, and follow through. Make a mistake? Pick yourself up and start again.

Many students who opted for the Center had been well-adjusted strong achievers in the parent school. Others, however, had been chronic underachievers. Of these, some, bored by school, lacked motivation; some felt socially isolated; and some had issues such as learning disabilities, dangerously low self-esteem, or drug addiction that got in the way. Many of those underachievers report that they soon blossomed after transferring into the Center. In addition to the turnaround in their high school experience, many credit the Center for setting them on a path to adult success. There are some striking examples: a psychologist who overcame severe learning disabilities (first recognized by the Center math facilitator) to earn her Ph.D. in psychology and a clinical and teaching career; an actress nominated for a Golden Globe and an Academy Award.

In my view (both as the parent of a student who opted for the Center at its outset and as a reader of this book) the Center was an unqualified success. For educators, parents, school boards and (dare I suggest it) government officials and legislators, this collection contains much wisdom. I would certainly recommend it to those thinking about founding charter schools. I would even recommend it to high school students.

How many adults in their 40s and 50s consider their high school experience to have been life transforming? How many would be moved to say so in fact-rich memoirs that leave no room for doubt as to their sincerity?

The book is a gem.

> *Ray Greenblatt served on the School Board of the Winnetka Public Schools (K-8) from 1969 to 1975, and during that time his son, Walter, was a student in the Center, class of 1974. From 1956 to 1994 he was a partner at Mayer Brown LLP, a large, Chicago-based, international law firm. From 1994 to 1998 he was a volunteer teacher at Providence St. Mel School, an inner-city Chicago private school, where he taught high school economics, started a Debate Club, and read and wrote poetry with first and second graders.*

"The Experiment was Clearly a Success"

Progressive education in the United States has waxed and waned over 100 years, finding its roots in the philosophy of John Dewey and being known for a focus on the "whole child." In the 1920s and 1930s, progressive education was at its height, spawning the biggest curriculum experiment in history known as "The Eight-Year Study." But at times it has also fallen victim to shifts in society towards more positivistic beliefs about schooling like the focus on math and science during the Cold War or the "Back to Basics" movement of the 1980s. Historian Herbert Kliebard has called this "the struggle for the American curriculum."

Becoming Self-Directed Learners offers a glimpse into a progressive school program in the 1970s. The Center for Self-Directed Learning was founded as a "school within a school" at the much larger and nationally known New Trier High School, located in Winnetka, IL. Both New Trier High School and the town of Winnetka are closely connected to the history of progressive education. New Trier was one of the 30 schools that took part in "The Eight-Year Study" and was one of the first schools to adopt an Advisor Program to support the social and emotional development of its students. Winnetka's elementary and middle schools are known for their own approach to progressive education, called "The Winnetka Plan," led by another well-known progressive educator, Carlton Washburne.

With these deep roots in placing the student at the center of learning, a group of teachers and students were given an opportunity by the school's board of education to create an alternative school. The Center for Self-Directed Learning opened its doors in the fall of 1972 to 150 students and six faculty members. Over the course of the next decade, hundreds of students were given the opportunity to control their own learning and help shape policy within the school and in the state. The curriculum was derived from student interest and curiosity. The teachers were given the task of coordinating that curriculum, often doing so "in the moment," and for making sure the students met state requirements for graduation. They also served as mentors for individual students and facilitators for weekly student town hall style meetings.

As is appropriate given this philosophy, the main focus of the book is the students. Now mature and successful adults, these alumni look back at their experience in The Center as seminal to their development and learning. They have strong memories and feelings about their instructors and classmates, solid evidence that the goals of building community and caring were accomplished by this program. Maybe more significant are the number of graduates who speak to their ability later in life to deal with adversity and problems using the creativity and rigor they learned in The Center. One of the more famous alums, Illinois Senator Mark Kirk, writes: "[The Center] provided a key set of tools and life experiences that have enabled me at significant moments of my life and career to work hard with a clear focus on learning difficult subjects." For Kirk, this included military service, foreign affairs, drafting legislation, and recovering from a stroke. These kinds of stories are repeated over and over by students and teachers in the program.

There have been too few books like this one about the actual practice of progressive education. It is an important historical document from the 1970s specifically and education generally. The decision to ask the students and teachers to write their own autobiographic story is especially appropriate. In style and content, this text is well grounded in its own philosophical tradition of guiding students to find and use their own voice, of putting students at the center of learning. For the students who experienced The Center, the experiment was clearly a success. For readers today, their stories may remind us that pre-packaged curriculum and high-stakes tests are not the only ways to learn.

> *Dr. Timothy Dohrer is Director of the Master of Science in Education program at Northwestern University. He is a former teacher, administrator, and principal at New Trier High School in Winnetka, IL. His research and writing focus on literacy, teacher education, school leadership, and curriculum studies.*

"An Inspiration for Today's Innovators"

It is a fitting time for the innovative educational practitioners of today to glean the lessons and best practices of self-directed learning from the student and teacher pioneers of the 1970s from New Trier High School's Center for Self-Directed Learning, thanks to the 50 former students (of 600 graduates in 10 years) and five former teachers whose rich memoirs form this book, *Becoming Self-Directed Learners*.

Those of us who have been involved in the movement for innovative 21st century schools and districts have attempted to develop practices and processes to promote and support self-directed and self-assessing learners.

But none of us who developed these schools in the 2000s knew about the Center for Self-Directed Learning. That's no surprise in education. Often great innovations come along, and either the context is not there to support them, they are ahead of their time, or they are not implemented fully. And then these innovations are forgotten, until they come back 20, 30, 40 years later.

The Center, as former teacher and book editor Jim Bellanca writes, "fit its time and was well ahead of its time." The Center was not a Summerhill or a Sudbury Valley School, free school models well known by the 1970s where students had complete responsibility for their own education. The Center shared some principles with these models, however its practices incorporated a well-defined seven-step process for student work and assessment where students would have to:

- Show their proficiencies to make an authentic goal of high personal importance;
- Find resources (from one course in the parent school per semester to internships, field studies, small group investigations, a research study or travel);
- Identify a facilitator/evaluator from the Center or the external community;
- Follow a self-planned weekly schedule;
- Produce evidence of learning;
- Assess that learning with criteria; and
- Show how the specific learning contributed to college, life and/or career goals.

It may sound contradictory, but self-direction in education, in my opinion, is best encouraged and implemented when supported by well-defined and common processes, systems, and structures. This was true of the Center and it is true today of the New Tech Network and Big Picture Learning, two innovative school models that prize self-directed learning.

Of course the second decade of the 21st century is a much different world than the 1970s. Much has changed—state standards, accountability, and technology. In the 1970s there were no laptops, internet, and smartphones. Today, Alan November in *Who Owns the Learning?* shows how new digital tools empower and enable students to be productive self-directed learners who author, produce, research, publish, and globally communicate and collaborate. But November rightly shows that this happens best when teachers, like those at the Center for Self-Directed Learning, facilitate, design, and enable self-directed learning experiences.

The stories and memoirs of this book reveal how the Center's students and teachers created and implemented a culture of self-directed learning and self-assessment. They are a treasure trove of lessons and an inspiration for today's innovators.

> *Bob Pearlman is a strategy consultant for 21st Century school development. He was Director of Strategic Planning for the New Technology Foundation in Napa, CA, which supports the New Technology 21st Century High School model in more than 50 communities across the United States; and he was President of the Autodesk Foundation, Coordinator of Education Reform Initiatives for the Boston Teachers' Union, and a high school teacher for 27 years.*

"A Blueprint to Find Ways to Increase Deep Learning"

Becoming Self-Directed Learners is a collection of memoirs that I, as a parent, teacher, staff developer, mentor, and urban school educational consultant, believe everyone in the educational world should read. Here is an incredible testimonial to the mindful growth made in an alternative school where these students, their teachers, and their parents all profited.

The many memoirs in this remarkable book attest to how this school embraced all students, not only those with handicapping conditions (as we now think of alternative schools), but the very bright, the very unique and those dissatisfied with traditional classes who were willing to risk "my way." This inspiring collection of educational success offers a blueprint to help all of us find ways to increase deep learning, and not just rote memorization, but deep thinking.

Long before the Common Core, these students were walking their own path to the future. I wish that all of us could have such an experience. As a parent, I would have wished it for my children; as a teacher, I would have wished it for my students; and as a teacher leader, I would have wished the opportunity for myself and my peers to "learn how to learn" as these students did and are still doing with a gift that will last forever. I am thankful at least to have read these stories.

Diana Mann was a New York City teacher for over 30 years. She is now a staff developer, an instructor of graduate courses for the New York State United Teachers Education Learning Trust, a consultant with the National Urban Alliance, and a certified instructor for the Feuerstein Institute.

"The Center Helped People Take Charge of Their Own Lives"

It is heartening to read *Becoming Self-Directed Learners*, especially now in 2013, when so much focus in education is on test scores and "accountability." This fascinating book chronicles the experience of a wide sampling of students and faculty and what is clear from the individual memoirs is that New Trier's Center for Self-Directed Learning helped people take charge of their own lives and their own education, and that for many, impressive achievement followed. As Illinois Senator Mark Kirk, a 1977 alumnus of the Center, puts it in his reminiscence, "I did have an intellectual life before the Center, but the Center catapulted me into the major leagues. It was there I built lifelong habits that showed me how to solve really hard problems."

This collection will stimulate debate, self-examination, and new approaches among educators of all sorts.

Julie West Johnson taught English in New Trier East's regular high school program and sometimes mentored self-directed studies by Center students. She is now a writer for The New York Times *magazine,* Chicago Life.

"When learning is self-directed, learners emerge as who they are."

This volume transports me back to the days when I worked and learned in a public alternative high school in the 1970s. The pieces by students and staff of the Center for Self-Directed Learning capture the aspirations, the challenges, the palpable spirit of such a place, and the lasting effect on participants. As editor and founding director Jim Bellanca writes, apart from the innovations and powerful learning, the legacy is to be found in the lives of the students and staff who brought the vision to life and then took that vision with them into the world.

The Center's story is about self-directed learning, to be sure, but it's about relationships, too. As Dewey pointed out long ago, when learning is self-directed, learners emerge as who they are, which makes it possible for teachers to know them better. Moreover, the commitment to self-directed learning calls for a transformation in the authority relationship between teacher and student—for a collegial pedagogy in which teachers and students are learning together and from each other. It is no accident that longtime teachers, launching the Center, soon realized that they would have to learn to teach all over again, and that teaching is a team sport.

In this second decade of the current century, the great irony remains that teachers are asked to foster 21st century skills in a 19th century work environment. Perhaps it wasn't so apparent back then, when this century seemed a distant future, but the Center for Self-Directed Learning offered a 21st century work environment for teachers. The evidence is everywhere in the testimony of these teachers, unleashed to pursue their passions, accountable to facilitate student learning, and joined by colleagues, students, and parents in their efforts to discover what's worth learning and why.

The questions that led to the Center remain with us today. Why are so many students disengaged? Why, in a transdisciplinary, problem-centered world, do we persist in dividing the "content" of education into "subjects"? Why insist on the same pace and the same content for everyone? Why shut out passion and interest? Why not foster self-directed learning in a community of learners? Some of us have been pursuing these questions in various ways for a long time. Others have just embarked on the journey. All of us, young and old, can draw inspiration from the lessons of the Center as conveyed by the powerful voices in this volume.

Rob Riordan is president of High Tech High Graduate School of Education, San Diego, CA.

Becoming Self-Directed Learners

Student & Faculty Memoirs of an Experimenting High School 40 Years Later

BECOMING SELF-DIRECTED LEARNERS

WINDY CITY PUBLISHERS
2118 Plum Grove Rd., #349
Rolling Meadows, IL 60008
www.windycitypublishers.com

An Off Center Press Production
940 Ridgewood Drive,
Highland Park, Illinois 60035
self-directedlearner@comcast.net

Published in the United States of America

First Edition: 2014

ISBN:
978-1-935766-90-2

Library of Congress Control Number:
2013954701

COVER DESIGN: JAMIE KEENAN
EDITOR PORTRAITS: KATHY RICHLAND PHOTOGRAPHY

BECOMING SELF-DIRECTED LEARNERS

STUDENT & FACULTY MEMOIRS OF AN EXPERIMENTING HIGH SCHOOL 40 YEARS LATER

JAMES A. BELLANCA, ARLINE PAUL, AND MARK PAUL

EDITORS

CHICAGO

AN OFF CENTER PRESS PRODUCTION

DEDICATION: IN MEMORY

This book is dedicated to those Center faculty and students
who have passed away.

THE FACULTY
Laura Daniels
William "Bill" Gregory
Vernoy "VJ" Johnson

THE STUDENTS
Mike Beliard
Ruben Borushek
Eric Burmeister
Mark Fucik
Peter Kidd
Greg Kowalski
Alex Markovic
Laird Peterson
Tom Trobaugh
Nicole Tuchman

*"Children do not need to be made
to learn about the world or shown how.
They want to, and they know how."*

~John Holt

TABLE OF CONTENTS

FOREWORD

Welcome to our house. This book of memories created by student graduates and faculty from New Trier East High School's Center for Self-Directed Learners (1972-82) turned out to be much more than we bargained for. Joyfully, we present you with the final and complete version. Now it is time for you to move inside the story with the many minds and hearts that collaborated to make these memories ready to share.

From its seeding at the first Center Reunion to a final touch of the last key, this book's production has provided a whole new set of learning experiences for all involved. These parallel the highs and lows that were the benchmark experiences from which Center students and faculty learned so much about becoming self-directed, but still very collaborative learners.

Indeed, this final product is more than a set of individual memoirs. As it progressed from rough manuscripts to edited pages, the book gathered a character of its own, capturing not only familiar recollections, but surprising insights and stories not before heard. Beyond the many Center incidents recorded for the first time, there are small brushstrokes and short takes, depicting the spirit and energy of those tumultuous and inspiring years where change outside the school walls did so much to push forward the changes occurring inside the Center.

As we worked with the various contributors of these very personal stories and noted the short glimpses and glimmers of others, we appreciated how much of what the inventors of the Center intuited about helping students become self-directed learners by risking many innovative teaching and learning practices well before their time.

It was extremely heart-warming to read the submissions that came from the memories of more than 50 graduates of those years. We know from e-mails, Facebook posts and other communications via social media, which were not even a ray of possibility in the Center's technologically bare decade, that many others with strong memories chose not to share their personal stories in the book, but noted, as the contributors did, that their self-directed learning did not stop at the beloved Bumpy Park graduation.

Although the many single stories told were fun to recall, it is the totality of what those stories say together that are the highpoint of this book. Starting as a small project, the book grew like Topsy and came to mean much more than we anticipated. As you read, we hope you will mark some of the key stepping stones that lead to that peak...the fond memories of VJ, Greg and Laura, the Town Halls, the community groups, the tin can mail system, the paddle, Bumpy Park...all contributing in one way or another to helping us all become more self-directed learners and to create a unique school experience that many thought was impossible.

We think every small memory that we waited patiently to receive, every little correction added by the many authors and proof-editors, every short take, every detail contributed to this wonderful story, a proud story of our house, the Center for Self-Directed Learning. We hope you take away as much as we have. Thank you, one and all for the shining memories of how you fared becoming self-directed learners.

~Jim, Arline, and Mark

FACULTY MEMOIRS

FROM THE CENTER: TAKEAWAYS FROM AN EXPERIMENTING HIGH SCHOOL

JIM BELLANCA

In September 1972, the Center for Self-Directed Learning opened its doors. One hundred and fifty volunteers, grades 10–12, flowed into Room 101, the new home of the new experimenting school-within-a-school. The room was located on the ground floor, southeast corner of New Trier East High School in Winnetka, Illinois, a suburb north of Chicago. Six faculty, volunteers from "the parent school," waited. More than 600 students would follow these pioneer risk-takers in the next decade.

For that time, Room 101 was literally and figuratively "The Center." As the stories included in this book attest, what emerged from the Center showed the power, the wonder, the limits and the bed sores of a high school experiment, as students, faculty and parents examined novel ways of teaching, learning, and assessing student performance during a tumultuous time in American education.

What emerged over time was transformative in 600, mostly remarkable ways which lasted well beyond each graduate's departure from the Center. The 600 ways were not a list of best practices, insights, axioms, or special features, they were all simple and unique stories.

Six hundred plus students walked into the Center with no more than their own dreams and the permission of their parents. Most were looking to do more with their high school education than sit passively in a classroom listening to teachers talk, memorizing information, getting top grades, or failing. Those dreams seldom were defined in a quick smattering and splattering of days or weeks. The definitions came, each different and distinct from the other 600, only after each student was immersed in the Center experience for many, many months, sometimes even years.

In a like manner, the faculty underwent significant changes in their understandings and practices. They had to rediscover what it meant to be a teacher. No longer in a traditional classroom with seats in rows, 50-minute bells, lectures, quizzes and tests, these six were in a substantively different learning place, one which re-formed each year as a highly collaborative community of learners, forever in search of new ways to teach. Like their risk-taking students, the faculty had to learn from doing what it meant to be self-directed learners.

THE START

After a summer of study and deliberation by a committee of teachers, parents, community leaders and students, plus visits to existing experimenting alternative schools and follow-up conversations with school administrators, the planning committee received the Board of Education's approval. The six faculty, governing themselves in a flat organizational style with only a coordinator as "intermediary" with the high school administration, were instructed to open the doors of the Center for Self-Directed Learning as an alternative school-within-in-a-school for 125 students and five faculty (the parent school's teacher-student ratio). The Center was to be housed on the first floor of New Trier East High School with open access to the world outside the walls and beyond the bordering streets of Winnetka.

The Center's definition of "alternative," reflective of that time in education history, was important. Unlike today when the title "alternative" most usually refers to a place to assign especially troublesome special needs students, this experimental program embraced all students who wanted to enter, providing they had parent approval. It was not a special education alternative for behavior challenged students, nor a haven for misfits, as some regular faculty contended when they tried to block students they liked from signing on. It was not a superficial experiment. It was a well-conceived alternative to traditional forms of education. It fit its time and was well ahead of its time. In its decade of existence, many of the innovations that made the Center work for the wide range of students who risked breaking from the norms of assembly-line high school education are just today fitting into broader practice. Others may never fit and some have yet to find their place.

During the six months which preceded the Center's opening, a series of open community forums were attended by hundreds of parents, students, and faculty. In civil discussions about the value of a program that was a paradigm away from the traditional, much-lauded education offered by New Trier—once dubbed a "lighthouse" by *Time* magazine—the school community wrestled with the giant college admission risks, about students going beyond school walls to study in the community, about non-certified volunteers supplementing instruction, and about a plethora of imagined fantasies of catastrophe that would befall those who might dare abandon the traditional New Trier way.

When all was said, 150 students and seven faculty applied while the initial budget could accommodate only 125 students and five faculty. New Trier East's Principal, Ralph McGee, and the school's Associate Director for Curriculum and Instruction, Mary Ida McGuire, two strong advocates for the alternative, proposed a lottery. Good idea, if unprecedented in the 1970s. So loud was the parent and student outcry when 25 were left on the waiting list that the surprised Board elected to accept all of the students and add a sixth faculty. When the doors opened there was a faculty director (yours truly) and one each from the English, Math, Science, Art and Social Studies (co-editor Arline Paul) departments, all assigned full-time to the Center for Self-Directed Learning. New Trier's teachers in the 1970s were hired for their "content" expertise. At New Trier, which had just recently split the venerable East campus into two, content expertise meant any new hires joined the faculty with several years of secondary teaching under their belts and a Master's Degree in a content area. The Center planning committee, however, called for something more—the faculty would "facilitate self-directed learning."

Although the six volunteers, along with parents and students, had spent a summer immersed in studying Carl Rogers's popular humanistic education theories which started with the belief that "A person cannot teach another person directly; a person can only facilitate another's learning" (Rogers, 1951), the Center faculty declared themselves novices in their new roles. Using Rogers's 19 propositions from *Freedom to Learn* (1969), the faculty conceived a concrete plan for facilitating self-directed learning. Ultimately, this plan became the foundation of the Center's unique teaching, learning and graduation process as the 156 student and faculty adventurers embarked on their new careers.

A DEEPER LEARNING PARADIGM

For students to earn a high school diploma from traditional New Trier, the Illinois State School Code mandated a list of required course work (e.g. a year of U.S. History, a course in driver's education, a course in consumer education, etc.) and left the remaining criteria to the local school board (e.g. four years of English, two years of lab science, etc.). New Trier's Board decided that Center students must only complete the list of state-mandated courses by whatever means the Center faculty approved. The mandates for district courses were removed. There were no seat time criteria. Instead, Center students would need to demonstrate they were "self-directed" by the founding committee's definition. Sometimes, this took less than the traditional hours mandated for a course; many times, it took more. It always required students to demonstrate their abilities to collaborate, think critically, and solve problems as they struggled toward self-directed learning.

The Center's ultimate definition of self-directed learning emerged from the assessment process with performance benchmarked to identify the competencies of self-directed learning. In a seven-step process, students would have to show their proficiencies to make an authentic goal of high personal importance, find resources (wherever or whatever those may be in a range of learning experiences from one course in the parent school per semester to internships, field studies, small group investigations, a research study, or travel to Italy), identify a facilitator/evaluator (wherever or whomever had the expertise from a Center, parent school, community college or university faculty member, practicing artists, parents, businesspersons, medical researchers, inventors, etc.), follow a self-planned weekly schedule, produce evidence of learning, assess that learning with criteria, and show how the specific learning contributed to college preparation, life, and/or career goals which the students were also forming at the same time.

Doubting Thomases bemoaned that all New Trier graduates already did this. However, what Center students and faculty discovered over the decade-long life cycle of the Center, that being a self-directed learner was easier said than done and much different than what students "did" in traditional classrooms. Certainly, it was not "do your own thing" and it was not marching to the beat of the same drummer. As the essays in this multifaceted memoir collection attest, even the best and most able students were challenged by the rigors of the process that was the Center's guiding light to find their own way of learning and to do it as Frank Sinatra had sung, "my way."

The faculty, with major input from students and parents, designed the "prove that you are a self-directed learner" standards. They also collaborated in forming the Center's structural elements that graduates would recall as the building blocks with which the Center was constructed. The first element was the community group. Each Center faculty facilitated two groups of 12–15 multi-grade, mixed gender students (Center students took pride in *not* identifying themselves by grade or gender). Once a week, the group met in one member's home, a field location, or in Room 101. Agendas varied, but the purpose was clear: mutual support for each member's emerging self-directed learning pathway. Peers and faculty talked about their current learning experience, challenges, missteps and successes. The group also formed smaller support groups so that peers could help each other in greater confidentiality and trust with issues that blocked learning. Often, these blocks were socio-emotional issues: family (divorce, abuse, sibling competition), personal motivation (self-direction, getting up in the morning, keeping a schedule) or adolescent issues (substance abuse, sexuality, friendships).

Early in a school year, the community groups focused on the practical problem of course selection. (Many Center students never found comfort using the all-inclusive "learning experience" to identify what and how they were learning. "Course" remained the convenient generic descriptor.) Course selection started with the popular and populist Town Hall during the first week of school each September. Each morning the entire community gathered in 101. A long wall (Room 101 was a former study hall, a double classroom with moveable tables, chairs, storage cabinets, and dividers replacing rows of desks) was cleared to post sheets of chart paper and the bubble-up brainstorming began. Over the five days, topics for study, means of study, places for study, and times for study were generated, grouped, and regrouped. By the second day, small groups would break off to investigate a common interest. By the fourth day, individuals, aided by their community groups or other friends, would begin to shape a schedule that might include ideas for an internship, a small group (at least two students), a project or a "what have you." Topics ranged from the traditional (Shakespeare, Burns, and Byron; The Civil War; Algebra) to the popular (music of the Beatles, alewives, Idi Amin) to individual interests (modern dance, geodesic domes, sign language, marijuana). The faculty, now facilitators, moved in and out of the groups, hand-holding, conferencing, observing small group discussions, and searching for those students, especially the novices, who were lost, frustrated, or overwhelmed.

At times, Room 101 looked like a chaotic beehive, with students buzzing in and out and around. But like a beehive at the height of the pollen-gathering season, there was hidden method in the madness, plus tears, angry words, and laughter. By the second week, individuals were at work with their community groups collaborating with faculty facilitators and early-onset volunteer facilitators drawn from outside the school walls. The planning process for each learning experience was at full force. Learning Groups planned their courses of study. Individuals planned their internships or research projects. Some groups fell apart. Others changed direction. By the end of the tumultuous two weeks, Room 101 became less and less populated and appeared more organized as students settled into their individualized routines and set off to their new learning locations.

From 7:30 AM to 7:30 PM, sometimes earlier and sometimes later, 101 never seemed to stop buzzing. Students consulted with facilitators, chatted in small groups, picked up mail messages from their Center mail boxes, studied alone, or practiced an instrument, held small group classes, met in their community group, napped, read a book, or wrote in journals.

PULLING TOGETHER

The Center's formal process toward self-directed learning picked up speed in the last month of each semester. The last month was evaluation time. This was the one time in the self-directed learning process in which the faculty applied external pressure. No matter how gently prodded, internal motivation gave way to the push for completed evaluations, especially from those in their "newbie" first semester who were half waiting, half hoping for the bestowal of that final grade, one which was never coming.

For each "study" in a semester, students were required to produce a multi-part evaluation. Part I was a self-evaluation. What worked? What hadn't worked? What was learned? Part II, a one or more page description, was compiled by the study or course facilitator. (If students had approval for peer reviews, those would count here. Faculty restricted peer reviews for those last year students who also had a graduation committee). First, the evaluator detailed what work the student had done, what goals were achieved, and what were the successes. Second, the evaluator gave feedback on the quality of the student's work.

After finishing these first steps for the semester's experiences, the student completed Part III in the synthesis. (See the Appendix for a sample) The student synthesized the semester's work, highlighting how the various studies developed their self-direction. It was this synthesis that was the frontispiece for the semester's official evaluation, which replaced traditional grades. The synthesis was filed as the student's transcript.

Any time after a full year in the Center, students could make a case to graduate. The requirement? Proof of self-directed learning. With approval of their community group facilitator, the applying student formed a graduation committee that included the facilitator, at least one other adult, and a peer. Occasionally, a student invited the whole community group to serve. For this committee, each candidate made a plan that would prove "I am a self-directed learner" as defined by established Center criteria and included a schedule of committee meetings, benchmarks, and descriptions of expected evidence. At the scheduled final meeting—the plan of action also determined how often the candidate would check in with the committee—the candidate appeared before the committee ready to demonstrate how the criteria had been met. In all cases but two, committees eventually gave the seal of approval. In June, the candidates appeared at Bumpy Park, a local green surrounded by grassy hills, where the Center graduation, limited only to Center students and the faculty, became a celebration tradition in which the special Center diploma was presented.

THE END OF THE AFFAIR

In spite of the intensive support from faculty and peers, the Center was not a rose garden for every student who entered, nor for the faculty. In its last years, this was especially true. From the first years, the faculty struggled with their own burnout issues. From the start, the energy that fueled the Center twelve hours a day, and sometimes more, drained the faculty. The constant flow of students to the facilitators' cubicles, logistical hassles created by a student's travel schedule, the lack of bells and breaks, adolescent angst and more, the challenge to counsel, advise, teach, facilitate, etc., etc., etc., took a toll even with individuals who, as many of the memories in this book attest, were especially committed. As Vernoy Johnson, a Renaissance-like teacher-facilitator who wrote poetry, taught mathematics, asked tough questions, and loved history, said in a meeting of the Center faculty team, "The Center is a place of extreme highs and lows. There's not much flatland in between. There are some days, I wish for a class bell, just so I can clear my head. But then, that would also remove the joy of being here day in and day out."

In its last years (the Center closed in June, 1982), the faculty struggled with an added burden. In those years, a change in what parents wanted from a high school education began to occur. The Back to Basics Movement was beginning. Parents' college acceptance concerns were increasing. In spite of Center students' admirable acceptance record at those colleges who examined more than grades, including the Ivies and little Ivies, fewer parents were ready to risk college acceptance on the values of the Center alternative.

In addition, without the strong leadership and support of the regular school's administration caused by the retirement of Mary Ida McGuire, New Trier's Director of Instruction, elements of the regular school faculty began to see the word "alternative" in a new light. It was a place, many believed, to dump those advisees who gave them trouble, didn't show up for classes, or lived in the drug culture. As more and more of these students applied for the Center, the workload and stress of the faculty increased.

From the beginning, the Center had attracted a few passive students each year. In the early years, the number was manageable and, as several memoirs attest, the faculty was able to turn many of these students around. It may have taken these students longer to buy into the demands of self-direction, but, as several memoirs attest, most eventually did.

With the new definition of "alternative" changing the Center's population, the voices branding the Center as an unsupervised "do your own thing" alternative with a perceived laissez-faire faculty grew louder and louder. Applications increased from those students who would extend the faculty's willingness to facilitate self-directed learning beyond the norm. The model with the high school's standard 1:25 ratio was insufficient for helping the increased numbers of passive and troubled students.

The number of parents who were able to put college admissions into perspective dwindled, especially as they saw the changing character of the alternative school. Burnout and slowly decreasing student applicants claimed additional faculty who returned to teaching in the parent school. With no new model emerging (the new School Board wasn't supportive of the costs to work with the emerging population and the program had lost its Central office champion), the Center began to die a slow death. In June 1982, the ten year-old died. Official cause of death: insufficient enrollment.

Although the Center ceased to operate, its spirit survived. This book is a collection of memories, written by those Center's graduates who responded to a bright idea concocted during the Center's first reunion in 2010, many decades after the Center's doors closed for the first time and last time. More than 100 of its 600 graduates and faculty attended that day in a forest preserve learning center in Highland Park. More than 50 from that group made contributions, some long and some short.

THE TAKEAWAYS

Reading the memories after more than 30 years, a number of common threads stand out. These are the most remembered takeaways:

The students' fondness for the Center's faculty. Most remembered are those faculty members who stayed in the program through its lifetime. Two who have passed, Vernoy Johnson and Bill Gregory, were noted time and again in the memoirs for the caring, support, and the inspiration they provided by helping students overcome blocks to learning mathematics, writing English, and becoming self-directed learners.

Two conclusions seem especially clear from these Center graduates' essays about experiences involving these two men and their colleagues. First, experience is the best teacher, especially when it comes with those who care so passionately about the individuals they are teaching. Both men came to the Center as seasoned and heralded classroom veterans with several decades teaching in the traditional lecture setting. Second, a school's structures, policies, and procedures do more to help students become life-long, self-directed learners when they encourage the teachers to be the best they can be and not impose restrictions that prevent teachers from serving as down-to-earth role models and mentors.

The value of preparing students to learn how-to-learn. Advocates of content, subject matter, and more subject matter would argue against this learn-to-learn proposition. However, the Center faculty showed the value of helping students learn how-to-learn in order to help those students become more effective learners. Whether a student came into the Center hating school or loving school, what mattered most in their memories was that the Center taught them learning-how-to-learn skills. As their stories tell, even those recalled by the most avid fans of the Center, learning to be in charge of one's own learning requires more than wishing it were so or having a single self-directed experience. Time after time, the authors speak of learning *how to* be self-directed learners as the most significant takeaway from the schooling they received, but a takeaway that was seldom easy to acquire.

The Center structures, the faculty interaction and positive relationships, and the peer connections in the Center helped students make the transformation and cement their new understandings in place for a lifetime of knowing-how-to-learn, not for a test of what they could memorize, but for a lifetime of inquiry pushed by learning for its own sake.

The value of discovering "my way." Frank Sinatra sang the song that could have been the Center anthem, "My Way." Threaded through each of the essays is what students learned from being serious about following their own pathways. Superficial judges would say, "It's just a matter of learning style." These essays, on the other hand, sing, "It is much more, much deeper than style." For these students it was the embodiment of Carl Roger's freedom to learn, about finding the right path to their persona, to the answer for the perennial adolescent question, "Who am I?" The starter seeds were chance after chance to pursue study of a personal interest or to learn in a new way such as through an internship, a model making, or a research study or camping trip. It was also chance to push ahead faster than the fastest classes, go slower than a turtle, or veer off in a different direction. It was one faculty person after another, or another adult who reacted to a crazy idea by saying "Now that's an intriguing idea. I would never have thought about that. Tell me more. Help me understand why you think you want to do that." Ultimately, the students report their discovery of two insights about the freedom to learn.

For these students, freedom seems to have meant, "First that nothing is going to be done for me. I have to do all the deciding. I have to do the digging. I am the one who is responsible to choose. Second, once I have chosen, it is ok to ask for ideas from others, support from others. But I will have to choose the help and support that is best for me." With these two discoveries, the students noted that not only were they free of any boundaries other than those they set to direct themselves, they were free to learn all they chose to learn because they knew how to learn. They literally could blow the top off what they had previously thought they might never learn.

The importance of caring and community. Story after story in this book reiterates this theme. It was not just the caring of faculty that mattered. It was also the caring of students for each other and it was the caring within a family of learners. The depth of the caring showed up most often in the tough situations where a parent or a peer took a hard, tough-love look at what a student was not doing.

In the Center, there was definitely the freedom to do, to learn, to go outside the walls, to walk beyond the limits into new frontiers of learning. There was also the freedom not to do, not to learn. This freedom, as several essays recall, was an absolute pre-requisite for the changes that followed, but was made possible only because it occurred in a community where students and faculty cared enough to provide the needed support so a student could make a significant turnaround. That freedom is affirmed time after time in these stories.

But what also appears is the freedom that students had to do nothing, to learn nothing. It was here that the caring was most pronounced. As students struggled with the opportunity not to learn, not to do, parents, peers, and faculty stood behind them, not as passive watchers, but as extended hands and hearts, supporting the struggle and encouraging the struggler to choose to go in some direction, any direction as long as it was a direction of their own making.

It is probably safe to say every student who elected the Center experienced a "fish or cut bait" moment at some time. As the stories tell, for some it came after the first exhilaration of being able to "do my own thing." For others, it waited, hidden for many months. For a few, it took the wall of the final graduation committee saying: "Where's the proof?" In all cases, again safe to say, each Center student not only discovered that he or she had the full responsibility of deciding, of choosing or rejecting the self-directed learning path, but that there was also a plethora of helping hands reaching out to say, "once you decide, we are here to help you go forward. You choose to walk and we will show you some great places to explore."

In the Center, the most advanced technology was the faculty's single IBM Selectric typewriter. Now and then, a group of students explored the digital world, but that world was still in its infancy. The 21st Century Skills which the faculty did facilitate were found in the development of a collaborative community in which students were constantly asked to problem solve. Sometimes this happened when all gathered on some Wednesday mornings to make governance decisions in Quaker consensus style; sometimes it happened in a community group when students were resolving relapses in learning commitments; sometimes it occurred when study groups were trying to fund a "big idea" like a trip to the Louvre (they did), building a geodesic dome (they did), cooking a Peking Duck dinner for 110 as part of a Chinese culture study (they did), or take a camping trip to Wisconsin (they didn't); and sometimes it occurred within literature, science, or interdisciplinary investigations when individuals or study teams sought to answer big questions such as "Who are the heroes in American Literature?" or "What can we do to end child slavery?"

Problem solving, critical thinking, collaboration, and communication, the 21st Century skills, not yet so named for these students, were the skills they used to think deeply about the topics and issues that concerned them or heightened their interest. The evidence of how deeply their self-directed learning experiences influenced them is found in these essays written more than a quarter of a century after. The most consistent takeaways reported are the values of self-directed learning, not just as a way to earn a high school diploma, but also as a life-long learning spirit that has driven them through their adult lives. In one very transparent memoir, the author discusses how a self-destructive addiction became the tool of salvation, driving him to a Ph.D. and a life-long research study. In others, experimentation with avant-garde film led to a successful documentary filmmaking career; extra heavy daily doses of music composition set the stage for conducting a major orchestra; full days as an intern in a special needs school resulted in the founding of an innovative elementary school.

A Summary

The stories in this book are our takeaways. These stories tell what these remarkable young people took away from a time and place that was itself remarkable. You may read these essays—one, several or all—and come up with your own takeaways. We hope you will. We also hope you will see how a school can mean much more than bricks and mortar, a piece of paper, or time spent sitting passively in a chair waiting for Godot.

Jim is a Senior Fellow, Partnership for 21st Century Skills (P21), editor and lead poster of the P21 blog, and author of a host of books on educational practice. He and his wife, Gerry, live in Glencoe, Illinois, and tend to their award-winning garden (Chicago Tribune, Garden of the Year, 2007). Their children and grandchildren live in Winnetka and Glenview, Illinois; Boulder, Colorado; and Sydney, Australia.

Short Takes

The first thing the Center did for me was to keep me in school until graduation and the best way the Center helped me was by encouraging creative thinking as well as problem solving. I was encouraged not just to succeed, but also to learn lessons when I failed in a safe environment.

I remember being asked why I was joining the Center because "You don't look like you do drugs, " and then just a few short weeks later being asked "Are you sure you are smart enough to be in the Center?" People just didn't get us.

I've done a lot of things since the Center. I joined the Air Force in 1987 and never looked back! I've lived in some amazing and not so amazing places. I loved every minute of the experience. I retired and started my second career as a system administrator for the Department of Defense and I love it.

~Nancy Holloway, 1978

Becoming Self-Directed: The Continuum from Student to Teacher-Facilitator

Arline Paul

Teaching was a mid-life decision, but finding myself at Opening Day of the Center's first year seemed as if I had planned it all along. That mid-life quest for a career began as my children grew increasingly independent and as I was increasingly dissatisfied with volunteer political activities. Realizing the lifelong effect of my education and my interest in different teaching and learning styles, I decided to become a teacher.

Once the decision to teach had been made, I enrolled in required education classes, including a TV course on teaching economics that actually included virtual field trips. A brief stint as a lecturer in Political Science at the new University of Illinois Chicago campus followed until I began teaching at New Trier in 1965 as a member of the Social Studies Department. With two partners, the newly formed United States History team teaching program was my major assignment. Facilities were specifically designed for the teams to maximize a variety of learning options: a large lecture hall, where the students from all three classes gathered, was used for films, lectures, debates, or guest speakers; each teacher had an individual classroom; and all three teachers shared a resource room with shelves filled with issue-oriented paperbacks in adequate numbers for a class. And all three teachers had the same extra free period to plan units and room usage.

Students enjoyed the opportunity to hear other teachers' approaches to the content and the variety of class sites. In a debate on the causes of the Civil War one day, our southern partner represented the South's views in his soft southern accent and I, with my fading Boston accent, represented the North. Here were some of the precursors to the Center, as students sometimes organized debates or presented some research to all the team's students.

New Trier also afforded me the opportunity to find new materials more appropriate for some of my students. Faced with restless freshmen in a civics class who were not very interested in a traditional text, I tracked down some project/activity paperbacks the University of Chicago Education Department was testing. The class was more involved with ideas when they could discuss them in small groups or have pertinent activities. Today, that observation might evoke a bored sigh accompanied by "Of course, what's new about that?" But it was new in those days, especially in traditional high schools and, to my knowledge, the material never made it into production.

As an advisor for a girls' homeroom, I found the system of required study halls to be of dubious value. The misuse of hall passes made the task of challenging "illegitimate" ones onerous. The complicity of seniors deemed mature enough to "supervise" study halls and maintain order had created an unruly system. At meetings with a dean and some faculty, I began to voice these concerns and eventually garnered a modicum of support. The dean finally capitulated and agreed to a compromise: he would eliminate study halls for all students except freshmen but maintain some voluntary study space. In return, I needed to provide an alternative known as "The Program for Unassigned Time." By that, he meant I had to develop programs to attract students in their free periods and prevent hall disturbances.

Gathering a committee of students, I turned them loose to develop and implement programs, certain that they were more attuned to their peer's interests than I. The committee invited bands and guest speakers, arranged for films and games with varying attendance levels until we invited Rev. Jesse Jackson and his colleagues from the Rainbow Project. This was circa 1970 and the men arrived wearing overalls and sporting Afros. The dean spotted them arriving as our largest audience ever was pouring into the Student Lounge. He was tense, fearing student rudeness at the very least. Not so! Rev. Jackson had them listening intensely, enthusiastically, but peaceably. He had the audience linking arms, swaying, and chanting, "I am somebody!" and "We shall overcome!"

I relinquished the (unpaid) role of sponsor of the "Unassigned Time Committee" when I became involved in researching the concept of alternative schools or a school-within-a-school that was then part of the dialogue about changes in education. New Trier had established a process known as "Bubbling Up" for a few Faculty Institute Days whereby the faculty members were randomly assigned to small groups to present ideas to improve the school environment. Fortunately, I was in a group with Jim Bellanca, an English teacher who came to the session with ideas about self-directed learning. This was fascinating to me and I supported the group's vote to have Jim's idea "Bubble Up' the ladder of administrators. So as I read the literature about self-directed learning, and thought about my decision to teach and the processes I was already using, I recognized these were elements of self-direction, elements I had absorbed from memorable educational experiences of my own that I had taken for granted for many years, experiences that did not include sitting in a row of desks.

While I was growing up, my father had used the Boston area as a classroom, bringing history to life during many Sunday field trips to Plymouth Rock, Salem, and other colonial and Revolutionary War sites. Informal roundtable seminars held by my high school American History teacher after school as additional preparation for the SATs introduced us to a different way to teach and a different way to learn.

Then Wellesley College provided extraordinary opportunities for experiential learning and small, informal groups. First, were internships, beginning with my participation in the first, and unofficial college internship program. A political science professor thought some of us could benefit from a summer of unpaid work in the bustling, exciting atmosphere of wartime Washington, D.C. She assigned me to a position at the Board of Economic Warfare, a section of the OSS and a precursor to the CIA! I was in Spyland at 19! I was entrusted with serious work, monitoring international cables for key names, places, or materials. I reviewed pre-war debriefings of businessmen as they returned from Axis nations because they brought knowledge of railroad lines, location of factories or shipments of raw materials. What I highlighted went to OSS analysts and ultimately, combined with chemical analyses and other information, determined bombing target choices. Since a few other Political Science majors had internships at various federal government departments, we would meet for dinner once a week to share our observations.

Deemed a great success, the college proceeded to officially sponsor no-credit internships the following winter when the college closed from the Christmas break through January because of a World War II fuel shortage. This time, I went to the Personnel Department of the Social Security Administration at a time when it was relatively new. There I was awarded a task none of the official employees wanted to do: reviewing the federally-mandated professional credentials of employees in the SSA's state offices, one of the real focal points of federal-state conflict. Under the supervision of the man who wrote the textbook on personnel management that I later used in graduate school, I discovered some irregularities as well as nepotism.

Learning about the civil service in this experience created an interest that continued with my master's thesis at the University of Chicago on a congressman who was considered the father of the federal civil service legislation. This internship in the Social Security Administration also was instrumental in my being hired after graduate school by the Institute for Psychological Services, an Illinois Institute of Technology unit that had a contract with the Veterans Administration to do vocational counseling for WWII veterans. This service was available to all veterans, but mandatory for those who wanted to change a course of study under the GI Bill or who had service connected disabilities. The director hired me because I had a working knowledge of the "Dictionary of Occupational Titles" gained at Social Security's Personnel Office. He said they were having difficulty in training psychologists who knew how to assign and interpret the batteries of tests but could not use the "Dictionary" accurately so he would try me from the other direction.

That was stressful for me because these men were older than I and most had seen combat. I often felt inadequate and questioned my right to do this. However, in one situation I was able to track the career of a veteran who was driving a taxi but followed my interpretation of his vocational tests and steadily climbed from a salesman at a major international corporation to become its president. That vindicated my assessment and validated my intuition.

Two other undergraduate experiences are embedded in my brain. One was a six-student seminar led by a noted German political philosopher, Herman Finer. We met in his living room and decided that we would each research a topic of interest, meet once a week to explain to the group what we had accomplished, and take questions to help us with our next steps. We were learning from each other. At the end of the semester, Professor Finer produced a long poem about each student as his contribution to the group. I have it still.

My mentor and the chair of the Political Science Department, Louise Overacker, was the only significant researcher into election campaign finance at that time, and after every presidential election she would establish herself in a corner of the U.S. Capitol Rotunda where the Clerk of the House of Representatives had his office and go through all the reports of campaign contributions. I was thrilled and honored when she asked me to be her research assistant. We had a great time tracing family ties among the donors, as that was how legal contribution limits were evaded. Also, each time the bell rang denoting time for a vote on the floor of the House of Representatives, we flew down the stairs to watch the action.

I developed a real understanding of the legislative process that summer as well as an appreciation of the dogged plodding and thrill of finding connections that comes with original research. Influenced by these experiences as a learner in internships, independent study, small groups, original research, and motherhood, I was also influenced by my experiences as a teacher who tried to bring small changes to the traditional learning experiences of New Trier students.

Now there was an opportunity to broaden the scope of efforts toward educational change. There were risks in that path. Our history team would replace me. Could I adjust to new colleagues from different disciplines? What about teaching in one huge room where everything I said or did could be public? What if I weren't flexible enough—dynamic enough—to meet expectations that were unknown? What if it didn't work for me or didn't work at all? What would my career be like then? In thinking this situation over, I understood that I had been wading at the shore for a number of years and it was time to dive in. My observations and interaction with students in classrooms and extracurricular activities had led to changes in my teaching and my memories of significant experiential learning in my education also influenced those changes. I wanted to make a difference, and I wasn't the only risk taker in this undertaking.

From the school administrators to the parents and students who applied, to my new colleagues, we all were taking a plunge into unknown waters. As Jim met with administrators, he also had a committee of faculty, students, and parents to create a specific plan. At the same time, the school's Curriculum Director, Mary Ida McGuire, and I traveled to Ann Arbor, Louisville, and Oak Park to observe and talk with students and teachers in their alternative schools, becoming more and more certain of the validity and value of self-direction for students.

By spring of 1972, the committee's proposal went to New Trier High School's Board of Education for discussion and won approval for the creation of The Center for Self-Directed Learning, a program for 125 students and five teachers. The faculty was invited to apply for positions on the staff of the Center and I waited anxiously for the news that I was selected as the Social Studies teacher. Jim Bellanca was the coordinator, Bob Applebaum represented the sciences, Bill Gregory came from the English Department, Vernoy Johnson taught Math, and Irene Niebauer was from the Art Department. I barely knew them. Fortunately, all of us turned out to be risk-takers like the student applicants, and willing interdisciplinary guides and co-learners.

Then began a series of parent and student evening meetings that resulted in serious dialogues about the purpose of education and the purpose of high school. We talked about the belief in high school as a safe place and time for the exploration of different learning styles and disciplines. We discussed concerns about students transitioning from the supervision of home and the oversight of daily assignments to the lack thereof on a college campus. Nothing seems to occur between senior year in high school and college entrance to facilitate that transition.

Lastly, we invited interested students, with parent permission, to sign up and to our surprise; we had over 150 registrants so a lottery seemed reasonable. However, those who did not have their numbers selected called on the School Board to increase the size of the student population and add another teacher. The Board complied and provided stipends for us to work together during the summer.

It was a busy summer. First, we worked with a consultant who helped us become a cohesive group that trusted and respected each other so we could talk about difficulties or problems that might arise from all the interactions and teaching occurring in one room. We had to be able to accept the fact that many students would gravitate to other facilitators and be glad they were able to find one of us to meet their needs. By learning through our own group experience, we had some techniques to help our new students form cohesive, supportive groups in the Center.

We also had to decide about room usage, but most important of all, we interviewed each student to explore what they were interested in learning and why. We also made some loose plans for opening day. So it was that on that anxious but exciting day in September 1972, I began the ten years as a facilitator and coordinator that were the most rewarding of my career. It was ten years filled with chaos, intensity, excitement, fun, worries, collaboration, trust, respect, learning, collegiality, affection, and always transparency.

Everything was ready, we thought. We had our large main room, a room for facilitators' desks, and a science/art room. Students arrived, full of excitement, some trepidation, and pioneer spirit, as we gathered together and dove into those uncharted waters. We had covered large areas of walls and blackboards with blank paper and had dozens of markers available for "brainstorming." After introductions, explanations, and ideas tossed out in the "brainstorming" session of our first Town Hall, we invited our students to use the markers to write ideas for learning groups and also to sign their names under other ideas that seemed appealing They could meet as a group in the following days to organize, or disband if there was lack of agreement or interest.

As facilitators, we posted a few ideas we thought would be worth investigating and that might alleviate student anxiety when faced with a blank slate instead of the traditional printout of courses, teachers, times, and places to meet. We were aware of adolescent angst as we moved about the room amidst excited conversation, with students milling around in apparent chaos as each Centerite searched out study groups of interest. We also moved about the room offering help to those who seemed confused or overwhelmed. "Are you finding ideas that appeal to you?" It was an offer and if accepted, our role was to ask questions about their interests, to encourage thinking beyond "English" or "History." The aim was to find specific issues or problems, to narrow the field. In the days devoted to the group meetings so they could clarify their goals and talk about how they would organize, as well as establish meeting times, we would circulate to see how well the groups were functioning and offer assistance.

Most of the assistance would be in the form of clarifying questions, helping with the process of developing a manageable topic and an agreed upon learning process, encouraging each one to express a view and all to listen to each other. For example, a facilitator would ask, "What do you want to learn?" Perhaps, "Why?" and "How will you demonstrate that you've accomplished your goal?" These questions could also be used for independent study, a traditional class at New Trier or another institution, or an internship. Some ideas never arrived at that stage or dissolved for a variety of reasons: some students decided they had to reduce the number of groups they had signed up for, some wanted to go in a different direction than the others, or they disagreed with the process.

Each semester I, as well as the other facilitators, offered some ideas for study or were asked to facilitate groups or help with an independent study.

My role varied with the topic and process the group selected. Ted Lowitz, interested in art, had heard about the great explosion in the art world in Germany between the two World Wars. Bruce Taylor wanted to focus on the economic situation leading to the rise of Hitler. I agreed to facilitate the two in a study even though my knowledge was basic. We read Peter Gay's *Weimar Culture* and Isherwood's *The Berlin Stories*, meeting once a week to talk about our readings and thoughts. We learned about German Expressionism, looking at paintings and the seminal film, *The Cabinet of Dr. Caligari*. We also read about the economy as Germany tried to rebuild after the devastation of war and reparations and the political experiment with democracy. We went to see a local production of *The Threepenny Opera*. We each found reading materials and agreed on the pace of reading. I was a co-learner, sometimes a guide, and then an evaluator.

To demonstrate what they had learned, the two Centerites decided to create a slide projector show (much before PowerPoint) covering the major ideas of our study. They photographed relevant pictures and text, adding slides of their own. Being present at the meetings, working and discussing issues with them, I had learned a great deal, too, and had a thorough grasp of their goals, process, and achievement for an evaluation.

The "Center Bill Group" was composed of students concerned about provisions in state laws about school attendance not being counted unless the students were on the school site. There were courses, also, mandated by state law that we were not "teaching" in the traditional way. For example, a few students completed the Consumer Education requirement by opening a "pop up" kiosk in a local store where they sold items made by creative Centerites. Fearing that the future of the Center was endangered, the group began to research laws in all 50 states about alternatives in education. They met with their state representative, Harold Katz, who had one child in the Center (and another one later) who told them they needed to make a strong case to him for legislative action because the law was not to be taken lightly.

During the time they were gathering data for the report to Rep. Katz, led by the determined Mike Kendall, I met with them to talk about the research and about the group's functioning. They had learned how and when they could use local law libraries and contacted 50 State Boards of Education. We made several trips to the state capital to meet members of the House Education Committee and other representatives, to observe the legislative process, and to discuss their issues with members they met. Bill Gregory, Center English teacher, suggested some changes to the group's report spelling out the case for alternative schools. The report convinced Rep. Katz and he agreed to introduce a bill to that effect.

On another visit, I introduced them to the Governor, a friend from my political days, who agreed to sign "our" bill if it became law. There was a glitch, however. One Education Committee member told our students some requirements had to remain in the bill before he could vote for it and they reluctantly agreed. The students gained first-hand knowledge of the legislative process, the research, and writing processes and provided a concrete demonstration of their learning. I wasn't teaching a class, I was only a facilitator, providing support, checking their progress, answering questions, and arranging the trips to Springfield. I still have a copy of *The Case For Alternative Schools* and Mike Kendall, now a lawyer, still checks the Illinois Law books to be sure "our bill" is still in force. It is.

The Italian Renaissance group, with me as facilitator, began as an interdisciplinary study with segments on the history, culture, and geography of that period. One day, a group member said, "It's great to read and look at pictures, but it would be more meaningful if we could see it in Italy." There was an immediate consensus and brainstorming began. Marty Heiser volunteered his mother, a travel agent, to provide information and costs. Linda Glass studied travel books to develop an itinerary based on our studies. Someone decided to learn Italian and found that Dr. Girardi, a Center volunteer from the community, knew Italian and was willing to teach some of us. I do not have an ear for languages so my fellow students were delighted with my struggle as they became more fluent faster! I was definitely a co-learner and not a star pupil at that.

Before long, these would-be travelers held a few bake sales for group expenses, wrote a proposal for the administration, and took it to the School Board where our learning adventure was approved. Five boys, three girls, and I left for three weeks in Italy in January and thanks to the "Center Law," they were considered in attendance at New Trier High School. People have been surprised that I was willing to take on such a responsibility by myself and my response has been "I believed that our mutual trust and respect would overcome any problems. Also, this was their idea and their plans." As it happened, we mostly stayed at inexpensive pensiones, and, as far as I know, no one cared to walk those dark side streets at night. At museums and historical sites, we would agree to move about at our own pace, returning to the entrance at a specified time. Anyone who wished more time would also return, ask for that, and the rest of us would wait, if at all possible. It worked every time.

Other kinds of small groups met differing student needs. A Play Reading group met at a table in the Center, took different roles in the play of the week, and then discussed the plot, characters, and their reactions. That worked for students who neither had the time nor the interest in reading books.

A few students were interested in art history and how to think about art. One found a great book, "What Is Art?" and asked me to facilitate a group using that book. In college, I had an art history course and had maintained an interest in art over the years. We planned our process and shared leadership, but there were times I had to help with the content and, as such, was a co-learner.

Court Watchers went to Cook County Criminal Courts a few times, decided that the fast pace of trials and the difficulty following the proceedings had provided them with enough of an understanding of the criminal justice system. Moving on to the federal courthouse where cases lasted several weeks or more, it was decided to focus there. A curious judge sent his bailiff to invite us into his chambers, asked the students some questions, explained the major issue before him, and gave a little lecture on law and justice. One defense attorney, having noticed us there before, came to our seats during a break, asked the students how they thought the trial was proceeding, and answered their questions. Another brought them brownies one day. We talked about the cases, differences in venues, federal law, the Constitution, and their dismay at the Criminal Courts. They did some reading in the criminal justice literature. I saw and heard, so I could vouch that learning was occurring, although in non-traditional ways.

Vernoy Johnson, in addition to teaching all levels of math, facilitated a group that read novels by Vonnegut and Hesse, as well as others, and then tried to write individual pieces in the style of the author. He sent the class's work to Vonnegut, who sent a note of appreciation back. He also facilitated some studies of Africa, having spent two years teaching there, and helped Eliot Neel build the planetarium with his workshop skills.

A number of students were out in the community with volunteer facilitators and that contributed to transparency. People outside the school could participate and understand the program. That was true of the parents who were co-learners or facilitators and people who took on interns. Besides having student teachers, we also were observed by a Northwestern University graduate student who came and went as needed for her doctoral dissertation. As a facilitator, and later the coordinator, I believed that this openness, rather than the closed classroom, had to be part of the atmosphere. Even though there was considerable chaos in our main room, not just during brainstorming and Town Halls, but also on busy days when a number of learners would be gathered around tables, with or without adults, focusing on the topic at hand. Others might be quietly playing a guitar, painting, reading, writing, or socializing. But there also could be a sense of chaos in students' lives and the facilitators' lives. So many were out and about—how could we keep in touch, how could we have a sense of community? How could all of us handle this freedom responsibly? We could ask each other for help. The students could ask us or their peers.

There was a two-fold system in place. First, there was the community group, ten or twelve boys and girls who were a mix of new and experienced Centerites and a mix of sophomores, juniors, and seniors. All groups met on Wednesday morning or afternoon. The task of the facilitator was to help the individuals coalesce into a caring, significant base where concern and assistance would be available to each member. It was to be a place where a sense of responsibility for each other developed to help each person cope with the freedom allowed. It was also a small group that enabled a facilitator and other members to sense or know how each student was faring in this environment. We would suggest each share their schedules with the group at the beginning of a semester and often someone would ask a new Centerite, "Do you think you can handle that much? That looks like a lot of reading." Another might say, "I couldn't find topics I was interested in."

Community groups met in various places—homes, parks, the beach, or the Chicago Botanic Garden. It was fun and active and, at times, difficult. Each facilitator had meetings that were disappointing in that a sense of trust might take too long to develop. A community group might not want to act to convey a message to a frequent absentee that this was not acceptable behavior and the message that he or she was missed. The facilitators had originally bonded in group development sessions before the Center opened, so we had an experience similar to what we were asking the students to follow. We had a facilitators' community group that met once a week, after school and outside school where we could share our feelings about issues, problems, or students and get feedback. If we sensed a student was floundering, we would ask the others about their perception or knowledge. I found it invaluable to hear my colleagues' concerns about effectiveness and know I was not alone.

It was in the support group that the individual student received the most attention. Selecting one adult and perhaps a peer or two, a student was required to meet with his/her support group at least twice per semester and a member could call one at any time if a need appeared. Early in the semester, each student talked about their goals for the semester, for both academic and personal growth, how they would achieve those goals, and perhaps seek advice or feedback. Then, at the end of the semester, the same group read the student's evaluations and talked about what was learned, what was not successful and what might change the next time. Despite our best intentions, there were a few students who opted to return to the traditional school. Interestingly, two were siblings of previous Centerites. A few have said emotional needs were not met.

Evaluation times brought intensity and anxiety. As a facilitator, I had to respond to the students' descriptions of learning experiences and their assessments of success in terms of their goals. I labored over the forms they completed in order to present a fair picture of each student's involvement in the group, learning, and suggestions for future or improvements. The students then gathered the completed evaluations and compressed them into a two-page summary of the learning experience (called a synthesis) with a balanced quotation from each evaluator. More times than not, I found the student had downplayed the positives and emphasized the suggested improvements. As advisor, I signed off on the completed document that was then filed in the Registrar's Office in lieu of a report card. Those were part of applications to college.

College acceptance was a major concern so after two years we did a survey of our graduates that reinforced our perception that smaller, liberal arts colleges were willing to consider our students but the very large universities were not organized to read non-traditional applications. For example, our students were accepted at Brown, Tulane, Vanderbilt, Vassar, and Yale, but denied at the University of Wisconsin-Madison and the University of Michigan. Both of the latter had programs resembling the Center and that was how one student argued her way into Wisconsin. Later on, the University of Michigan did accept one of our graduates into its program.

After a few years, the flexibility of the program became apparent, as the students and the facilitators adapted to the evolving nature and needs of the student body.

Early on, a student brought an old couch for our "office" followed by someone with floor beanbags because they liked to hang out with us. Feeling a bit crowded, the faculty proposed to a Town Hall that we move our desks, chairs, and files into the large main room, room 100, turning the "office" into another room for general use as we had a lot going on over the years—a fruit fly experiment, a maze for rats, a jumble of wires somehow connected to a "Vogelback," an early computer actually installed at Northwestern University, and various art projects, including one that involved a discarded bathtub and, of course, the planetarium. It was agreed that the move was a sensible one. Town Halls emphasized community decision-making in order for students to have a serious role in the operation of the program.

Another early student proposal at a Town Hall was to liven up room 101 and put our stamp on it by painting a huge mural on a huge wall. Ted Lowitz designed our "yellow brick road" and with his colleagues' help executed a cheerful and symbolic mural. A number of years later another group of Centerites decided they needed their own mural, the Town Hall agreed, much to the chagrin of earlier grads who, when visiting would exclaim "What happened to *our* mural?" Other aspects of the program changed as students developed responses in Town Halls to needs or issues they raised.

Communication was a perceived problem with students off at internships or other learning sites so Town Hall adopted a student suggestion that we have a wall of large coffee cans, one for each student. Before long we had well over 100 of those three -pound cans, alphabetically arranged and labeled, serving us well for many years as ample mailboxes. Other changes would include a newspaper, a literary magazine, a yearbook, play production, and PR materials for students who decided to visit regular school homerooms to publicize the Center. These developed as students decided they wanted to have them, were willing to produce them, and then disappeared when there was no interest.

The longest lasting innovation, beside the coffee cans, came with the development of "Bumpy Baccalaureate," also known as the Center graduation ceremony in a nearby park. Early on, graduation arose as an issue because many of our seniors did not wish to participate in the large, formal ceremony for those in the traditional school. Some would participate, but also wanted a small, informal Center graduation. "Bumpy" park is a beachfront park a few blocks from campus with a number of berms and was often used by Center students. That was selected as the site and seniors planned the program, classmates provided live music, facilitators, and students spoke, and eventually a Center designed diploma was bestowed.

Town Hall itself underwent some changes as time went on. At first, students waited to be called on by whoever was trying to move the group toward consensus, raising hands, but after a while several people would talk at once. Ultimately, a student brought in a paddle that was passed from speaker to speaker and that made listening and thinking easier. Many times, we facilitators had to bite our tongues to avoid playing "the sensible adult" and railroading the process when the discussion seemed endless and we could envision a compromise.

There were also times when Town Halls were called by small groups of students who wanted the community to gather without weighty issues to discuss. One time they had an ice cream social with long tables end to end piled with all the ingredients for ice cream sundaes. Another time they served huge sub sandwiches. The sense of community was evident and strong at a Town Hall that was asked to decide on how we should use a $500 check from a parent appreciative of her son's graduation committee arriving (with his assent) at the decision that he was not ready to graduate as yet.

Students were asked to bring any project ideas they had. The most well organized presentation was Eliot Neel's plan to build a small planetarium. Town Hall arrived at a consensus: Eliot should get most of the money. One student, Carol Amir-Fazli, was so excited by the proposal and Eliot's knowledge that she jumped up to volunteer money from her savings account and others volunteered to help him realize his dream.

The Center faculty maintained their sense of community despite changes in the group. Irene Niebauer and Bob Applebaum returned to the traditional program after two years, replaced by Laura Daniels and Pamela Wood. Then Jim decided to join an educational consulting partnership and resigned. We agreed, with the administration concurring, that I should replace him as coordinator, and Bev Miller Kirk filled the empty staff slot. We thus continued with the same basic ideas and structures. This was such a self-governing group that no one—from the School Board on down—was concerned when I took the Renaissance learning group to Italy for three weeks. The only drama during those three weeks was a blizzard that socked Chicago.

There were so many adventures, so much learning and growth in the ten years I was privileged to be a part of the Center. But most of all, I remember those intrepid students who struggled with the awesome challenges we placed before them: learning self-direction and self-evaluation while creating a community of caring learners. It's been a great joy to reconnect with so many alumni after all these years and to hear about the life-long influence of "lessons learned." As it happened, I was the only person to be present at the Center for Self-Direction's birth and its sad demise. I eagerly await its rebirth 40 years later.

> *Arline was the sole faculty person who taught in the Center from its alpha to its omega. During the past three years, she has facilitated organization of two Center reunions where the seeds for this book were planted. Over the several years since the first seed planting, she organized the memoirs, raided the New Trier archives, communicated with recalcitrant contributors and double-checked the edits. She resides with her husband, Stanley, in Highland Park.*

Short Takes

The Center was the culmination of my '70s education that included experimental teaching methods throughout. I loved the freedom and responsibility it offered so I went on to Brown University, a school that took pride in letting students design their own program and also to forgo grades if they liked. I liked. It was good for me to know I could survive without someone else planning my life for me.

I remember some interminable Town Halls that sure were a lesson on the insanity of the consensus process. I still prefer consensus. I also started writing a book that I still haven't finished.

~Mary Minow, 1976

Purposefully and
Self-Consciously Involved

William P. Gregory

*In November, 1972 "Mr. Greg" spoke about the Center at the
National Council of Teachers of English, three months after
the Center doors opened.*

All last summer I was eager for September because then I would be with
five of my colleagues and 155 randomly chosen students, all ages and
abilities, in our new Center for Self-directed Learning. The Center has been
in being for nearly twelve weeks now, and I have experienced a wider range
of human activity and relationship than ever before. The "highs" are so high
and the "lows" so low they are difficult to imagine or describe. Frustration, joy,
chaos, spontaneous planning, exhaustion, boundless emotional and intellectual
energy expended, hours of discussion, exciting perceptions, joint decision-
making. Students fanning out across the city to experience and to learn, adults
coming into the Center to lead and to share their specialties, the Center faculty
developing trust and concern in community groups. A senior student in the
Center said: "For the first time in eleven years of education, I feel that I am the
same person in the school as I am outside it."

In 1984, in a self-assessment, Bill wrote the following:

Upon the creation of the Center in 1972, however, from that year on, my
development as a teacher and a person took a major turn. I became involved,
purposefully and self-consciously involved, in the education and development
of the whole person, interested in the simultaneous growth of a student's
cognitive and effective skills.

William arrived at the New Trier High School English Department in 1957 and joined the Center for Self-Directed Learning as part of the original team of facilitators. Prior to that, Bill trained Navy pilots during World War II, received his B.A. degree from Wesleyan University and M.A. from The Breadloaf School of English at Middlebury College. He also taught at two private boys' schools. While at New Trier, Bill was active in the 1960-1970 civil rights movement.

Short Takes

The University of Michigan would not accept my transcript from my senior year in high school because of my participation in the Center. MIT, Rhode Island School of Design, University of Illinois Champaign, Illinois Institute of Technology, and University of Toronto all accepted me. University of Michigan said that written evaluations did not constitute a "grade," and as far as they were concerned, I did not attend school my senior year.

I am a licensed architect, practicing in the Chicago area. My career began with a Center internship with a local architect. Educators continue to look today for successful strategies for educational programs, and the Center's ideals are more relevant today than they were back then.

~Richard D. Hayes, 1973

MY GREAT ADVENTURE...
TEACHING IN THE CENTER

BEV MILLER KIRK

*"We have a marvelous student teaching assignment in a
fourth grade classroom for you, Bev."*

*"No thank you! I have already fallen in love with a bunch of
scruffy teenagers at New Trier's Center for Self-directed Learning,
and I mean to do my student teaching there,
and they have already said 'Yes!'"*

Thus began my five-year Great Adventure in a most wonderful but difficult-to-describe educational experiment, the Center for Self-directed Learning. Skeptics would often ask me how it was that Center kids could possibly learn anything if they didn't take Math or Science or English or History! My favorite shorthand explanation was always to tell about our course on "Bridges." A group of kids and I formed this class as a gentle spoof to an established course in the Center called "Rivers" where every year the kids would study a different American River and learn about the implications of these waterways on American History. So, "Bridges" came to be. Even in pre-Google days there existed a plethora of fascinating bridge information including everything from engineering to poetry.

Here is a partial list of our class curricula: Bridge structure: building bridges out of toothpicks and straws and balsa, collapsing bridges (including one that oscillated itself to death). Famous bridge literature: *An Occurrence at Owl Creek Bridge*, and *The Bridge on the River Kwai*. So we read books upon books, built sturdy structures, and composed poems, and we also needled the "Rivers" class with our bulletin board filled with bridge facts and myths. Naturally, they retaliated! And both classes learned more from the competition. And finally, we took a field trip to Chicago, a city whose very life has depended on bridges. On a blue-sky sparkly day a gaggle of teenagers with me in tow explored the edges of the Chicago River. A bunch of hardhat steelworkers invited us up on a beautiful old iron bridge they were dismantling. "Yup!" they said "Lucky you got to see this beauty before she was torn up and sold for scrap." And she was indeed a beauty with stars and moons cut out of her ironwork, and we felt so sad that progress had forced her to be turned into trash. But it was a beautiful day, and we continued along the riverfront admiring a trunnion bascule bridge…. Oh yes, and yet another trunnion bascule bridge, and then of course the Michigan Avenue double-leaf double-deck trunnion bascule bridge. And then I would peer at my skeptic questioner and say "Oh really! You didn't know this about Chicago's trunnion bascule bridges? Hmmm!" I would arch my eyebrows and give a pitying sigh implying the sorry incompleteness of their education.

And then of course, as educators we like to talk about "the whole child." We know it is difficult for your brain to function if your heart is hurting or you have self-doubt. Is there a teenager or an adult who does not have self-doubt? Just as I was about to begin my teaching in the Center, I overheard a conversation between two young men on the train to Chicago. One young man was explaining his decision to go into teaching rather than the ministry. He said "If I am a teacher I can have an impact every day of the week, not just Sundays." And yes, the calling to be a teacher in the Center was for me every bit as strong as a calling to ministry could be. Every day we Center facilitators were able to connect to the hearts and souls of our kids because we made time, and we believed that this time was vitally important. I call these connections "God Moments" because in them we can clearly experience the other person's soul. Perhaps others would not use such religious terminology, but for me it helped me to recognize how extraordinary and important the ministry of teaching truly is. And time…the gift of time! In our hurried life, we made time for important moments in the Center. And it takes a lot of time!

I particularly remember one September as we began our process of building community. We were sorting out what academic subjects might be of interest, and how to form community groups, and how does consensus work, and how to form support groups, and it was all such an intense vital exciting learning experience. Then Arline Paul got a phone call from an angry parent. He said that he understood that his son was not yet going to class, and he wanted to know exactly why, and as Arline started to explain, he chastised her by saying, "*My son will be behind a week for the rest of his life!*" I personally am so very happy to "Be behind for the rest of my life!"

THE REST OF MY LIFE: AN ADDENDUM

So, is there life after the Center? We all better hope so, or the Center will have been an abject failure! And lucky me who had the dream job of teaching in the Center for five wonderful years…was there life after that? Every year in the spring, I was fired from New Trier. They called it "being riffed" or "reduction in force," and every year I was heartbroken until Tah Dah! I was hired back to teach one more year.

Not so on year five. In 1980, teachers with 17 years of tenure were fired. No chance at all for me. So, I collected unemployment and pretended to look for work.

August 1980 still no job, but my friend, Don Monroe, Superintendent of Winnetka Schools, asked me at church one day "What do you know about teaching television production, Bev?" Well, full disclosure here: I knew nothing! I didn't even watch television. *But* it was August! *And* the two other candidates were professors who were techno geeks and didn't know much about kids.

So, Don in his wisdom hired me figuring I could learn the equipment but the professors could never love the kids.

So, for 26 years I got to have a whole lot of fun in the Washburne Television Studio teaching cooperation, bravery, group process, and gumption to try new things.

But back up to year one. It was *awful*! The kids were *awful*! The equipment was *awful*!! I hated it! One day in November, I was walking down Washburne's front steps and another New Trier riffed refuge teacher was walking with me. I said to her "Wow! It sure is different teaching middle school from teaching high school." And she said, "Yes it is, but don't you just love the kids?" *Love the kids*? No, I did not. That in three little words was my problem.

And then I fell in love with the kids. There is no explaining this. You either love middle school kids or you don't. People always ask Junior High teachers, "How can you stand kids that age?" and we always secretly smile because we love the kids.

And other cool things I got to do at Washburne: I was a department chair. I was a Winnetka's Teachers Union President. I negotiated for salary increases and medical coverage. And I taught with excellent colleagues. Twenty-six years. A great job.

But not all of life is defined by work. When you read bios in books such as this there are always lots of achievements listed. But I say you don't know the person, until you also know their tragedies. So here is my short list:

Happiness of 30 years with the love of my life, Frank Kirk, who sadly died of idiopathic pulmonary fibrosis. The joy of being related to eight wonderful kids. Sadness at some of their difficult divorces, and of course abject terror as my stepson Mark came close to dying with a massive stroke. And more recently, big worries as my daughter has been diagnosed with lupus and a persistent lung infection. Amazing, eight grandchildren who are growing into adults before my eyes and struggling to make it. Sadness that my oldest grandson chose drugs and flunked out of college. Happy that he is working for Americorps and trying to turn his life around. Prayers for the younger grandchildren as they run into the inevitable snags of growing up.

And now that I have reached the ripe old age of 73, I feel so lucky to be alive, to be blessed with family and friends and neighbors and church. Life is good. May life be good for all of you too! Much love to all you Centerites wherever you may be!

> *Bev's life-long love of teaching began after she earned her certificate at National-Lewis University. Five years in the Center were followed by 26 more at Washburne Middle School in Winnetka, Illinois and then...retirement and grandchildren.*

Short Takes

I taught in the Center for a limited time, but those years have a fond place in my heart. The intensity of the relationships with my fellow faculty members and with the students was at times contentious, but always exciting! I learned a lot about myself during my time in the Center, a lot about what it meant to really listen to people, and a lot about the skills that I had (and lacked!) and a lot about learning to respect and honor the feelings of others.

In my last 15 years at New Trier, I taught only physics, a good deal of that I learned by helping to "facilitate" a small learning group in the Center; the truth is, we were all learning it together. The other truth is that I left the Center because I could not in good conscience expect students to construct 25 hours/week of learning when I knew that I (as an adult) could not meet such an expectation.

After retiring from New Trier, I have been actively composing choral music and still play piano professionally—little jazz trio things in wine bars and restaurants.

~Robert Applebaum
Facilitator, 1972-74

The Worst Educational Invention

Vernoy Johnson

*I was given a chance to make a presentation to the parent school
mathematics department concerning grading procedures.
My recollection is that people were polite, but uninterested.
Nothing ever came of my suggestions, as far as I know.
21 February 1977*

There is nothing to be gained by a Lobatschewskian and a Euclidean debating their differences at the point of conflict of a theorem—say the angle sum of a triangle. The place to confront each other is at the level of one's assumptions. Likewise, a pro- and anti-abortion supporter can ultimately only come to even understand each other by wrestling with each other's assumptions. The same is true for the hawk and the dove, or the pro- and anti-busing exponent, or those who support the issuing of grades and those who, like myself, oppose it. I think one of the assumptions of those who support letter or number grades is that they provide a level of objectivity for measuring students' abilities. But I think the evidence is abundant, including the numbers that the mathematics department head has given us today, that that is just not so.

The numbers suggest strongly that there are those of us in this room who issue Cs to students who another of us in this room would give Bs to, and yet another, a D. Look, for example, at the grade averages and their spread for Geometry 213, the only course I'm currently involved in. With a grade average spread of 1.36, my C could be your low A or his borderline failure. And that's a difference within people in this room, to say nothing of what would happen if that student took the same course at XYZ high school. There are national studies to show that the spread in grades assigned to Geometry tests by 100 grading teachers is wider than the spread assigned by teachers reading English themes. There are studies to show that if you graded the same set of your own papers two weeks apart, the grades could easily differ by a full letter grade. And think of just yourself, as you grade papers from Algebra 212 to Geometry 214, and from morning to evening, or before and after a headache. And this takes no account of the letter grade turned in being determined by other factors—attention, attitude, effort, neatness, and if the student smells nice. So, any fiction that grades offer an objective measure of learning is just that—a fiction.

Secondly, the assumption that grades are a necessity for admission to, and a predictor of success in, collegiate studies is just not so. National studies, in addition to our own experience in the Center, show that only about five per cent of colleges and universities in this country insist on grades, GPA, or RIC. We have Center graduates all the way from Hampshire to MIT, from Johnston to Yale (including Illinois' only Rhodes Scholar this year). National studies show only about a 0.6 correlation between high school grades and collegiate success, and a 0.09 correlation (that is, virtually none) between high school grades and success (whatever that means) in occupational involvements beyond that.

Thirdly, the assumption that grades somehow act as a positive motivational device for genuine learning has virtually no support in fact. The national studies show that the fear of failure tends only to spread the grades—the good get better and the poor get poorer. I do not attach research significance to the New Trier News editorial page, but a recent one does point out a germ of truth when it says: *"It has long been recognized that senior slump is the inevitable result of four years of high school work. This problem continues with consistent severity despite teachers' and administrators' attempts to quell it. Before this problem can be solved, it is important to know the causes."* The most important cause of the SS [senior slump] rests in the very system of education existing at New Trier. Intense importance is placed upon grades and competition. This often creates a situation where learning becomes secondary to grade attainment. During second semester of senior year, seniors no longer have any incentive to work. As a result, the work stops. As one senior put it: "for four years I bullshitted my way through school. Now there is no need for the bullshit any more."

Fourthly, the assumption that we must in some way prepare our students for a competitive world "out there" is backwards, to me. I do not see my role as one of helping students to accommodate to a world of which I disapprove in large chunks. I see it rather as my function to help them modify that world. And a part of the hoped-for modification involves a reduction of competition "out there."

Let me offer briefly then not a solution to the grading dilemma, but my assumptions dealing with it. I believe that the person being evaluated must be as involved in the process of evaluation as any "official" evaluator, and that without that input the learning experience will be marginal at best. And I believe that process lends itself most naturally to subjective evaluations. I am not only interested in being a partner to creating a climate of competition, but I am interested in actively suppressing what I think is the emotionally destructive atmosphere of grade competition. The value of subjective evaluations, for re-thinking, for modification of position, for improved analysis, is enormously greater than for single-letter (or number) grades.

> *Vernoy was born in China to missionary parents and served in the U.S. Navy during World War II before receiving his B.A. from the University of Chicago and M.A. from Northwestern. In the Center, Vernoy was resident poet, Renaissance man, woodworker and handyman, math teacher, North Woods guide, and community group facilitator. When the Center closed, he returned to the Mathematics department until his retirement in 1986. With his wife, Lois, he retired to California where he lost his battle with Parkinson's disease in 2001.*

Short Takes

I think the biggest impact from my attending the Center is that I always looked beyond "regular" for the best education for my two children and never shied away from alternatives. Getting to know all the teachers on a personal level made a big difference.

~Alice Bowers Anderson, 1977

STUDENT MEMOIRS

THE YEAR OF THINKING DANGEROUSLY

REBECCA ARMSTRONG, 1973

In the spring of 1972, I had no intention of joining the Center for Self-Directed Learning. My success at New Trier High School was assured, my grades were excellent and senior year promised to be an easy slide towards graduation. But there are two great forces that are the undoing of the best-laid plans—Love and War—and it was (thankfully) the former of these that pivoted me off my chosen path and into a year of thinking dangerously.

Love had blossomed, a secret, unrequited love for the president of student council who seemed to my hormone-addled brain the living incarnation of the Greek Adonis. I adopted a passion for school politics completely out-of-character to my previous goody-two-shoes, teacher's pet persona. For his sake, I forsook classes and took to the lawns to join student protests against the war and marched off campus for demonstrations at the local parks. When I learned of his interest in supporting efforts for the new "free school" I naturally took his side. In this frame of mind, I attended a meeting where teachers would introduce the Center to the parents of those students who had already expressed an interest in becoming part of the experiment in learning.

Jim Bellanca, Bill Gregory, and Arline Paul were there, as well as several other teachers whom I did not yet know. They gave an eloquent presentation and then opened the floor to questions. I don't know if anyone was prepared for the active hostility and vehemence with which some anxious parents expressed their horror at the idea of a "free school." The terror that their darlings were sacrificing a chance at Harvard for some harebrained scheme of self-actualization made the room crackle with tension. The main argument emerging from the parents was essentially this: young people cannot be trusted to direct themselves because they are irresponsible, capricious and ignorant of what is best for their own lives. They require a strong hand from above until they are safely ensconced in a prestigious university. Annoyed as I was with this demeaning profile of students, it did not occur to me to speak out—until I saw the dismay written across the handsome face of my unsuspecting beloved. What lover would not leap into the fray to protect the loved one? And so, thus inspired, I leaned into the battle and saw an opening in the barrage of the parental assault.

With courage I did not know I had, I raised my hand and was acknowledged by, yes, the president of student council who was chairing the meeting. Turning to the parents, I threaded my way through their argument with a subversive suggestion. "Why," I asked, "do you have so little faith in your own parenting? Do you really believe that your own offspring are so ill-prepared to meet the real world? That they have learned nothing from your own good examples of self-discipline? That they are not capable of expressing those virtues that you have instilled in them through all these years of child-rearing? Surely, you cannot have so little faith in yourselves? Would you be so cold as to lay odds against your own progeny? With all of these privileges that you have provided, are we then, really no better off than if we had been rudely born and raised?"

With trembling knees, I took my seat and waited. I don't want to flatter myself and suggest that my counter-argument won the day, but there was certainly a surprised stillness in the room and a shift of tone to the remainder of the meeting. More importantly, there were warm, appreciative thanks from the Center teachers and a document was thrust into my hands which, with a single signature, sealed my fate as I agreed that, yes, I would be interested in becoming a member of the first class of the Center for Self-Directed Learning.

I tell you all this because, as with most enterprises, the opening chapter sets the tone for all that follows and so it was with my Center year. Although sweet Adonis graduated that year and was never seen again, he had played his role in my drama, and I had learned an essential lesson about education: motivation matters.

The second great lesson I learned came early in the fall of 1972. The school-within-a-school had been assigned several rooms at the far southeast corner of the building and one of the former study hall rooms served as our gathering place, being the only one large enough to accommodate the 120 of us who'd signed on for the first sailing of the untried ship. We were to learn, slowly, that the pedagogy for the Center was closer to Paulo Friere than anyone had suspected, and that the very methods by which we were to self-govern would have to be created by the students from scratch. And so, at the first Town Hall meeting, we all sprawled into the carpeted space, flung ourselves on chairs and couches or floor, and debated how we would make decisions that affected us as a group.

For some of us it seemed patently absurd to make so much out of this question. After all, we had been ruled by authority for so long that few of us had any experience in self-government and found it hard to warm to the finer nuances of the debate. The model that we did all acknowledge was the bedrock of primitive democracy: one person—one vote. A first straw poll revealed huge support for a simple "majority win" in questions of group decisions. I was ready to move on.

Then, a short, dark underclassman took the floor and, slowly at first, began to challenge the very assumption of majority rule. "Isn't it the case" he argued, "that most of us are here in this room because we do not fit easily into the majority? Haven't we all experienced the discomfort of having our own views and desires overridden because we express a minority opinion? Even worse, haven't we found ourselves doubting or disowning our own opinions because they did not fit the model of the majority? Why did we join the Center if not to have the chance to find out what it is that we actually believe and want? Are we bucking the system only to conform to its assumptions right out of the starting gate? Frankly, I've spent too many years being the odd-man-out. At least here I'd like to be the odd-man-in!"

I was stunned by what I heard. Something clicked open in my mind that afternoon—a key in a lock to a prison door I was not aware I stood behind. In the outer world of Center politics we arrived at an astonishing decision that day—we would not use majority rule but would make decisions by consensus, no matter how long that took, in order that no minority opinion be lost. In the inner world of my heart and mind, my own repressed minority came out to report on the state of the union and I was shocked to discover that I had abdicated my powers to authorities known and unknown before I even knew what those powers were. I had no real pleasure in learning because I had never connected learning with anything authentic to my own desires or inclinations. I was not an autonomous actor in my own life drama but a player speaking lines handed to me by others and living only for the applause of "getting it right." And so, I made the dangerous passage from "slave mentality" to "free woman" that year. I started thinking for myself. I questioned authority. I challenged assumptions. I searched for the minority report. And, I experienced learning for the thrill of it, for the pure, unadulterated pleasure of learning something new, without attachment to praise or grade. I got the single thing that every philosopher and educator has pronounced to be the bedrock of civilized society—an inquiring mind. In the process, I began to learn something else. I began to learn to love the world and the person I might become within it.

Rebecca went on to work in arts and education through Urban Gateways for 18 years where she brought music, art, and storytelling to school children in the 800 schools of greater Chicagoland. For 12 years, she served as the International Outreach Director for the Joseph Campbell Foundation. In 2004, she earned her doctorate in ministry at Chicago Theological Seminary. Today she teaches classes in ethics and religion at DePaul University School for New Learning, and business ethics in the M.B.A. program at Purdue University.

Short Takes

The brainstorming sessions helped to transform my way of approaching a situation or problem. They taught me to become a good problem solver and strategic thinker, useful in my work as a lobbyist in Wisconsin for AFSCME, the public employee union.

I was very lucky to be a part of a unique educational experiment which was a groundbreaking model of inclusiveness of all types of people, different learning styles and ability levels.

~Susan McMurray, 1978

THE ONCE AND FUTURE LAW

MIKE KENDALL, 1973

What we early Centerites called the "parent school" hadn't been too bad for me. My grades were fine and second semester junior year I was elected Student Council President, a position that would continue for half of my year in the Center. But I had become really, really bored with the traditional classroom routine by then and that made me increasingly restless and resentful. The final straw came in English class. Our teacher had passed out a student essay that he said made his mouth water every time he read it. It was putatively about food, but to me its sophomoric double entendre was obvious: warm, glistening buns; sweet, popping cherries; oozing this, spurting that, and so on. When I pointed this out and wouldn't back down, I was permanently expelled from the class. The teacher would brook no alternative reading—apparently due to a singular affection for baked goods.

After that, I spent my time brooding or arguing with the school administration when it did things such as trying to bar a student-run film festival from screening *Juliet of the Spirits*. This Fellini work was totally incomprehensible to me at the time, but I felt we had struck a blow for artistic and academic freedom when the administration relented and let the film be shown.

Then, near the end of the year I started to hear talk of what was variously described as a new "school without walls," a "school within a school," an "alternative school," a "self-directed learning program," being proposed by a committee of New Trier faculty and students. It sounded revolutionary and it turned out to be so. At the time, I thought there was no way I'd ever get to participate in it. For one thing, I didn't think it had a chance of being approved. For another thing, I thought that even if it were somehow given a green light it would take a couple years to establish and then comprise only a small group

45

of honor students. As it turned out, I was a member of the first Center for Self-Directed Learning class. In fact, I became deeply involved in one of the Center's most celebrated small group projects, namely, the successful effort to have the Illinois School Code changed to recognize and explicitly permit alternative educational programs like the Center. The law is still on the books today.

It almost didn't happen because I almost didn't get into the Center. Students were chosen by lottery for 125 places. There were no preconditions for participating in the lottery (except for parent permission) that I remember. My name was *not* chosen and I felt like I was being unfairly excluded from educational heaven. When I approached Jim Bellanca to express my crushing disappointment and to plead my case he—never one to waste a teaching moment—said, "Well, that's just the way it goes sometimes." I thought that was a little cold quite frankly.

Fortunately, this was not the last word. In response to the persistent nagging from the students who didn't make it, the fact that the number of students who applied but didn't get in was not that large, and an anomalous situation wherein the selected student body was disproportionately female, the Superintendent proposed that the Board of Education take up the issue of expanding the Center at its next meeting. The room was packed and I sat right up front. The Board quickly decided that the best thing would be to let everyone in who had applied, thereby increasing the Center from 125 to over 150 students. This new number included me, of course, and apparently I let my feelings show because right after the vote the Superintendent said to the crowd, "It appears we have a very relieved Student Council President tonight." And I was relieved. At that point, the prospect of spending another year in the regular school was just too dismal to contemplate.

The Center's population was diverse and the cross-pollination of ideas and perspectives that was an intrinsic part of the Center experience was fantastic. I think one of our students that year went on to become a Rhodes Scholar. The Vice-President of Student Council, who was both a top student academically and a top athlete, joined the Center, as did the President of Tri-Ship, New Trier's boys club. There were musicians, visual artists, writers, and dancers along with students interested in science and math. Some students were delightfully eccentric, some were proudly nerdy, a couple were jocks, and some were early 1970s lost souls, which the Center did a better job of helping along than the regular school could possibly have done.

Being Student Council President first semester of my Center year kept me exposed to a broad range of New Trier's faculty, some of whom were more than a little hostile to the whole "learn in your own way" concept. This unpleasant slice of the faculty was quick to say how happy they were that so many "troublemakers" (their word for nonconformists) were gone from the regular school, but at the same time did not tire of pointing out that the whole experiment would soon collapse because it did not comply with state law. They were right about the law thing.

It wasn't that the Center excused students from meeting the state requirements, at least not during its first year. It was just that the Center did not chop up the school day into formal classes of 40-minute periods. Center students working with their teacher advisors came up with all sorts of creative ways to study the required subjects, but that did not impress those who just kept repeating, "That's not how the law says you have to do it." A number of us were worried about this and had no doubt that someone who was unfriendly to the idea of doing anything differently from the way it had been done for 50 years was going to file some sort of complaint.

A group of us got together to discuss the graduation requirements issue. We couldn't believe how rigid the state requirements were and we began to wonder whether other states' laws were the same. We were interested in learning how other experimental schools in both Illinois and in other parts of the country were dealing with these potentially fatal impediments to the existence of more flexible and creative educational approaches.

We formed a class with Arline Paul as our sponsor and teacher. The research we did, in a relatively short time, was impressive. We wrote to state departments of education and alternative school programs, collected education requirement statutes, got copies of articles about the self-directed learning philosophy, and started to develop a case for adopting more flexibility in state educational mandates. We kept all of our research in a beat-up metal box that I carried around as if it were a briefcase. The group would review the correspondence we drafted, talk about the responses we received, and write up summaries about what we were learning. None of us knew how to write a sophisticated formal letter before becoming involved in the project, but we wrote many of them as part of it.

One of the most interesting things we did was visit alternative programs at other schools, public and private. Oak Park had a school-within-a-school, which had many similarities to the Center. When we went there and referred to New Trier as the "parent school" the director was aghast. He emphasized how important it was for students and faculty in the alternative program to maintain negative feelings about the larger institution. I certainly had little affection for the regular school, but even at the time, it seemed to me that there were more positive ways to maintain solidarity among the Center community.

In the city, some alternative schools had been opened up in storefronts. It was a different world from the suburbs. One of these urban schools without walls, Metro, particularly stands out in my mind. The students and teacher-facilitators at Metro didn't seem to worry about state requirements at all, probably because they didn't think they were being scrutinized by anyone wishing them ill. When we walked into the business offices they were using for their headquarters, there were students in the halls playing instruments, reading, holding discussion groups. They said the city was their classroom and apparently spent a lot of time at Chicago's museums. The person "running" the program (he would have eschewed the characterization) told us that if not for Metro many, if not most, of the students would have been dropouts.

These city alternative schools had programs that were even more free form than the Center. They may not have worried about the state requirements, but we became worried for them. By then, we had a pretty large file about alternative approaches to education that simply could not be squared with the then existing law. The more we thought about it the more we realized that the only way to protect experimental programs throughout the state was to do something about the existing statute. But what and how?

That was when Mrs. Paul suggested that we talk to Julia Katz, a Center student whose father was State Representative Harold Katz. Arline's major role is what made everything possible. Of course, she advised us and helped us strategize. But her teaching genius lay in her ability to stimulate us into figuring out what logical steps to take without just coming out and telling us what we should do next.

It also helped that she had strong political connections. She knew Rep. Katz, for example, and along with Julia, facilitated our introduction to him. The first time we traveled to Springfield to meet with Rep. Katz he was wearing a pair of brown pull-on rubber rain boots and a navy blue suit. He was eating his lunch out of a brown paper bag. He didn't strike me as a typical politician, which I now fully understand is a good thing, but at the time made me wonder if he would be able to haul the mail. He was so courtly and soft-spoken I thought he'd just get bulldozed. After all, the only reason it was even possible for him to be a Democrat state representative from the Republican North Shore was because in those days, every district elected three representatives and only two could be from the same party. Several months later, we came to learn just how effective a legislator this unassuming gentleman was.

Mrs. Paul also knew Dr. Michael Bakalis, the State Superintendent of Public Instruction. When we first heard about the position, the group wondered why there even was such a thing since local school boards ran public schools. We made some jokes about unnecessary Illinois government jobs, but Mrs. Paul set up a meeting with him and he turned out to be extremely dynamic and articulate. Best of all, he supported our plan to work on legislation to change the Illinois School Code. A few years later, he was the unsuccessful Democratic candidate for Illinois governor.

Last but not least, Arline personally knew Governor Dan Walker and his wife. She had helped Walker revive the Democratic Party in Lake County and she, along with her husband Stanley, had worked closely with him during the Kennedy campaign in 1960.

On that first trip to Springfield Arline arranged for us to meet with the governor. In response to our very direct inquiry he told us that if our eventual bill passed he would be inclined to sign it, but said that he never made a commitment to sign a piece of legislation until he could see it in its final adopted form. Somehow, Arline also persuaded Mrs. Walker to give the group a private guided tour of the Governor's Mansion.

Governor Walker never saw the original legislative language we drafted. The proposed legislation we showed Rep. Katz was a long, ringing, teen-pompous declaration of the universal right of students to cast off the shackles of oppression and learn pretty much what they wanted to when they wanted to however they wanted to…if they wanted to. I'm sure Arline knew we weren't going anywhere with this manifesto, but she didn't want to quash our creativity. When Representative Katz finished reading he looked up at us, gave us a warm, indulgent smile, and said, "That dog won't hunt" or something to that effect (he was originally from the South).

He was much more impressed with the report we wrote in support of the proposed legislation. Mrs. Paul helped us with the language so it was a little more toned down. The document reviewed what some of the other states were doing, quoted educational experts, and argued that a one-size-fits-all approach to high school education was contrary to traditional American, consumer choice, free-market principles. We didn't want to sound radical.

The report went through many revisions and because so many people contributed the document had to be edited repeatedly to ensure consistent style. We had to iron out disagreements among ourselves about what needed to be included and what could be omitted. Mrs. Wirple, Rep. Katz's legislative assistant and mother of a Center student, checked some of our facts for us.

We showed our document to a number of people before distributing it more widely. It was then I learned the importance of having someone who is not too close to a project review a draft. I have continued to follow this practice throughout my career with motions, briefs, and even letters. We had a sentence that said something like, "the time for a monolithic approach to public education has come." Of course, that was the exact opposite of what we meant, but nobody picked up on it until Center facilitator and English teacher Bill Gregory read it and said, "that sentence flows very well from the language before it, which is probably why you didn't catch this, but what I think you really mean is that the time for a monolithic approach to public education *is past.*" Good catch. We made the revision.

Mrs. Paul guided us, explaining that to be effective a document like ours had to be interesting and balanced. The interesting part we understood, but the balanced part was a little harder to accomplish. We were, after all, impassioned advocates driven by the knowledge that unless the law was changed the future of self-directed learning programs like the Center was tenuous. We struggled with the concept and eventually saw the strategic benefit in conceding a few non-critical points and the value of anticipating and addressing opposing arguments by acknowledging them in our discussion.

In order to create a complete package we enlisted a Center artist to design our cover. Using arrows, straight lines, and dots he created a graphic representing the expansion of educational thought beyond traditional boundaries. It was quite common during that first year in the Center to seek the talents of Center students not otherwise involved in a project to help with a particular aspect of it.

We took another trip to Springfield, where we watched the Illinois House Education Committee discuss the bill Rep. Katz had introduced. The bill's language was low key, technical, and brief, but its effect would be to give local school districts the ability to establish alternative and experimental programs free of the otherwise rigid and detailed state requirements.

We had to give on one point. Perhaps the most conservative member of the Illinois House at the time, Weber Borchers, was on the Education Committee. He was very nice to us and I think was actually quite taken with the fact that we had become so involved with the legislative process. "You can have this law as far as I'm concerned," he said, "but you have to agree with me on one thing." He was adamant that the U.S. History requirements remain inviolable. We were fairly certain that without his support the bill wouldn't go anywhere so, putting into practice Mrs. Paul's lessons about practical political compromise, we agreed to preserve the state's U.S. History requirement. For me personally, the fact that we had already beaten back the gym teachers' objections to making gym waivable made keeping the U.S. History requirement much easier to swallow.

On that same trip the group visited the House gallery. We saw then Majority Leader Henry Hyde strutting around at the back of the chamber like he owned the place, a gargantuan unlit cigar sticking out of his face. He went on to be the Republican point man in the U.S. House for the impeachment of Bill Clinton.

The vital role Harold Katz played in this practical education as to how America works was an example of one of the Center's most valuable aspects, namely, the willingness of motivated parents to serve as educational resources. Another example that I took advantage of was the Mandarin Chinese class taught by another of our student's mothers.

But I think every former Center student would agree that it was the faculty's dedication that made it possible for the students to get the most out of their Center educations. There were students and teachers in the regular school who thought teachers in the Center didn't have to do much. Nothing could be further from the truth. Rather than sleepwalking through 15-year old (or older) lesson plans, Center teachers had to adapt constantly and learn new things themselves in order to guide us toward the learning goals we had set for ourselves. Truly, each of us received a customized education.

Arline Paul was the perfect facilitator for our legislative project that year. She had extensive political connections, was a history teacher who was intimately familiar with the practical workings of government, and she knew how to write compelling advocacy pieces. It was apparent that her time at Wellesley, where she earned her undergraduate degree, and at the University of Chicago, where she earned a Master's Degree, had served her well.

In addition to all that, Mrs. Paul's enthusiasm for life-long learning was infectious. I'll never forget the gourmet dinner group she sponsored and the great conversations she stimulated about dozens of subjects during our get-togethers. I feel completely confident in saying that none of my contemporaries in the regular school had an educational experience as rich and as lasting as the one I had in the Center.

Governor Walker did eventually sign our education bill after it passed both houses of the Legislature and we were there to see him do it. Forty years later, the legislation still resides in the Illinois Compiled Statutes as the last paragraph of 105 ILCS 5/10-19.

There certainly doesn't seem to be the thirst for more fulfilling ways to educate and to be educated that there was when I was in the Center. I'm sure that there will be someday though. That's why I think of our little statute as the once and future law. It protected self-directed learning programs decades ago, and it will be there to do the same thing when the need arises again.

Mike earned College of the Atlantic's (Bar Harbor, Maine) only degree, a Bachelor of Arts in Human Ecology. He returned to Chicago, earned a law degree and practices in the Intellectual Property field. He is President of Interstitial Systems, Inc., which manufactures a multi-level, raised floor electro-mechanical distribution system for use in data centers and similar environments.

Short Takes

It was a fun, empowering, crazy time and I thank Arline for believing in us. I left early as an exchange student in Japan and now I'm an internist and infectious disease specialist.

~Joel Katz, 1976

WHAT'S A YEAR WORTH?

JIM MCKAY, 1973

After a truly disastrous junior year, in which I got straight Ds in the second semester, I entered the Center for Self-Directed Learning. My mother was all too happy for me to try another way. As a senior, I had essentially lost all interest in academic work, and just wanted to play guitar. My distant memories of my year in the Center largely included playing electric guitar in a band called "Bogus Thunder." I did study classical guitar pretty seriously that year and I stayed in school. Recently, my mother gave me copies of the two syntheses I did with my advisor Bill Gregory at the end of each semester. I had no idea they still existed. In addition to a lot of guitar playing, I also appear to have taken a bunch of psychology courses in the Center, and at least one music course in the parent school. The psychology courses did not seem to have impressed me much ("most of it seems like stuff that high school students could have figured out" I had written in my evaluation). I'm afraid that I did not always use my time in the Center very productively; there was quite a bit of alcohol and drug use too, that year. I also made no preparations to attend college, instead deciding to continue playing guitar in rock bands.

After leaving New Trier, I did play in Chicago-area rock and blues bands for five years and continued to study classical guitar. I ended up managing a local business, Gary Gand Music, which sold electric guitars, amps, keyboards, and PA systems. By the time I was 23, however, I had pretty much had it with the rock and roll business; too much alcohol and drug use, too many gigs in lousy bars with bands that weren't going anywhere. I started taking courses at a community college. After a year of that, I quit my job at Gand Music and began college full time at Loyola University, where I majored in psychology and minored in philosophy.

After finishing up at Loyola in 1983, I entered a Ph.D. program in psychology at Harvard University, which was followed by post-doctoral training in addiction treatment research. I joined the faculty at the University of Pennsylvania in 1990, and have been there ever since.

At Penn, I direct a center on addiction treatment research, as well as a second center at the Philadelphia VA Hospital that focuses on the development of addiction treatment policy in the VA and training for VA clinicians in new treatment approaches. Much of my time is spent writing research articles and grants, and developing new interventions to help people achieve more durable, long-term recoveries from addiction.

What about the music? I sold my electric guitars before going to graduate school, and only kept my classical guitar, which I continued to play pretty seriously. One of my high points of graduate school was making a recording of all the classical guitar concert pieces I knew at that point. My recording studio was one of the bathrooms of the Psychology building at Harvard. I had to wait until the middle of the night to make the recording, so no one would interrupt me by walking into the bathroom or flushing a toilet on the floors above or below where I was set up. The great acoustics in the bathroom (all tile, terrific reverb effect!) made my effort worthwhile. Over the years, I've continued to play classical guitar, without thinking much about the electric stuff. However, about two years ago, I suddenly became very interested in electric guitar again, and got back into it in a big way.

Now, I'm playing in a band with a couple of other guys in their 50s, and just loving it. It's been a great pleasure—and relief—to find so many people my age who still want to crank up the amps and play. I probably play some sort of gig, concert, or open blues jam a couple of times a week these days. My kids thought this was all pretty weird at first, but they now seem amused by having a dad who is in a band.

I'm also playing classical guitar regularly at the U Penn medical center hospital as part of a program organized by our local progressive rock radio station to provide live music for the sick. After getting back into playing the electric guitar, I had a kind of midlife crisis, prompted by the clear realization that I was much more excited about playing music than I was about my addiction work. Fortunately, I have somewhat better judgment now than I did 37 years ago, so I didn't quit my day job. I know I have to pay the bills, and, unlike when I was 17, I hadn't completely lost interest in the academic stuff. I'm back to a more balanced place at this point, which all-in-all feels pretty good.

So what is the moral of the story? What does my story have to do with my experiences in the Center? With the "documentation" supplied by my own long forgotten semester syntheses, it is now clear that my Center experience consisted of equal parts guitar playing, psychology, and alcohol and drug use! Somewhat amazingly, the latter two turned out to be instrumental in my choice of graduate studies and a career—although the progression was anything but linear and smooth. And, electric guitar has reemerged as a great passion and is a very big and rewarding part of my life these days. So, it seems that all the stuff I did during my Center year has ended up profoundly influencing the directions my life has taken. It may have seemed like insanity at the time, but something positive was clearly going on.

Moreover, at least in my case, the value of that year in the Center was not immediately clear. In fact, it would have been easy to conclude when I was in my early twenties that it had been a wasted year—or worse. I'm sure now that the combination of the experiences I had that year were educational and ultimately life transforming. For that, I'm very grateful.

Jim is a Professor at the University of Pennsylvania. With funding from the NIH and the Department of Veterans Affairs, he conducts research and writes about treatments for addiction. He is playing a lot of guitar these days, and greatly enjoying it.

Short Takes

Most schools teach you how to learn by study. I went to a school where we studied how to learn by teaching.

~David Humphrey, 1976

The Risk Factor

Mimi Diaz, 1974

In my junior year, I took a big risk. I joined the Center and I plunged right in. During my first self-planned internship, I worked at a school for the developmentally disabled. I was asked to start a young boy who was thought to be "autistic" on a toilet training program. I remember spending lots of time with him in the bathroom, giving him M&Ms to modify his behavior. It was an amazing experience that inspired me to become a public school teacher and administrator.

Today, I am a lead partner in the Green School in Denver, implementing my research on green schools and renewable energy along with a best practice 21st Century learning model. I may seem a far distance from the Center in Winnetka, Illinois, but in spirit, I am very close.

It's always been a matter of risk. During my internship, I was presented immediately with awesome responsibilities. No sitting in a desk listening to someone tell me about teaching difficult students; no reading about autism in a book. It was the direct experience for me.

As a high school student, I developed strong relationships with the staff in my internship. They guided me. They were my mentors. They even nominated me as volunteer of the year for the City of Chicago in my senior year, affirming that I got the most out of my experience there. Not only did I learn to toilet train students, but I also learned to collect data on student behavior, to develop relationships with the students' families and take daily risks.

To link my internship to my Center goals, I developed a photography journal with a photo essay for my self-evaluation. I took a photography class to improve the quality of the photo essay. It turned out to be incredibly powerful in terms of what I was asked to demonstrate about my learning there and led me to my path of becoming a special educator, a teacher leader, a public school principal and eventually a partner in the creation of a very Center-like charter school; the Denver Green School.

After my Center graduation, my next step was to get an undergraduate degree in what was then called "education for the lower functioning students." I selected that program of studies with the confidence of knowing this was exactly what I wanted to do. My passion had been fostered by the staff who mentored me during my internship, giving me supportive feedback. I knew from the feedback I had received that I was really good at working with youngsters at the low functioning end of the spectrum. The responsibilities, the feedback, and the hands-on experience all had set me up for success in my early college years in an extremely difficult field.

Later, I earned a Master's degree in literacy and elementary education so I could teach in the regular classroom as well. Besides influencing my special education career choice, the Center helped me develop self-leadership skills. In those two years in the Center, I had to find my way in numerous uncharted territories. Where did I want to go in the Center? What did I want to pursue? How was I going to get there and how would I know what I was doing was worthwhile? How would I challenge myself so my learning would have value for me?

The Center forced me to tackle these questions over and over. Once I was in the internship, I was faced with a lot of responsibility. I had to step up to do things that I wasn't necessarily asked to do or knew exactly how to do, but knew that they were my responsibility. My self-direction, my self-leadership skills, as it were, led to the development of my "other" leadership skills. As a teacher, I have always been on the leadership teams of my schools, been outspoken about my beliefs, and not afraid to say what I thought. My values and beliefs were built around kids, how they learn, and how we differentiate.

In the Center, we all spent considerable time talking about our work and our learning as well as how to do things together as a group, a team. So, I always felt obliged to express my beliefs and values and if it appeared that I could not, then I needed to change that. Rather than sit back and teach in my classroom knowing that this or that way of helping kids was not working, I needed to participate in and help informed change make the situation better. Most teachers never have the opportunity to step out of their role. I did and I learned how to use those skills.

I have taught in only two schools in the Denver system. In the first school where I taught for ten years, I worked with two fabulous principals. In the second school, I also worked with one who almost ruined the school. Disturbed by the vacuum this principal had made with her laissez faire approach, I took the lead. I made the point that after one semester, it's obvious this is not the direction we need to go in. I gathered together a group of teachers and parents. We ended up taking control of the school and making changes that needed to be made so that the kids were getting the education they deserved. This experience created a "wow" moment for me. If this person can lead a school so ineptly just by having a certificate, then I wanted to become a formal leader and have a bigger, more positive impact. I realized I had spent seven years as a Special Education teacher with severely and profoundly limited students. I was helping to integrate them into regular classrooms based on their individual needs. I also realized that I had spent those years teaching with teachers and coaching teachers how to integrate students. I knew the power and importance of collaboration. I decided that I would get my Master's Degree in Literacy, teach in the regular classroom so I could be on the opposite end of the spectrum, and be a model for teachers the other way around. I would actually be able to "walk the talk" instead of asking teachers to do what I had never done myself. I became a regular education teacher and then spent the rest of my teaching career integrating special education students into my second grade and kindergarten classrooms.

All went well until I went to another school, only to find an extremely poor leader with a staff that was an amazing learning community despite the principal. It was a very high-needs inner city school that was tanking because we had a super ineffective leader and no one dared step up and take the bull by the horns. I had heard from colleagues about ineffective leaders in their schools. Now, I was in one of those schools. The pattern, well-documented in the research, but seldom acted on by school districts, was clear. The jargon is "*not* an instructional leader." What that means to someone who came from a school that had strong instructional leadership was that the principal didn't know what should be happening in the classroom because she or he had been an ineffectual teacher, had very limited teaching experience or never taught at all.

Without strong knowledge and direct experience about what makes good teaching, something research is very clear about, such leaders don't recognize what is or is not happening in a classroom. Not being able to support and guide teachers, these ineffective principals develop divisive cultures. They select favorite people to collaborate with, excluding all others. They don't build a trusting, cohesive culture, nor have the ability to create a learning community that is collaborative and based on mutual trust. Without that collaboration, everyone gets left to do their own thing without a shared goal for improvement.

In this environment, I knew I couldn't have the maximum effect if I didn't get my principal's license. As soon as my last child finished high school, I decided it was time. In a remarkable confluence of events, the Public Schools created a leadership program in conjunction with Denver University called the Richie School for Leaders. That was an amazing opportunity to get a principal's license within this cohort that was very similar to the Center's community groups. The Richie School had four instructors, it was project based, and lasted a year. We developed a portfolio and interned at a school while we worked at full time jobs. Sometimes, I felt I was back in Evanston with my mentors. The internship required 8 to 12 hours a week at a school so I left classroom teaching and took a job as a Special Education specialist in a district where I was coaching teachers and principals at 15 schools about special education issues. I was on a team with a literacy specialist, an assessment specialist, and a variety of other specialists who worked together to help support change in these schools.

It turned out that one of my future Denver Green colleagues on that team, Andrew, was also in the Richie program.

We had often talked about education and change a year before the Denver Public Schools introduced another "confluent change" for broader school reform through the "Beacon Schools." Any current Denver school could apply and submit a design, laying out how they would tweak their school to be innovative. I was asked to be on the taskforce that reviewed the applications and selected the ones that would become "Beacon Schools." As I looked at all the proposals that came in I said, "None of these are innovative. This is all tweaking, like adding an after-school activity or changing the calendar. There is not a single paradigm transformation in the lot." I couldn't vote for any of them. It provoked me because I was really interested in creating a completely different school.

Then another remarkable event occurred. Colorado passed the "Innovations School Act" that allowed for schools, either existing or new schools, to apply for innovation status. The State could waive a lot of board policies and state statutes that dealt with everything from curriculum and instruction to assessment, school year, school calendar—pretty much everything. Andrew and I decided that if we were to try to create an innovative school we would spend the year researching and thinking about our mission, our vision, and our model. We decided that since not only the governor and mayor, but also the whole world seemed to be moving into the "Green Movement," we would start with that.

However, for us that was not enough. It had to be about sustainability, changing how we live in our society in order to sustain what we want to have in our lives. We began to research all over the world, searching specifically for green schools. We found that Australia had implemented a statewide policy of environmental education as part of a sustainability curriculum for all schools. We continued our research and continued to define what we wanted kids to know and to do, ending with a whole child assessment as opposed to just a drive toward piecemeal outcomes in a summative assessment.

We then developed our mission and vision that were really about sustainability and created values like community, equity, stewardship, and all those things that we valued in terms of the whole child. That summer, Andrew died. He was just 33. He died suddenly. I was stunned and for months I kept wondering how I could move forward with this, how I could find some other people who shared my vision, how I could fill the giant gap his absence made.

Out of the blue came another man that Andrew and I had collaborated with and who had taught in the district. He contacted me and said "Mimi, believe it or not, there is a group of guys in this middle school who've been talking about the same ideas as you and I think you all ought to meet." We did meet and it was just amazing that we really did share the same vision and mission. We committed to working together and nine of us, working collaboratively, created a 132-page "Request for Proposal" that was presented to the school board and the Colorado Board of Education for approval. That experience of working together created a bond and defined us as a group. We were accountable, not just to ourselves, but also to each other to drive the mission, vision, and values of this entity that we were building. Like the community in the Center, we had a commitment to drive the model of the program as individuals, but also as a group.

This partnership model worked so well in the development phase that we decided to keep it going in the school for administration and for the students.

The leadership of our school is a partnership of three lead partners with no one having a final veto. Seven of the founders are partners. Two of us have administrative licenses so we handle the tasks that are required in a public school system, all in collaboration. We teach, as well, and lead in our areas of expertise. We opened this first year with 215 pre-school, kindergarten, first grade, second grade, and sixth grade students because we wanted to grow the culture from the elementary and the middle school.

We will fill in each year as we go along, adding a fourth grade and a seventh grade first. We have a diverse population of students who speak fourteen different languages. Approximately 56% receive free or reduced cost lunches. We are a neighborhood school so we serve the neighborhood students first, after which we take in "choice" students if there is room. This past year was our first year. Our student leadership model has been focused on the sixth grade taking part in decision-making. Kids have been researching the food service program, speaking with the food service administration of the Denver Public Schools and doing surveys of what kids eat. They are trying to get recipes from the district to see how healthy they are and how they might participate in building healthy menus. The sixth graders also helped develop this school year's energy plan for our building to determine how we can green up the building. There were probably other issues they participated in. They will also have a say in what the dress code looks like.

Last year we focused on curriculum. One of the reasons we wanted to be an innovative school was because the traditional textbook curriculum is not viable, despite the progress the district leaders thought they were making. We chose to purchase a literacy curriculum and a math curriculum that was different from the District's. In our urban district, we had relied on a traditional scope and sequence as the curriculum's foundation. It left huge gaps because teachers didn't understand that a systematic approach for teaching skills and knowledge around reading, writing, and math was necessary. The standard curriculum also did not help with our sustainability missions.

We are working with the Cloud Institute for Education in New York to develop our sustainability standards. Those education-for-sustainability standards are our aspiration. They encompass a variety of topics around sustainability that include environmental as well as economic and social sustainability. We also have common core standards. The teachers are creating units that are interdisciplinary and meet one of the standards for education for sustainability, inventing and affecting the future. We look at the Colorado State Standards and see which could be integrated into social studies or science. Now students can integrate non-fiction writing skills as well as reading books at their grade level that fit the topic. Maybe math fits in now, maybe not. We try to include a service-learning component in each unit so kids can impact our community. We created three or four units this year and will develop more, as more teachers understand the Backward Lesson Design template that we use to design our units.

Some came in understanding that and took off while some took longer. The consulting model we have with Jamie Cloud (Cloud Institute) is that she has contact with our teachers and grade level teams, every month, either here or on Skype, so they know every month they can tweak their units. Our aspiration is to continue to create more interdisciplinary learning. For our second year, we plan to focus on summative, formative, and developmental assessments. I've spent considerable amount of time this summer designing our professional development in order to use performance criteria for the project-based learning.

We are also planning to implement a data management system for these assessments after we use Google Docs to collect the data. We will also have what we call Instructional Conversation Cycles, a form of professional development. For example, one week we will do data analysis, and another, peer coaching, where a team of teachers will observe each other and provide feedback on specific goals and strategies. We are planning a Knowledge and Development week when we will look at school data to look for gaps that we can focus on.

As I look back at these 20 years of teaching and leading, I am astounded at the constant presence of the Center in my career and in my life. All that I have done in my life, as a teacher, has been influenced by my experiences in the Center. I took big risks in the Center, as we all did, by simply enrolling and then doing what we believed we should be experiencing in school. Step by step as opportunities have arisen, I have chosen to take the risks and the advantages that present themselves.

While shaping me as a risk taker, the Center also shaped me as an innovator and leader. All these things I took into my 20 years of teaching, trying, within the parameters of the schools I was in, to follow the project-based and self-directed model that I practiced in the Center. As I look at the structures such as portfolios, projects, internships, study groups and the collaborative models of schooling that I experienced in the Center, I see their offspring falling into place in the Green School. I realize that it is not the structures themselves, but the value system that underlies what is built on top and has us thinking in a different way, in creating a different paradigm of schooling that aligns with the Center's paradigm or risk-taking. I've challenged myself and pushed myself into new ventures, a risk-taking approach was derived from my experience of creating my own curriculum in the Center, pushing myself forward, listening to my mentors and colleagues and then holding myself accountable for the outcomes.

In the Center, I found my passion and received the encouragement to follow that passion, setting me on this journey as part of my career and who I am as a person. I believe it is essential that kids have opportunities to learn their passions and meld knowledge and skills into real-world application. That thought is always at the center of my motivation.

After 20 years as an elementary and special needs teacher, Mimi became the founder and Lead Partner in the Denver Green School, an innovative public school molded after the Center. Today, she continues in these roles as Denver Green expands.

Short Takes

Three out of four of my children went to a high school program like ours. Part of the Center is the togetherness and synergy, like the way a spark lights a crackling fire of laughter. Teen years are a tapestry, and the Center helped weave my life into a magic carpet.

~Julie Doyle James, 1977

Finding the Work of the Soul

Sylvia Fuerstenberg, 1974

When I graduated from the Center, I received the "unseasoned peripatetic traveler's award." I was restless then. Since then, I have traveled in 49 states, backpacked most of our major mountain ranges, and gone around the world. It took traveling on many roads to find the work that seasons my soul and calms my restless spirits. I elected the Center because I was bored, bored, bored. I was bored with the traditional high school. I was forever restless. I just couldn't sit in a classroom anymore and do traditional listening as learning. It was time to move on.

My mom was extremely supportive. She was a director of Head Start when Head Start was a new idea. Her philosophy about education was that people will learn if you give them an environment that invites them to learn and give them resources with which to do that. She was gung ho about the Center, I think probably more than I was. She knew me well. In the Center, I favored internships.

My first were at Greeley Elementary School and the Oak School for children with emotional difficulties. At Greeley, I often played the guitar for kindergartners, being a mother duck with my small ducklings following me around or sitting for a sing-along. Between my internships, I sought out other ways to learn. One of the opportunities we had allowed us to figure out how to organize our learning. I took this open door as a chance to design some creative ways to meet state graduation requirements. To meet one requirement, I joined a government learning group that would satisfy the Illinois Constitution requirement. We researched state requirements for graduation and attendance, traveling to Springfield, Illinois's state capitol, observing the state legislature in session, meeting with a number of our local legislators and inviting one to help us work through the law changing process.

From the start, I knew I loved lobbying. I came to know my legislators personally. It was an "aha" moment for me to realize the relationship between legislation and my life, my education, to understand how laws are written and who writes them. Learning about all that firsthand in high school was amazing. I could drive down to the state capital and talk to people who write laws! I remember thinking "Wow! This is really cool!" I have passed that love onto my kids. Both of my children worked at the legislature as legislative pages during high school and they too knew their representatives personally.

We had some lively discussion groups. We read and discussed our picks such as Carlos Castaneda, Kafka, and Sartre. Even as we argued and debated in a seminar fashion, we developed our own criteria for great literature. It was these wonderful teacher-facilitated conversations replacing teacher-dominated class time that rekindled my love of reading.

By the time January 1974 rolled around I was done and needed to go. The more I followed my instincts into new internships and study groups, the more interests I had that I couldn't get to. I was restless again. Miss Niebauer was the faculty member on my support group/graduation committee. She asked me lots of questions before she was able to say "Yeah, you should go. You need to move on and pursue all these interests now." That was pretty phenomenal. I don't know anything about the story of the beginning of the Center, but I know the faculty was visionary. Each shared patience and love with students every single day as they put up with our immaturity, our flailing about, our jumping from subject to subject, our learning things that were really difficult for young people to learn…confidence and self-expression, how to evaluate ourselves, and deciding what we wanted to do. I did move on and the kernels of interests that appeared to me in the Center are the things that have moved forward with me.

When I left the Center, I went to California with my mother who sensed I was restless again, but also noticed I did a Gestalt class in the Center. She said, "Let's go to the Esalen Institute for a Gestalt workshop." After that, I hitchhiked to New Mexico and backpacked in the mountains. I had backpacked in Wyoming the summer before my high school senior year and fell passionately in love with the mountains and the environment. I wanted to spend as much time as I could outdoors, backpacking. I found that I could do that studying environmental education at Prescott College, a small desert college in Arizona.

At Prescott, all new students and new faculty spent the first month backpacking in the wilderness for a long time without coming out. One gets to know people well under those circumstances. At the end of that course the instructor recommended that I apply to work as an intern from Prescott at an intervention program for delinquents set up by Willie Ensoeld from The Evergreen State College.

"Operation Breakout," was run by the Christian Brothers in Southern Missouri, functioning out of a Christian Brothers Retreat Center. Less than a year after graduating from high school I was an instructor working with delinquent teens from the inner city who were about a year or two younger than me. The other instructors were only two or three years older and we enthusiastically took kids rock climbing, canoeing, and backpacking. We were also doing transactional analysis workshops under the tutelage of one of the older Christian Brothers who was trained in that discipline.

It was phenomenal that I had such an opportunity so early in my life. Without the Center experience that was so freeing, I don't think I would have had the guts to go to Prescott, nor would I have worked at Operation Breakout. I am not surprised when I look at my syntheses to see the seeds of life-long interests that I have pursued as my way of life to this day. The kernel of who I am is there. I can read and hear my voice in what I wrote. What strikes me clearly in the face is how incredibly young I was and how new the exercise of learning to evaluate myself and assess my learning was. The gentle suggestions from the teachers are similar: Do things more in depth, comment more in depth, evaluate more specifically. I wanted to explore so many areas because it was about a sense of discovery for me at that point. It was a matter of discovering my interests, trying things out and figuring out how I learn. Each semester my synthesis became more specific, a bit more in depth as I track the path of self-discovery through those three semesters.

After working in the field for fifteen years, I decided to go to graduate school. I picked Hunter College in New York, where I was living and working at the time. A different kind of wilderness adventure! I entered into a program called the one-year residency in social work for 100 students with prior field experience. They reduced our field placement to one year because we were all professionals. We had to be self-directed in order to work full time in the field while going to graduate school. I had learned to organize myself by then, to focus, and get things done.

The program required intensive self-reflection and self-evaluation so it wasn't the regular social work program, but perfectly suited to my experience. I still had to take tests and be graded for the first time since sophomore year in high school and I faced the fear of testing. But I prevailed and I am still a self-directed learner. If I want to learn something, I get a book or I find someone who can teach me and occasionally I take a class. I am in charge of what and how I learn. When I look back to my Center days, I realize that there were so many different kinds of students, some dismal failures, some bored by traditional classrooms, some extremely bright and some with a clear focus on a specific pursuit. When I hear of all we have done in the ensuing years and the ways in which we have pursued our lives, I realize the positive impact of learning self-direction through self-assessment.

Being the restless person that I was, becoming a self-directed learner was not easy. Some think "just doing your thing" is self-direction. I don't. I put more weight on learning how to take control of the many interests, to set goals, to regulate choices and then to look back and assess what I did so I can learn from it. Otherwise, I think, restless activity stays just that without a guarantee that any learning ensues.

As I've looked back at my Center experience I am struck by the way I picked up the threads of those learning experiences in high school, carried them all the way through my life and am still carrying them. The interest in government, in people and human interaction, in music and the Gestalt workshop, children with disabilities or behavioral issues—these all grew in personal and professional importance throughout my life because I learned to assess and regulate what I was choosing to do.

Today, I am an executive director of a non-profit. This type of work has allowed me to merge my large number of interests. My position with The Arc of King County allows me to lead, assess, direct, learn, and continue to grow. I will be there until I retire. I am a bit less restless and I think I have hit on the work that feeds my soul.

Sylvia was appointed executive director of The Arc of King County, Washington, in March 2008. Throughout her career, Sylvia has been a champion for students with disabilities She continues her passion for travel, climbing, and the great outdoors.

Short Takes

The Center liberated me from the rigidity of the parent school. I had an instinct that I would really thrive in an unstructured environment, and that instinct was right. Ever since those two wonderful years of freedom in the Center, I have tried to create a life for myself in which I always have the freedom to explore ideas, and to take on new projects, almost all in the art world.

The Center really did help me learn how to learn. I recall many specific experiences that had lasting impact on my approach to pursuing new ideas and making sense of them. I recall studying the Weimar Republic with Mrs. Paul—the first time I ever studied history with enthusiasm and a sense of personal investment; with Mr. Bellanca, learning to research and write a strong essay on the Bauhaus; with Mr. Johnson, learning to follow the trail of footnotes in a book on topology all the way to the John Crerar Library at IIT; with Ms. Niebauer, vastly expanding my understanding of art in our "Art Composition" group; with my classmates, creating our "E-Lit" English literature study group senior year; designing and making the scenery for Man of La Mancha; producing the play I Never Sang for My Father with Prissy Howell, Terry Greenblatt, Phil Seitz, Cynthia Jaffe, Sue Ringel Segal, Lucy Heller, and others whom I momentarily don't recall. And I remember the Center Store above Fell's in Glencoe, painting the mural in Phil Hall (Room 101), practicing calligraphy with Bob Saunders, and the Gestalt Theater workshops.

After college, I began studying to be a rabbi, but I left the program after the first of five years. Then I worked as an assistant to the curator of the Museum of Contemporary Art in Chicago, got an M.F.A. in painting and sculpture, organized drawing and art appreciation classes in an aborted attempt to start my own art school, sold furniture, worked with my brother on some real estate projects, and then, in 1989, started a handmade decorative tile company which, for the past 20 years, has been an unexpectedly gratifying endeavor.

~Ted Lowitz, 1974

Professor Chang, My Dad, and The Peking Duck Dinner

Walter C. (Terry) Greenblatt, 1974

Thirty-five years after graduating from New Trier East's alternative program, I continue to operate in a totally self-structured, self-directed work environment. I think it's fair to say that the Center instilled a lifelong practice of seeking out a self-directed milieu as the most fun, most productive, and best suited to how I like to work, even how I like to live. Perhaps if I describe how my father and my daughter, the generations before and after me, came to view my experience in the Center, my own perspective on it may make more sense.

My Dad's Perspective

For my father, 79, his account of my going into the Center remains perhaps the only "you were right, I was wrong" anecdote in his entire—and extensive— repertoire of stories from my childhood. Now, when he talks about our experience with the Center to my friends or his, he explains how I came to him toward the end of my sophomore year wanting to enroll for my Junior and Senior years of high school in the new "school-without-walls" program that was starting up at New Trier High School.

Dad was then president of the School Board of Winnetka. It is there where the famous dictum of legendary superintendent and educational innovator Carleton Washburn, that "children learn by doing," was still gospel in Winnetka's public schools, and dad believed it. However, when he discovered that the Center program would be ungraded except for "narrative evaluations" co-written by the student and a facilitator/teacher; that participants would

69

have no class rank; and that the curriculum would—except for a few meager state-mandated requirements—be entirely at the discretion of the students, Dad began to worry. He was concerned that Center kids (and more particularly his son) would never be admitted to a "good" college.

While somewhat concerned myself on this score, I continued to insist that I wanted to enroll in the Center. I assured Dad that I would develop a curriculum for myself that covered all the academic bases—literature, history, math, science, and so forth. After attending informational meetings for parents and students conducted by the faculty, he reluctantly gave his permission. His worries crescendoed when I explained that the Center desperately needed to raise money in order to support the many idiosyncratic student projects underway. (including my own) He grew pale when I told him that my contribution to the fund-raising effort would be to organize 14 friends to prepare a Peking Duck and Dim Sum banquet and sell 150 tickets. As he predicted, this project sucked down enormous amounts of my time, displacing more pedestrian academic pursuits like Calculus and French and Russian Literature. I just had no idea how much work it would be to organize the planning, shopping, preparation, and service for the banquet, to say nothing of the selling the tickets. Academic subjects took a backseat for several months and Dad began to feel that his worst fears were justified.

His parental despair became absolute when, after the banquet occurred, a number of the attendees asked me if I would prepare Chinese meals in their homes for guests on a catering basis, and I responded with the birth of "North Shore Oriental Catering." I continued to run it throughout the rest of high school (where it served to fulfill my Illinois state "Consumer Education" requirement) and for four years after I graduated from the Center. During this time the company served to provide me and six or seven friends with summer employment through college).

Imagine my father's shock when, on April 15th of my Senior Year, a handwritten letter came back from the head of admissions at Yale apprising me that "Professor Richard Chang of the engineering department, who was this year's faculty representative on the admissions committee, impressed upon the rest of us what an undertaking it was to prepare Peking Duck and Dim Sum for 150 people and you promptly set a new culinary standard for the applicant pool. Congratulations on your admission to Yale." To this day, Dad shakes his head in wonder that things worked out with my college application, apparently against all odds. Even at the time, I thought Professor Chang realized something pretty basic about how the Center experience would prepare a high school kid for college.

When I got to Yale after the Center, I quickly realized that my experience of the first semester of college was very different than most of my classmates. Most of the other freshman were struggling with all the freedom to structure—or fail to structure—their own work time and play time, whereas I was chafing somewhat under the structure of having a "pre-fabricated" curriculum handed to me by the professors. I felt that I learned many of the most important project management and time management skills in the crucible of working to make my education happen in the Center. I also learned a new respect for my father and his ability to let me take my chances in the Center; now that I'm a parent of college-aged kids myself, I admire him all the more for this.

Since leaving the Center, I've completed degrees at several highly regarded educational institutions: After graduating from Yale College, I went to Oxford University and then Harvard Business School. At Oxford, the education was radically unstructured—each student met once a week with a tutor and one classmate for each of two courses. Other than these two one-hour tutorials and writing the essay to prepare for them, one's time was utterly free—the British kids were struggling to mine their education out of the rich but imposing resources on offer in this milieu, but it was perfectly adapted for a Center alum. My time in the Center eased my way through these programs, where academic success demanded taut time management and an "it's-all-on-me" approach to personal organization.

My Daughter's Perspective

My daughter, age 16, does not suffer high school gladly. When I tell Susannah tales of my years in the Center, her face assumes that far-off, wistful look that I could once conjure when she was a small child by reading charming stories of elves in fairyland. To her, the Center is a Never-Never Land where a mind can soar effortlessly on wings of unforced learning. Susannah, a sophomore now, recognizes that Princeton High School provides her with superb teachers and bright classmates. She's a talented student and she loves learning, but she bridles at how the traditional high school structure thwarts her efforts to delve into areas of academic interest.

There's so much time spent in class and so much time required to complete—even in a minimal way—the assigned homework (to say nothing of the pedagogical time frittered away "teaching to the test") that she cannot go "above and beyond" the assigned work and follow her intellectual heart. She tells me she longs to "learn for learning's sake, not because it's required" but finds this is impossible within the structure of the school. She despises it when anyone—including herself—is working for a grade. Then I tell her that the most important lesson I took from the Center for Self-Directed Learning was an approach to a learning experience rather than a place or institution or even a "program-without-walls." That being so, I shared that a person matriculated into the Center by entering a state of mind, not by enrolling in an alternative school. "It's not some kind of Zen paradox," I explain. Pretty much everything I did could be transformed into an opportunity to learn; each experience could be milked for either a positive or negative learning experience, if I came to it with that frame of mind. The principles, I say, are generalizable. Then she treats me to one of her Olympian eye-rolls.

Like many classmates in the Center, I came into the Center already predisposed to self-directed learning. That's why we were attracted to it in the first place. But after two years in the Center I came to believe that the truth is this: The concepts of a "Positive Learning Experience" and a "Negative Learning Experience" form a ying/yang constellation in which both, of course, are positive at the meta-conceptual level. Certainly, we joked about this and reveled in the absurdity of it, but it was nonetheless the paramount idea to me and my classmates, as Centerites.

When Susannah and I explore further her fantasies of what it would be like to be a Center student, she imagines that it is easier than being in her traditional high school because you are studying things that interest you and *only* things that interest you. Think of the time saved by blowing away all that chaff! But I tell her that if you're in the Center, before you can rid yourself of the chaff, you have to grow your wheat from a seed, including all the tedium of tilling the ground, sowing the wheat and all the many other steps that the Little Red Hen—the most self-directed of fowls—undertook to produce her fabled bread. That means, that even to focus on only what interests you, you have to think through what you want to study, create a curriculum, and find teachers and/or the other resources required to pursue that curriculum. When you're in the middle of this planning, it often seems that you are wasting more time on the process of creating your educational experience than you would if someone did all this stuff for you (the way they do in a traditional school) and just let you focus on learning the material. Instead, you're playing phone tag with someone who's supposed to facilitate your seminar on "my favorite books." Or you're trying to convince fourteen of your best friends (in the days before text messages!) to come work for most of a weekend filling dumplings for a Chinese banquet. So the timesaving aspect of the Center is utterly illusory—you still do grunt work, but it's just lavished on different tasks.

Admittedly there is some comfort in the notion of "a poor task, but mine own," but not really all that much comfort, as I tell Susannah. And I'm promptly treated to another magnificent eye-roll. As I think she understands, however, I really believe it all passionately! I emerged from the intense crush of designing my own curriculum in the Center and then beating the bushes for the resources (teachers, reading materials, lab supplies etc.) needed to pursue it, converted to the belief that the entire process is bona fide learning. Developing the curriculum is more than half of mastering it, as any experienced teacher will attest. It's a corollary of the old saw that "the best way to learn a subject thoroughly is to teach it." And, not surprisingly, developing a curriculum takes a lot more time to do than merely studying that curriculum once it's developed.

MY PERSPECTIVE

For me, the Center was mostly about the projects we each dreamed up and implemented. So what did I do besides plan and cook Chinese banquets? One friend and I conducted a two-year experiment running rats through mazes to see whether they could learn faster with extra ACTH (Adrenocorticotropic *hormone,* a pituitary hormone) than they could without it. We had to build a wooden T-Maze, procure some rats (and all the cages and other rat-care equipment); inveigle a Northwestern professor (our "community resource") to teach us how to hold rats, train rats, inject rats and draw blood from rats; conduct statistical analysis; and write up experimental results. (By the way, rats injected with ACTH acquire appetitive-learning tasks 66% faster than their untreated brethren.)

When I got to Yale I shared our paper with my freshman Psychology professor. She had doubts about our sample size—only about seven rats in each arm of the study, but we went through about fifty rats to get there! Another friend and I collaborated on staging a production of the musical *Man of La Mancha*. To do so, we had to assemble potential cast members (many of the Chinese banquet sous chefs participated); audition them; rehearse them (and piss them off in the process, of course); get a small orchestra together (we originally planned on a seven-piece group but ended up with a piano and a percussionist); design and make costumes; build sets; create lighting (a hand-held slide projector); and get an audience together. Quixotic every way you looked at it.

I researched the civil war by driving each week from Winnetka to the Chicago Historical Society (itself a learning experience for a couple of high school Juniors), reading microfilmed newspapers from the 1860s and writing about the war based on the accounts in the contemporary Chicago newspapers. They say no man is a saint to his valet, and Lincoln wasn't a saint to the Chicago Tribune readers. This was a revelation to a 17-year-old in 1973.

A group of six formed a "French and Russian Literature" class and recruited a long-suffering, well-read mom to be our discussion leader. When some of us opted to make a film of Kafka's "The Trial" as our project, our attendance at class discussions was compromised. Another group of us studied space-time physics without first having studied classical mechanics (probably a mistake, but as long as you learn from it). And that's only a sample of the many great Center projects almost all done in partnership with terrific people from whom I learned a whole lot of important stuff, including how to work in partnerships. We "fulfilled" state education requirements informed by the anti-authoritarian sensibility of the mid-seventies era we inhabited.

My girlfriend and I sincerely attempted to see if the thirty minutes or so we devoted to sexual activity, every day could be counted towards the state requirement for that amount of vigorous physical activity. No dice. I successfully counted the Chicago Historical Society microfiche newspaper reading towards the Illinois U.S. History requirement, but when it came to the SAT-II in that subject, I read the textbook used in the regular high school cover-to-cover over two weeks, which turned out to produce a perfectly respectable score.

The procedural elements of this education were just as peculiar and learning-laden. Just how do you write a narrative evaluation (in lieu of a grade) of a year-long "negative learning experience"? And how do you "co-synthesize" your own narrative with that of your evaluator to present a blended view of the quality and scope of a Center project (and, hopefully, convey the worth of it to colleges)? Moreover, what does the chameleon word "consensus" come to mean when every Center-wide Town Hall could only adopt a resolution by reaching this so-called "consensus?" It turns out, I learned, that a consensus is actually a heterogeneous sausage. Like a sausage, consensus comes from a mishmash of many ingredients. In the process of reaching consensus, the ingredients include enthusiastic embraces of some ideas, grudging accord with others and exhausted capitulation to the rest

This Center objective—forging consensus—was in stark contrast to my experience of the daily (graded) class discussions at Harvard Business School (HBS) during that first boot-camp year. At HBS, eighty, hypercompetitive, would-be masters-of-the-universe seated in the horseshoe-shaped theater vehemently debated their views on case studies, each with the ardent goal of never, ever surrendering his or her original position in the discussion. In any event, the most important lessons of the Center (and perhaps HBS too, come to think of it) were learning to make things happen instead of waiting for them to happen and learning that you could do it.

A coda to the Chinese banquet/Center fund-raiser that engendered North Shore Oriental Catering followed. After I graduated from Harvard Business School, I started up a much more ambitious food service in Manhattan, which I founded and ran for ten years, ultimately employing 130 people, until I sold it to a much larger operator in 1995.

Indeed, that Center fund-raiser eventually cascaded into a business that provided a livelihood for me, my family and a lot of other people for many years. Now I run a life-science-focused boutique investment bank that I founded in 1998 to raise capital for early-stage companies developing therapeutics, medical devices, diagnostics, and/or pharmaceutical services. My company is Walter Greenblatt & Associates (still "Self-Directed," no?), and I have a handful of associates who work with me, some full-time, some part-time (including my son, Daniel, who is a research analyst). We have helped a number of very early-stage life science companies take technologies out of universities and develop them into marketed products and services, including several that have gone public.

The best part of my job is that I get to work with brilliant scientists who are trying to make significant improvements in the medical field through important innovations. We help them translate their scientific vision into the language of investment and help them convey to investors the value proposition of commercializing that scientific vision. I love what I do and it draws heavily on skills I developed in the Center, like learning a lot of new science on my own for each new project.

One more legacy of my Center past: When I interview people to work with me, I value self-directedness above almost all else. When I find someone with the ability to structure a project or task from its initial chaotic form (combined with the persistence necessary to execute, of course!) I'm always eager to try teaming up with them. It's powerful stuff. I am never surprised.

Walter lives in Princeton, NJ where he is Managing Director of Walter Greenblatt & Associates, a bank that he founded in 1998. He works with scientist-entrepreneurs to raise capital for developing companies. He has three grown children and spends his leisure hours cooking and reading.

Short Takes

I'm guessing that my intellectual curiosity preceded the Center, but the confidence to follow that curiosity was fostered by the Center. I never would have gone to an Ivy League college nor had the courage to study something as unemployable as classics. I might not have had the courage to push back against some situations, and if I'd not done that, maybe I'd have lacked the courage to be an entrepreneur. In the end, the only conclusion with 100% confidence is that I'd do it again, and wish it on my children.

~Preston Kavanagh, 1977

DAN MCNERNEY, 1974

The early seventies were years of rapid change in America; likewise in my hometown, Winnetka, Illinois. The education system participated in those changes. So did my best friend, Terry. So did I. So did our families. Because of these changes, I embarked on a lifetime journey marked with milestones of the heart. I cannot remember whether my friend Terry, now Walter, came to me before I came to him. One of us surely asked the other, "Have you heard about the Center For Self-Directed Learning?" Since Terry and I talked about everything, it wouldn't have been very long before our conversation blossomed into "Would you consider signing up for this Center?" followed with "Yep, I'm thinking about it." Thus began a journey that would forever impact our lives, my relationships with my parents, and with the career I choose.

It was the spring of my sophomore year. Either my Dad or I was the first to think about inviting my New Trier advisor for dinner to hear his perspective on this innovative school-within-a-school. Bob Ward sat in our dining room as we reviewed what any of us knew at that point about this fledgling school. As Mr. Ward answered our family's questions, I could tell that my dad was feeling more and more comfortable with this bizarre idea. I already knew my mom was the less resistant parent. That dinner ended on a wonderful note. With my dad's conclusion that he thought the Center was legitimate, a good idea for me, a subsequent discussion with my dad and my mom led to my decision to put my name in the Center's lottery.

One of my clearer memories of those exciting days was standing in a big study hall. Room 101 would become our school-within-a-school. There were 150 or so waiting. All were counting down the 125 promised spots. I remember thinking that this was not based on any merit. No interview, no application. No favors. Just someone picking a ball out of a bowl. The minutes dragged on.

Both Walter's number and mine were picked. A huge milestone. I immediately knew I had one friend that was going with me on this adventure. Even though I was Vice-President of Student Council, I don't remember other student leaders entering the Center. Neither were many of the athletes from the hockey and football teams. But, happily, my friend Terry was there. I was there.

The day this tiny school opened, I recall being thrust into an arena of people I wouldn't normally have met. For me, that was a positive thing. Vernoy Johnson was the one of six facilitators I knew. He had been my sophomore geometry teacher. It was a rich environment of brand new personalities and possible new friends with peers and teachers I did not know. I passed the second milestone. The next challenge in the first week was for students and faculty to create classes and other ways to learn. I was amazed that four or five ideas percolated quickly for me. From that moment, I recall that I always had five or six things going at a time. I don't remember floundering at all. The lack of traditional structures like timed bells, assigned classrooms, and a daily schedule didn't bother me in the least. I loved the experimental frontier. I loved the fact that this ship had never sailed before. Some people might have been nervous, but I enjoyed the feeling that we were making history. I dove right in.

Having my friend, Walter, with me in the Center, was a greater boon than I expected. One of my first Center learning experiences, The Rat Experiment, involved a partnership with Walter. Even though we had this history of conversation, talking about who knows what, I was always amazed about what he was up to. At this early point, he had been over at Northwestern University doing some research about one of his many curiosities. I remember the day he came and said, "You know, I am really wondering about this pituitary gland, some of the hormones, and its effect on learning." Then we launched into one of our precocious conversations. From middle school, that was the kind of relationship we had. We shared what we were reading, thinking, our philosophies, and whatever we found that we thought was new. He was more of a scientist than I, but I said, "Okay, you want to do this experiment? Sounds interesting. I'm game."

We approached this experiment with our most earnest seriousness—two young scientists studying how rats learned. We started our project by reading articles. At this early stage of our Center lives, the only self-direction noticeable was our motivation to answer questions raised by articles we read. There was not a careful plan, goals or the other things I learned about self-direction over my years in the Center. We just took the first steps that seemed so right. More Huck Finn than Jonas Salk, I think. After our reading discussions, we got into the car and drove to Kankakee, Illinois to get the ACTH drug that we had to administer to the rats. Walter inveigled permission to use a school lab. We set up the experiment by establishing our norms.

As we progressed, we became more disciplined in following through, making sure that we were fairly even handed and not biased in what we did or the observations we recorded. When we were finished months later, we submitted the results to some of our peers and faculty. Our precisely documented conclusion noted that there was an enhancement of learning with this particular drug.

Although Walter had initiated the rat experiment, my long and emerging interest in China called me to another milestone study. China had a particular, undefined quality that was very appealing to me. The group we formed to study China included Vernoy Johnson who had taught several times in China. Vernoy facilitated our strong bonding. Our common thread was our shared impossible dream of going to China. We organized ourselves so that each week someone would present a paper about Chinese history or culture. After the presentation, we asked questions and talked about what we had learned. More often than not, our conversations on any evening ended with discussions in which we were exploring possible ways to obtain visas for China. One of the highlights of this study was the presence of my mother, a contributing member in the group. It was special for me to study with my mom, watch her read about China, and then prepare her paper. For the first time, I experienced a group study that was a mirror reflecting the values and thinking of our school-without-walls.

Here, for the first time I discovered how a learning community reflected life. Ours was a learning lab and we were all learning together—parents, kids, faculty. We were learning the topics we studied, but we were also discovering each other and our new community. The Center environment allowed for students to get to know the faculty as individuals and as co-learners. It also allowed them to see each of us as a unique person. And it fostered an environment in which I could get to know my mom, not just as Mom, but as a student and fellow learner. Age and position did not matter when it came to our self-directed learning in this community.

We never did get to China. In spite of sending some money to a Canadian travel agency that we picked because it was having some results getting visas for

Canadians, the barriers to travel there were too great. It wasn't the right time. Years later, I did answer the next call and travel to China on my own.

A third highlight of my maturing self-direction came through my projects at the Chicago Historical Society. I gained a great sense of accomplishment in downtown Chicago. The whole idea of original research was brand new to me. I clearly recall the excitement of being at this venerable library in downtown Chicago, looking at original documents, using a microfiche, having the freedom to select and study topics that really interested me in as much depth as I determined. World War I became my favorite study.

To this day, I remember the contents well. I would do the research and once a week, Arline Paul, our social studies facilitator who also made sure our studies qualified for the state required U.S. History credit, reviewed what I wrote, made suggestions, and provided guidance. When I was finished, I had produced a 40-page paper and a feeling of pride that I could do "big" research.

There were two English groups that stirred my budding enthusiasm for literature. One was guided by Bill Gregory, a Center faculty member who had taught at Marshall High School in an African-American Chicago neighborhood, while on leave from New Trier. In this group, we read books by African-American authors and discussed them in the light of social changes that were dominating the news of the day. The other was a group we called E-LIT. We read various books and discussed them, but the highlight was writing haiku. I had never written poetry let alone haiku, and I remember thinking how fantastic it was. I recall times I sat in a park or outside my own house or wherever it was, and imagining it was a Japanese garden. I ended up writing a lot of haiku, enjoying it, and loving the opportunity to share it with others.

In addition to our small group studies, there were a number of ways the Center facilitated rich interpersonal interactions so that we could get to know people at a deep level. I recall both Town Hall and Community Group meetings. I wasn't a leader, but I recall enjoying the feeling of community, a feeling that blossomed into my positive feelings about the importance of community today. The fact that people felt community at a psychological and spiritual level was a significant thing. I don't remember the wrangling for consensus, what we discussed, or how the meetings were advanced. I do remember Jim Bellanca, the Center coordinator, challenging the students and, with other faculty, building community for us, helping us listen to each other, share ideas, resolve disagreements and respect each other. Community groups were especially valuable for developing a feeling of belonging in an important place. Guided by a faculty facilitator, each of these groups met once a week in a small group session. Once, in my community group there was an issue about how well our group was functioning. The air was filled with tension. Bill Gregory, our facilitator, teared-up saying, "I feel that I haven't done this well. Tell me what I need to do to help." I thought that getting to know teachers at a very different level, at this very human level, was special. His tears needed to happen for that community meeting to advance to a very rich, very honest level.

In retrospect, I admire my mom and dad's willingness to go on this journey with me and be willing to take the risk of whatever impact it might have on my future. My parents had the integrity not to make my Center time about the ever-present concern of college admissions. My non-Center friends did that, as they made concrete in often repeated and significant questions. "How will colleges interpret the Center?" "How *can* they admit you when you don't have grades or a grade point average?" "Aren't you risking your future on a lark?" I applied to Harvard, Yale, and Stanford. I was accepted at all three. The Center faculty must have been right on the mark, writing seriously and well about what and how we were learning how to learn. I recall my own self-assessments, as painful to compose as they were. There must have been some valuable kernels in them. Not only was I admitted to Yale, but also Walter, Sarah Ball, Ann Garvin, and David Abell, Center classmates, were accepted and attended with me. When I got there, I majored in History and I earned a Bachelor of Arts.

After college, I embarked on new journeys. Each new path was marked with signposts that I had stuck in the ground in my Center days. First, I started my adult work with the Cargill Corporation. I traveled throughout South America while living in Minneapolis and Toledo, Ohio as an agricultural commodities trader. As I flew to Guatemala, the Dominican Republic, or Venezuela to buy or sell sugar and molasses. I discovered that I was far more interested in the cultural aspects of the countries than in the business deals I was making.

The business was fine, but what I defined about myself during those years was more important. I thought if I were going to be honest with myself, I had to acknowledge that I was far more interested in the history and cultural issues of those countries. I enrolled in South American and Central American history classes at the University of Minnesota. I didn't have to. But probably because of the Center, I wanted to continue my cultural explorations.

In my social work and psychology classes, I made friends with an increasing number of people serious in their Christian faith. Many issues came to the fore. I realized that intercultural, anthropological affairs and people interested me more than making money in business. I was also wrestling with the question of what was true about life. With increased church attendance, my philosophical, historical, and ultimately theological reflections deepened. The twenties were very fertile years for me. I was determined to figure out why there is a God, what is the relationship between God and people, and what does the Bible have to say about it? Is this truth or is that truth? I found it satisfying to wrestle with those questions and yet very easy not to. At the same time, I felt a spiritual call to this unknown thing called "ministry."

As I looked around the trading floor, I increasingly wondered about motivations. Is it possible to earn a lot of money and be spiritual? Could I be in business and not necessarily be motivated to explore those questions? Did I need a complete separation?

It was then that I had another talk with my parents. "Dad, I feel a call into ministry. I'm not entirely sure, but I do feel this call to Costa Rica." As he had done when Bob Ward came to discuss the Center, he listened carefully and asked questions before offering his ideas. I went to Costa Rica with the little money I had earned, lived with a Costa Rican family, and studied Spanish. I learned about the Christian faith, mission work, and about Costa Rica. It was a way of testing my wings and missionary ministry work.

My next step was my next milestone. I graduated from Trinity Seminary in Deerfield, Illinois, in 1989. McCormick Seminary at the University of Chicago followed Trinity. I finished an internship at Winnetka Presbyterian Church in my hometown and remained on the staff there for seven years. Thirteen or fourteen years ago, I left the Winnetka Church. I started my work with international missions for the denomination with a little group, Presbyterian Frontier Fellowship. It led me into the frontier areas of the Presbyterian Church round the world.

Throughout my ministry career, bringing people from North American culture into other cultures, from one ethnicity into a different ethnicity has been a huge part of my life. Now I am well into the global church and believe that if Christians aren't careful, they can let their culture override their understanding of the Bible and see it through just a very narrow lens. By mingling with people from different cultures, their understanding of old ideas of faith and religion can become brand new.

When I take people from Winnetka or Glencoe, well-to-do communities where there is so much "hyper individualism," and plop them down in the middle of Kampala, Uganda or Chiapas in Mexico, their eyes are completely opened. They discover how people survive on so little. They're awaken to see a whole other way of life, one they have never seen before because the layers of wealth in our country give us the resources to be isolated as individuals. They meet people in a community who have no other option but to rely on each other to survive. They see close-knit communities that pick up all the loose ends when there is no health care system or outside help.

Looking back, I see why the Center was such a blessing. Intuitively, it created that community within a community. That community was a safe place to step away from the motivation of getting good grades, performing hyper-well in school, climbing to a top class rank, competing in every aspect of life. It provided the freedom to pursue something vigorously with no external pressures. I cannot recall anyone saying, "You must do this" or "this is due."

In the Center, we just swam or sank with our own dreams and drives. I may have had a degree of self-direction within me that was strengthened when the faculty modeled it and helped us build strategies for guiding ourselves. What I gleaned was so instrumental in my having the courage to leave that business career and go off into the unknown. Later, I know it was central to my selection of my ministerial career and my belief in the power of community to transform. I am extremely grateful that I made that initial choice, passed the first milestone, and the many after choices in which I was true to my heart, always electing for a career that was joyful.

Dan is an ordained minister with the Presbyterian Church U.S.A. At age 27, Dan made the decision to leave his business career trading agricultural commodities with Cargill, Inc. and answered a call into ministry. For the past thirty years, Dan has had one foot overseas doing mission work for the Global Ministries division of the Presbyterian Church, U.S.A and one foot involved with ministry among the people of the Winnetka area. Dan can still be found playing adult hockey in the Winnetka area, or watching his children play in the travel hockey program of Winnetka.

Short Takes

I went into the Center because most of the classes I took were boring, so I was learning very little except for Communication Electronics with Mr. Rocky. My frustration level was so high I was planning to drop out on my 16th birthday. The Center gave me an education that could not be matched by the parent school. I worked hard and learned more than I can express. Within a year of graduation I was hired as an electronics and software engineer—not bad for a 19-year-old—and I have progressed in that field ever since.

When I went on to college, I attended and dropped out of some of the best: Worcester Polytechnic Institute, Harvard, Scripps Institute of Oceanography at UC San Diego and more. I learned more in the Center than in college and graduate school. It prepared me for the rest of my life.

~Bill Nugent, 1978

LEARNING TO LIVE

PHILIP-FRANZ SEITZ, 1974

As I remember, an orientation meeting for future Center students and their parents took place at the end of the school year in June 1972. My father took me to the event, which was held in a basement room at the high school, where my friends and I played cards during lunch periods and the cheerleaders trained after school when the weather was bad. I was, of course, miserable to be in public with a parent, and my father's enthusiasm and uncharacteristic attempts to work the crowd made me all the more uncomfortable.

Because my parents had been divorced since I was seven, my mother was not there; she and my father could not be in the same place at the same time. My broken family was, in fact, the main reason I decided to throw in my lot with the Center, though I didn't understand it that way at the time. When I graduated two years later, my identity had more to do with me—my personality, values, and choices—and less to do with the family in which I had grown up. Had the Center not given me the opportunity and encouragement to "work on myself" during those two critical years, I would have lived a different, and less happy life than the one in which I find myself now, at age 53.

Growing up in Glencoe, going to Central school from kindergarten through the eighth grade, the youngest son of educated parents from "good" Illinois-German families, I should have had—I felt I had a right to have—the most stable and secure childhood anyone on the planet at that time could have. Until I was seven, when my parents split up, that is what I did have.

In 1963, I began to have a life that was all wrong. My father remarried and lived in Chicago's Old Town neighborhood while my mother moved into an apartment in Glencoe. My older brother and sister were already out of the house. My parents had evidently waited to split until they were both safely away in college.

Every Friday after school, my father would pick me up and take me to Chicago, where I would live with him, his wife, and my step-sister until Monday morning. Then, my father would drop me off back at school. Monday through Thursday nights, I lived with my mother in Glencoe. Until I started ninth grade at New Trier East, I had never even met another kid (other than my year-older step-sister) whose parents were divorced. I was ashamed of my family situation, and it's not surprising that my few friends were nonplussed by it.

Shame, however, was not the main theme of my life. I looked at my brother, the winner of the Illinois Math Contest for high school seniors, who went to MIT; at my sister, with her legion of boyfriends, new car, and comfortable life in an exclusive private college; at my friends, who didn't have to disappear from Glencoe every weekend and miss the ball games and other fun; at my step-sister, who got to stay in her Chicago neighborhood all the time in a two-parent family, with my father...and I was angry, resentful, and envious. This was all wrong; this was not my life, not the life I deserved. It's hard to concentrate in school or get into any hobbies when you're angry and resentful all the time, plus shuttling between two families. The only stable activity I had was Scouting, which my parents treated as a sort of demilitarized zone. I had entirely normal Cub Scout and Boy Scout careers. Thanks to scouting, I learned some wholesome habits and avoided mischief. I was, however, an extremely poor student.

My parents gave me a pass in regard to my underachievement in school, I suppose because they could see that I was struggling emotionally with my family situation. Many of my Central School and pre-Center New Trier teachers, though, could not help comparing me to my math-whiz brother and super-perky sister, who had been their students a few years earlier. No doubt meaning well, they asked me endlessly if everything was OK at home, and in the case of a couple of hipster types, asked me if I wanted to "rap." Their efforts were fruitless. I just didn't pay attention in class or study at all. When I could get away from my parents, I took long walks by myself, usually through Turnbull Woods in Glencoe or Lincoln Park when I was in Chicago. My parents and teachers probably thought I didn't care about my near-failing grades, but that was not the case. Every bad report card affected me deeply. I grieved for weeks over every one.

But I was still not able to rouse myself to pay attention in school or to study. I don't remember how I heard about the Center, but somehow I knew immediately that it could be my lifeline, my way to get out of the rut I was in. There was a lot of talk at that time about how the Center could damage one's chances of getting into a good college, and some parents were reluctant to agree to let their kids join the Center based on this concern. My parents weren't worried and were perfectly happy for me to join the Center; after all, no grades had to be better than failing grades. I'm sure they also recognized how unhappy I was, and were receptive to anything they believed held some promise of relieving my unhappiness.

In the fall of 1972, the other Centerites and I started our great adventure in self-directed learning. The excitement and intensity of the first weeks left me without the option of tuning out, as I was accustomed to doing in school. With the Watergate hearings droning in the background, teachers and students brainstormed, some furiously, some in a more leisurely fashion, but all with the sense that we were together on a journey into the unknown. (In Vernoy Johnson's community group, we actually adopted the slogan, "We're all bozos on this bus.") What effect did these early Center experiences have on me? I almost immediately began to discover that I had a personality buried under my anger and resentment. I had more interesting and urgent things to think about than how unfair my life was.

The new friends I was making, who didn't know anything about my family and me, didn't expect me to be the morose, withdrawn person that my old friends knew. The Center teachers were thankfully not among those who knew my siblings, and even if they had known them (maybe they did?), I'm sure they wouldn't have compared me to them. We all understood implicitly that comparisons between Centerites and non-Centerites were as senseless as comparisons between, say, an Inuit and an Inca. We were a sort of isolated, primitive tribe with evolving customs and mores entirely opaque to outsiders. As a member of this tribe, I could and did re-invent myself. My friend Lee Sandlin, who these days is the getting the fame he deserves as the foremost author of "lyrical history," had an enormous influence on me the two years we spent together in the Center. There, our intellectual relationship had the space and time it needed in order to take wing.

During my senior year, I had an unrequited crush on a fellow Centerite, a girl of sublime intelligence, artistic creativity, sensitivity, spirituality, and beauty. My father egged me on terribly, pressing on me Goethe's Werther and Gide's White Notebooks, as though I needed more pathetic romanticism. Maybe he thought I should get it out of my system before I left the nest. In any case, what I admired in my beloved was, I think now, an indication of how far I'd come after one year in the Center.

If I'd continued in the depressed rut I'd been in before the Center, I imagine I would have fallen for a girl in her own depressed rut. Because in the Center I continually discovered the intelligence, creativity, empathy, and spirituality within myself, I yearned for a soul mate with the qualities to which I aspired. This wonderful girl and I did not become soul mates, but just by being my friend, and treating me with tenderness and respect, she had a profoundly positive effect on me. I trust she knows that. Because of my romantic preoccupation during twelfth grade, my college applications were almost an afterthought. I had managed to get such high SAT and ACT scores that I half believed they were a mistake, but they meant that I got accepted at most of the colleges to which I applied.

My parents were surprised and pleased, and, reasonably enough, considered this a vindication of the Center. I recognized how my learning activities in the Center contributed to my doing well on the standardized tests: Indefatigable reading of Dickens, Joyce, Mann (mostly in translation), Emerson, Henry James, Nabokov, Durkheim, Kierkegaard, and others in the 1970s pantheon of "deep" fiction and non-fiction, dictionary and vocabulary lists always at my side...and, crucially, the teacher-facilitated discussions in which I flaunted my growing vocabulary. Through Vernoy Johnson's teaching I was also able to attain a mathematical fluency I'd never thought was within my abilities. But I also understood that the personal growth I achieved was more important than test scores and colleges' offers of admission. I decided to go to Occidental College in Los Angeles—a city I'd never visited.

My father was apoplectic. His second marriage was breaking up and he had started having financial problems. He might have been OK with the high tuition at the University of Pennsylvania (where I would later go to graduate school) because it was a family tradition to go to "dear old Penn," but going to an equally expensive private liberal arts college (that was far away to boot) was not OK with him. He insisted that I go to the University of Illinois. I reminded him of his promise to "pay for me to go to any college

I can get into," the same promise operative for my brother and sister. In fact, I was most inclined to go to Urbana, but I was perversely intent on skewering my father.

After a blow-up that I remember as something like John McEnroe's reaction to a bad call, my father wouldn't talk to me or let me in his house for several weeks. That was a relaxing time for me despite not knowing where, or whether, I would go to college. My father finally relented. Then I had to come to terms with my choice. Although my personal life in Los Angeles was far from copacetic (as my friend Lee, who was there for a while, could attest), I was a diligent student and got almost straight A's, which was no joke at "Oxy," an infamous grind school.

Leveraging my aptitude for foreign languages, I majored in German and Linguistics, and in my senior year was offered a full scholarship in the Ph.D. program of the Department of Linguistics at the University of Pennsylvania. In Philadelphia, I continued to wage a campaign of self-destructive personal relationships, but excelled academically as a protégé of the linguist William Labov and the sociologist Erving Goffman. I received my Ph.D. and decided to go into research instead of teaching, though I was really quite tired of both after several years as a research and teaching assistant. But I needed a job. For the next several years, I was a scientific hired gun. I worked at Oxford University in England, the University of Quebec, Gallaudet University, and finally for the U.S. Army at Walter Reed Army Medical Center.

Although I was having success getting grant funding, publishing, and so forth, I came to the conclusion that I was not temperamentally suited to research. I wanted to deal directly with people, lead teams, and solve immediate problems. A diplomatic career beckoned. Since receiving a Presidential Commission as a U.S. Foreign Service Officer in 1999, I have served in China, Germany, Vietnam, and Afghanistan. I finally started a family, and my wife and I have two children, now ages 8 and 3. We're living in Frankfurt, Germany—our second assignment in Germany, having served a few years ago in Berlin—where I'm the Chief of American Citizen Services at the U.S. Consulate General.

We have a good, happy life, but don't be surprised if I resign from the Service, move back to our permanent home in Glenview, and start yet another career. I learned in the Center that happiness and success come from doing what I know really comes from inside of me, from the values and talents that make me the person I am. Having children has made me discover the part of myself that is deeply rooted in my native place and strongly connected to my family, friends, and community there. Do I think often of the Center, of my teachers and peers, of what we did there? Of course. How could it be otherwise?

> *Phil graduated from Occidental College and was later awarded a Ph.D. in Linguistics from the University of Pennsylvania. This led to a 15-year career as a researcher within the federal Civil Service, He has been stationed in Shenyang, China; Berlin, Germany; Saigon (Ho Chi Minh City), Vietnam; the Zabul Provincial Reconstruction Team, Afghanistan; the Kandahar Provincial Reconstruction Team, Afghanistan; and now in Frankfurt, Germany with his wife and children.*

Short Takes

I often spoke of my Center experiences to my two boys because it was an opportunity I wished for them. Because of the Center, I was able to create and produce a charity marathon on the school radio station, learn business while earning money for college and participate in reading and analyzing some great works of literature. Although I am an Episcopal priest, I still create and produce commercial, entertainment radio/television, and my wife and I wrote and produced two children's books for charity.

My first adult book, *How to Pray When You're Pissed at God*, was published in spring of 2013 and I appeared on the "Oprah Show" to talk about it.

~Ian Punnett, 1978

A New Direction from Self-Direction

Susan Ringel Segal, 1974

It was the spring of 1972. For me, all was not well in the academic world. I was just finishing my sophomore year at New Trier East and had continued to do poorly in most of my classes, getting C's and D's in English, History, and even Physical Education, which I tended to "ditch" most often. My favorite spot on the school grounds was the smoking area, known as the "ashtray," right next to the tennis courts hidden behind a row of tall Arbor Vitae in front of the main building. My one beacon of light was Biology. I did really enjoy Biology and had an interesting teacher who was passionate about his subject and presented fun labs as well as lots of collaborative activities. Go figure that his style of teaching would spark my interest in learning, which I had hidden quite well since the sixth grade.

Enter the New Trier School Board and a new initiative they approved for an experiment; a school within a school, based on an alternative education idea that was popularized by Herbert R. Kohl's 1970 book, *The Open Classroom: A Practical Guide to a New Way of Teaching*. I don't recall the details of the creation of this program or its approval by the School Board, but I knew I needed a change.

The Center for Self-Directed Learning opened its doors in a converted study hall in the fall of 1972. Since I had failed traditional learning or it had failed me, I was eager to try the new method. I signed on as a "Centerite" for the start of my junior year. I think I had read Kohl's book somewhere along the way. Aside from poor academic performance in the first two years of high school, the "sturm und drang" of adolescence had hit me hard. I was bored, insecure, angry, and unhappy. Sounds lovely, doesn't it?

The new Center offered a sliver of hope. It ended up changing my life. I became a participant learner rather than an observer sitting at the back of a classroom being bored, looking out the window and daydreaming about what I could do after the bell rang announcing the end of class.

From the first days and weeks that were spent getting to know each other and the teachers as well as deciding how we would attend to learning, I felt the change. These hours and hours of brainstorming sessions became the basis for what the Center was all about, individualized learning in a collaborative environment. We had sophomores, juniors, and seniors who talked, planned, figured out (with the encouragement of the teachers) the classes we would have, the method of teaching, the curricula and the materials to be used. The brave teachers acted mostly as facilitators, to help us begin to take charge of our own learning. We forged relationships with a diverse group of students; some like myself who had been on the road to failure and some who were completely successful in the "parent school," but who wanted the challenge of self directed, experimental learning and an escape to something that would invigorate their lives. In fact, in that first year lottery, winners included the New Trier Student Council President and Vice President, the President of the Boys' Tri-Ship service club and many other high ranking students and athletes. For the first time, I met a whole new group of people.

That first semester my class choices included Geometry (taught by my loving and patient "Community Group" leader, the late Vernoy Alfred Johnson), Psychology, Art Composition, Political Science, and Ingmar Bergman film group. In addition, we were each assigned to a "Community Group" which was the "parent school" (the regular New Trier) equivalent of advisory (homeroom to some) except Community Groups were co-ed, half the size (15 vs 30) and had one of the Center teachers as the leader/ adviser. While advisories began each school day in a 15-minute time slot, the Community Groups met once a week for several hours, usually in a student's home.

I learned so much during that first year, both academically and socially. My self confidence and love of learning began to sprout and grew exponentially as did collegial relationships with students, teachers, and other adults who participated in helping the Center to grow and evolve. All this, and it was really fun too!

One of my best Center experiences evolved from my first year Political Science class. Dealing with the State of Illinois education requirements was a bit tricky. All students in Illinois had to complete a certain number of hours of specific classes to graduate. That was easier for some of the seniors who had gone through three years in the "parent school" and completed the requirements before entering the Center. For others, it required the innovative teaching and student direction on which the Center was based. In Political Science class, we discussed the rigidity of State graduation requirements in all subjects, including physical education. We wondered how we could address these requirements to meet alternative school needs and we decided to pursue writing a bill to be introduced in the Illinois State Legislature.

With the help of one pioneer Center facilitator, Arline Paul, we began to research, document, and write a bill. It became House Bill 1813. The bill was presented to the Legislature by State Rep. Harold Katz, whose daughter happened to be a Center student. Rep. Katz served as our expert guide and resource during the months of our study. The bill's intent was to make it easier for alternative schools to keep state aid even if specific graduation and attendance requirements were met in alternative ways.

We researched graduation requirements in all 50 states and spent hours in law libraries. We visited the Illinois Legislature in Springfield a number of times and watched the legislative process, while compiling research and rationale to support our bill. We discussed our ideas with Rep. Katz and Mrs. Paul. The bill passed the State House and State Senate and we sat in as the Governor signed the bill into law.

Another memorable event in my senior year was the Peking Duck dinner the China Study group prepared and served in the New Trier cafeteria. This was a benefit to raise funds to get us to China. The group effort started right after President Richard Nixon had opened the lines of communication with and had visited China. We thought we would be able to get visas to go to China, chaperoned by Vernoy Johnson, who spent many years there with his parents who were missionaries. We were never able to get visas, so we abandoned the cause after the dinner and the many days of bake sale tables in the front hallway of the school.

A favorite experience was a month-long internship with local silversmiths in their small jewelry shop, learning to make jewelry. They took me and another Center student under their wings and taught us the craft. I worked at the store all through my senior year and cemented a lifelong friendship with Mike and Maureen. They took me to work at the big craft fairs in Chicago, during the summers, where I got to meet a diversity of artists and craftspeople. To this day, I love creating jewelry and have even started a small home jewelry business.

However, it was not all easy sailing as getting in to college was a bit difficult. There were no grades in the Center, just extensive written evaluations. Center students had no class rank when we graduated and had to rely more on our SAT and ACT scores. My scores were awful. I was determined to go to the University of Wisconsin and, literally, had to beg my way in by interviewing, writing essays, securing personal recommendations, and pleading my case. I was accepted to the University of Wisconsin and found there was a long-standing alternative program, Integrated Liberal Studies (ILS). ILS is based upon the teaching methods of Alexander Meiklejohn, an educator in the 1920s who founded the "Experimental College," a living and learning model. ILS provided the core college courses for freshman and sophomores in a small learning environment and had a similar philosophy to the Center. ILS had approximately 60 students out of a total student population of 35,000. That made my transition to college less stressful.

As in the Center, ILS helped me develop a love of learning in small, collaborative groups with complete access to the professors. There were no 300-student lectures like in entry-level courses outside ILS. We had discussion groups with five to ten people! I received a B.A. in social work and eventually completed a master's degree in Social Service Administration from the University of Chicago.

My area of choice was working with the elderly. I had wonderful grandparents as role models and also volunteered at a nursing home during my Center days. My social service career, which was the first of several, was highlighted by securing a large grant as the director of one of four State of Illinois model projects to determine the extent of and services to deal with elder abuse and neglect in the community. Our project oversaw the research and subsequent publications that became the elder abuse model in the state.

I can truly say that I was in the right place at the right time when I joined the Center. I am so thankful that the opportunity was available. There are so many teenagers today who would benefit from such a program, but it is not available. I can only wonder how different my life would have been without the experiences of the Center.

Sue has interests in many areas and is still evolving. She started her career after undergraduate and graduate degrees in Social Work, working in geriatrics. Her current career(s) include real estate brokerage, jewelry making, and various volunteer positions in the community. She resides in Winnetka with her husband and two wonderful daughters who would have thrived in the Center.

Short Take

I learned how to learn in the Center. It legitimized unconventional thinking, and at the same time, I came to see how much effort it took to make it work.

I've worked as an illustrator, sound engineer, editor, programmer, and producer for multimedia presentations and advertising.

~Guy Palm, 1975

Short Take

The Center allowed me to survive high school as a closeted gay guy.

I've worked as an administrator for a variety of non-profit arts organizations.

~Evan Kavanagh, 1978

Moments of Judgment

Jennifer Armstrong, 1975

I always thought of myself as bright. I was not the sharpest crayon in the box, but certainly not all wax and no wick. I had friends. I had enough coordination to play music, ride a bicycle and I do well in school. That is to say, until high school, I did well in school.

My freshman year at New Trier East was a baffling nightmare. As a ninth grader, I was overwhelmed by the sheer mass of humanity and the unrelenting pressure to be part of a dominant culture. My main interests being traditional fiddle styles, yoga, a vegetarian diet, and weaving on a floor loom made fitting in to this culture extraordinarily difficult. If I add the debilitating fear experienced in my history class, my world was all the more frightening.

To this day I can't think back on approaching the glass doors to my history classroom without the classic symptoms of sweaty palms, clenched jaw, staring eyes, and labored breathing. Somehow, in history class I was 24 cents short of a quarter. I could never answer correctly. I wilted beneath the undisguised contempt of the history professor and I was horrified when I received a D at the end of the semester. I had never ever gotten a D in any subject before, especially not in history where I had always gotten As. I was totally demoralized. At the end of my freshman year I was ready to drop out.

When the Center For Self-Directed Learning appeared on the horizon, it was like an oasis to a parched and desperate traveler. I was saved! I created many wonderful independent projects and participated in numerous scintillating classes during my three years in the Center. I did projects in fiddling, traditional singing, bagpipe playing, yoga, vegetarian cooking, and weaving. Some of my favorite classes were a Herman Hesse discussion group, a Gestalt Theater workshop and being in the musical, *The Man of La Mancha*.

During my Center sojourn, the most important lesson I learned had to do with making judgments. We were not graded by teachers in the Center, but were asked to evaluate our own learning. I was extremely hard on myself. I was worse even than the evil history professor from freshman year. I remember my mother saying to me, "Why do you judge yourself so harshly? Look where that project took you! You've learned so much." "Yes" I said, "I ended up learning some great things, but I failed at my original intention didn't I?" At that moment, I remember quite clearly the instant when my judgments were blown to smithereens and a new way of experiencing life and learning became possible. That moment was followed by others of equal importance for my search.

One such moment occurred when Mr. Johnson was conducting a "fun with math" afternoon. I was there because I couldn't believe the words "fun" and "math" could be used in the same sentence. He had done some mathematical magic tricks with a magazine (I didn't understand how he knew what was on certain pages even though he explained it through numbers) and then he had us sit in chairs in rows, like a graph, as he put equations on the board. If our number (our place in the graph) was the answer, we had to stand up. The patterns we created were fabulous! Everyone in a row would stand up or we would make an X or a row on the diagonal. You knew at once if you were standing when you should be sitting or sitting when you should be standing because the pattern would be off. Although I didn't understand what we were doing, we were all laughing and having a great time. I've tried to explain that afternoon before, but without much success. I'm having just as much trouble now because I still don't know what we were doing! I learned absolutely no math that day. I did however learn something of great importance.

I remember sitting there feeling happy and relaxed and part of a group when suddenly with blinding clarity, I realized Mr. Johnson loved math the way I loved music. I was stunned. The world opened up. Judgments exploded into rainbow colored lights. I looked at everyone in the room with new eyes. They all loved something with the same passion I felt for music and I didn't have to know, learn, understand, or judge anything about it. I could just be grateful for the myriad ways we humans find to bring love and meaning to our lives.

There are hundreds of ways to kneel and kiss the ground."
~Rumi

Thirty-five years later I am still grateful for that moment in Mr. Johnson's "Fun with Math" workshop. I am also still struggling with moments of judgment. My most recent non-judgment strategy has been to embrace mistakes. With all best wishes, here is a recent poem on the subject:

> Flagrant Inaccuracy
> This is it then
> Life full of flagrant inaccuracy
> The two slopes of the bridge meant to meet in the middle
> Don't meet
> Is this failure?
> Or is this a stunning opportunity for a moonlit swim?

Jennifer is a musical storyteller with a lifetime involvement in the folk arts. She works as an artist-in-residence and performer in schools, libraries, theaters, and festivals all across Maine and around the country. She's been featured at the National Storytelling Festival, been interviewed on NPR, performed as far flung as Hong Kong and has seven (many award-winning) recordings of music and stories to her name as well as two children's picture books. She is happily married, the proud mother of two grown daughters and co-owner of 17 laying hens.

Short Takes

The Center allowed me to learn about social justice issues, and to be able to recognize the need for working in community settings helping underserved populations. Most of my professional work has been in the GLBTQ community and in health care and policy making.

~Laird Petersen, 1975 (deceased 2010)

BEYOND A MUSIC GEEK

CAMILLE AVELLANO, 1975

As a high school student, I had already decided on a career in music; my parents are both professional musicians, and I had been seriously pursuing studies in piano and violin (as well as ballet) since I was five years old. By my teen years, I had narrowed my focus exclusively to the violin and was performing as soloist with several local orchestras, including the Chicago Symphony. During my first two years at New Trier, I tried to balance my competitive work on the violin with my academic classes, but it was very stressful. I had always driven myself to excel in school, and learning was just as important to me as winning music competitions.

Stanley Ackerman, the New Trier music teacher who taught the orchestra students, began to tell us about a New Trier program called the Center For Self-Directed Learning. In this "school within a school," we would be able to have more flexibility in planning the time devoted to practice, performance, and academics. That sounded very appealing to me and several other music students who also joined.

When I was accepted into the Center, I remember feeling a sense of relief that I would be freed from time and grade pressures as well as the tyranny of the bells that regulated all students in the parent school. There was also the excitement of participating in a program that accepted us for our differences. I was no longer the "music geek" who had to be excused from certain PE activities because it was risky for my hands; I felt supported and celebrated for my successes and was encouraged by the staff and faculty to explore new and interesting areas of study. I remember a class in Hermann Hesse, where we sat in a circle discussing *Narcissus and Goldmund*, and truly understanding and enjoying the interactions of that class. I enjoyed my American history independent project, where I created a ten-foot long timeline that compared the events of James Michener's *Centennial* with actual historical events.

Musically, I spent my junior and senior years participating in four orchestras (two at New Trier, the Youth Orchestra of Greater Chicago, and the Civic Orchestra of Chicago), and numerous chamber music ensembles, all that would have been next to impossible had I remained in the parent school.

Although it has been a long time since I graduated (1975), I remember a unique feeling of support, respect, and fun in the Center. I had the support of my small community group where we all supported each other, and an individual "support group" focused on me, my goals, and my path to achieving them. Occasionally I also had fun just being able to sit around the Center and be a "hippie" with my macramé headband.

Had I not had the opportunity to be a part of the Center, I may not have been able to make the advances that I did at that pivotal point in my musical life when I sensed that to become a professional violinist I needed time to focus on practice. The Center encouraged and celebrated individuality, creativity, and the joy of learning in a noncompetitive, nurturing atmosphere; something that I am trying to find for my own son in the current toxic educational environment of funding cuts and overpopulated classrooms with uninspired teachers "teaching for the test." I feel proud that New Trier was insightful enough to experiment with an alternative and progressive idea that became the Center, and I am thankful that I was a part of it.

Camille is a violinist with the Los Angeles Philharmonic since 1981. She attended the University of Cincinnati where she studied violin with Dorothy DeLay and then played with the Rochester Philharmonic.

Short Takes

The Center validated curiosity as a lifelong pursuit.

~Janet Gould Nolan, 1975

A Test of Time

Nancy Budwig, 1975

I think of the Center as a precursor to my work here at Clark University. I am a developmental psychologist. My current responsibility is in the academic administration as an associate provost. I am working to rethink university education in light of 21st Century Goals. By the clock, I am a long time removed from those two and a half years I spent in the Center. Conceptually, I can trace what I have learned in my developmental science research back to those days. I can also trace my growth from a shy, non-risk taker to a confident researcher comfortable with the ways of thinking essential in my profession.

When I think about what was central during my Center years, development of the understanding that learning is much more than rote memorization and the superficial buildup of isolated facts, stands out as a highlight. My experiences from my sophomore to my senior year taught me that true learning takes place when learners come to think deeply about what they are learning because they are engaged and motivated by what and how they are learning.

For me, this opportunity to experience such engagement wasn't happenstance. It was in the Center that I learned to take risks, make significant connections among topics, and reflect more and more deeply on what and how I was learning to work collaboratively. Because we were immersed in interdisciplinary problem solving day-in and day-out, making what we were doing in one course connected to what we were doing in other courses, our learning went deeper and deeper. Because of how multiple teachers in the Center promoted making these interdisciplinary connections and engaged us in real-world problem-solving and serious reflection, our learning took on new shades of meaning that would last over time.

Although the program was called the Center for Self-Directed Learning and we clearly were engaged, motivated and being scaffolded to take responsibility for our own education, we also were part of a community, a community of practice around learning. That community was the glue that tied all the pieces together, and even if it was intuitively constructed, it proved to be a forerunner of many of today's conversations about 21st Century school reform.

Today, the big, enduring questions about our society and our globe come down to collaboration—learning to work with teams and recognize our own roles in a larger project. From my first small group study in which I was the baby, if you will, the youngest student in the Center with my summer birthday, I felt very challenged to have the wealth of experience of the older juniors and seniors as well as the faculty.

My peers weren't really peers; they were more teachers for me, scaffolding me and teaching me how to work in a team. This prepared me for difficult times when I was a senior and faced with newcomers in the community or a class. Some were disengaged new kids on the block who didn't necessarily want to be part of a team. They came to be self-directed. They didn't yet have that experience of community building, a process which reoccurred each year in the Center. They had to learn that teamwork was central, with everyone helping others. It was a powerful experience to learn how to help others to engage with a project by seeing what different teachers had to offer and what members of the study groups had to offer. We had to learn that a teacher wasn't the automatic source of singular wisdom and we had to learn about collaborating through brainstorming with our peers and teachers as we solved problems together in a community group, Town Hall, or a small class.

Town Hall became especially important to me. Town Hall was the place I grew a special skill that proved valuable to my professional life: consensus building. From my days in the Center to this day, people often ask me "where do you get that ability?" I always tell them "in the Center at the Town Hall meetings." However, it didn't happen easily.

As a high school sophomore, I was a very shy kid, I don't think I was socially adept. I was a good listener and I learned to listen for the different perspectives in Town Hall. Even with the faculty prompting all of us to take over the Town Hall decision-making, it was a very hard skill set for me to learn. It was so easy to get wrapped up in my view within an issue. The "consensus builder" was a role I carved out over time and was such an important skill to bring to future activities.

I gradually became more adept at stepping back to help facilitate this large group's decisions. While not in the classroom and while there was no assigned homework, I learned powerful lessons about the art of consensus building from watching the Center faculty. I gained new insights about what our teachers, our facilitators, did as they engaged us in Center governance issues by modeling that collaborative process.

And there were always issues, especially in Town Hall. Whether we were going to have mailboxes for everyone at the end of the room, have a Halloween Party, require everyone to check with their advisor each week, mandate graduation committees or not, hold our own Center graduation, paint a new mural on the back wall, require X and Y, small or big—these were the issues that became the meat for our full community's weekly gathering to make decisions.

Today, I find it easy to encourage groups to hold broad dialogues and consider several options. Regardless of what I think I want, I encourage the group to hear the different perspectives. I will step up and try to outline the points of view to see if that tactic can move us to a second ground with commonality as opposed to having each one of us stay locked in our own ideas. The ability to come to consensus, drawing on the wealth of ideas packed in group thinking, helping others realize that the sum of our individual ideas can lead to the best solution has been an important skill I learned in the Center over my three years of time.

With my community at my back, I was able to develop my abilities as a self-directed learner; I balanced my learning time in internships and real-world activities outside the Center's walls with group studies inside. The "beyond the walls" opportunities were very good for motivating me to think about the connection between the content that I was learning in my group studies and how I could apply it.

I remember in particular an internship that took place at the Grove School and my literature study group. Grove was a school for developmentally delayed children, and children with various kinds of pervasive developmental problems. And at the same time, I was part of the group that was working with a professor from Northwestern University. We were reading *Walden*. It was a wonderful book about education that taught me how we can have a philosophy of learning, but unless we think about the actual learner as opposed to the philosophy of learning, we are far from the heart of the matter. For the first time, I was combining what I was reading, a book that made good sense for my own learning and that of my fellow students, with what was going on in this internship. How soon I discovered that some of the best sounding ideas just didn't work when I had to teach a hyperactive child who didn't fit the theory.

Other opportunities in the Center led me to other discoveries that impacted my lifelong thinking. In my first semester, a group of junior and senior students invited me to join a Philosophy of Existentialism course. To be honest, when they asked me to be in that group, I don't think I knew what either philosophy or existentialism was. I was clearly the youngest in the group, but felt included from the first meeting. I recall how we roamed around the bookstore at Northwestern, searching for texts. We contacted various people we thought might help us understand the material. I soon learned that I wasn't the only one who had no idea what we were getting into, making mistakes along the way, getting in over our heads. It also was humbling to realize that I could not control my destiny as easily as I dreamt.

Some might say that we lost months of important time in our first go at this course. In the traditional school, we would have been told "No. No way. Not allowed," by teachers who had already picked our reading list. By second semester, we realized that we could not push ourselves quite as far as we wanted, switched that course around, found an instructor, and learned to focus our energy. This professor from the Philosophy Department of Northwestern was intrigued with us. He came in the evenings to one of the students' homes where we met and I began my first deep inquiry study.

I still recall how rewarding that experience was, less perhaps for what I discovered about existentialism and philosophy, and more for what I learned about the value of risk taking. The risk taking started the day we applied for this experimental school-within-a-school, especially for the seniors. I remember that a potential class Valedictorian had to give up her standing if she got a place in the Center via the lottery. I remember meetings at our house with groups of parents who weren't sure about this idea. They said it sounded intriguing, but they were getting cold feet. They wondered about their kids taking that risk to do something that intuitively made sense and would be a better learning experience, but might hurt their chances for college. Remember this was a school and community that was very focused on college admission well in advance of the frenzy that we see these days.

Luckily my parents knew the teachers well and completely trusted that an experiment they were behind would be a powerful experience for me.

Those that did take the risk had to be those from families who really cared more about their kids learning than they did about college admissions. This turned out to be a range of kids from those who were at the top of their class to students who were floundering and could really be inspired by this program. Ironically, as it turned out, all of those who took the risk did very well. My case was no exception.

It was difficult to consider where I wanted to go to college. Two sorts of schools appealed to me: an alternative school built on premises similar to the Center and a more traditional liberal arts college. I went out to visit schools on the west coast, some set up in ways identical to the Center. I remember vividly one interview at an experimental school with no grades that my father and I visited. The Dean of Admissions looked at my material and let me know my candidacy would not have a chance due to the lack of grades. This seemed ironic since the school itself had no grades and used a similar narrative evaluation like the Center. This taught me a powerful lesson about the ways particular units can be tied to broader constraints of the larger entities of which they are a part. I ended up deciding to apply to Vassar College early admission. I remember the feeling of complete joy to know that the risk I had taken had paid off—I got into a traditional liberal arts school without grades in part because they valued the learning that had taken place at the Center.

Not having grades carried more risks than just a rejection from a college. I would put the allowance to fail in first place as the biggest of risks. It was a risk that we took each day we were in the Center. As with my existential philosophy experience, all the safety nets were taken away. We were allowed to fail. We always had the sense from the start that intellectual inquiry was about risk-taking. Our risk-taking involved more than not getting to where you want to go, doing what you wanted or having a project fall flat. It was about picking yourself up and resetting the course. I can't count the way that the allowed risk of failing gave me a kind of springboard for testing out some things that I would never have tried. Nor can I count the times I had to learn *from* these seeming failures as part of the Center's process for moving forward.

In the conventional school, failure had not been a bad thing. I just didn't take any risks. I stayed with the safe status quo and rather did okay because okay would be okay. In my classes in a traditional platform when a course was over, I tucked the course notes away and moved on to the next course. I never thought that anything I learned in one course might have something to do with what I did next. Least of all, I never thought I was supposed to learn as much from what I didn't accomplish as from what I did. In the Center, I learned from each and every failure as much as from my successes. I applied my new insights to the next situation and developed the habit of making connections. I didn't have to do these for a grade. I learned that what had tasted sour might be as strong a medicine as the honey.

My learning from failure was helped by two *modus operandi* in the Center: the inquiry rich courses and the self-evaluation process. As I moved through my years in the Center, I learned the value of taking risks in order to ensure that my readiness to inquire and my willingness to evaluate that inquiry were helping me challenge the quality of my own learning.

I have strong memories of very deep inquiry-based learning coming from my Center classes. The memory is less about content—the names, the dates, and even the ideas—than that process of asking serious and deep questions. That was as true for Geometry as it was U.S. History or some other subject. All my studies were so different from the traditional program's courses. Instead of memorizing and spitting back the knowledge the teacher gave us, we actually got into discussions that took place, not only in the class time, but in the common room, in the corridor, on the phone at night. Those perpetual out of class discussions switched my views about thinking and learning. I discovered how fun curiosity and questioning could be for a student and how posing and answering questions was more intellectually exhilarating than showing off my memory powers.

The Center's evaluation practices reinforced the inquiry processes and skills our facilitators built during those fast paced, deep meaning classes. The Center evaluation process was quite simple. It was difficult for non-Centerites to grasp how a no-grades approach worked, but it didn't take long for me to grasp how difficult self-evaluation was and how risky.

A lot of what the evaluations let us do, and the inquiry and the failure let us do, and the community groups let us do, was to reflect. Today I see reflection as central to the most meaningful learning. What was terrific about my experiences was the chance to be given a space with others to reflect on each and every experience, learn from constructive feedback and make sense of the totality of what we learned, not just about the facts of a course, but about risk and failure. During our community groups, our class discussions with peers and our one-on-ones with our advisors, we were given a space to make mistakes as long as we would think about what we might do to bring about change based on what we had learned.

Reflection started at the opening day of each semester. In those opening Town Halls, we had to think about what we wanted to learn. As we became more adept, we slid from "wants" or "would have fun with" ideas like my first group on existential philosophy, to what we needed to learn. My advisors, my parents, and the Center facilitators all helped with that. Inquiry wasn't just about course work or an internship. It was about who we were and who we wanted to be. What were our aspirations? As I became more adept at asking these questions, I became more skilled at determining what was most important to learn.

At the end of each learning experience each semester, I had to prepare my self-evaluation. For this, I had to get written feedback from my peers in the study, and the adult who was my course facilitator or intern mentor. I shaped that information into my self-evaluation, reflecting on what I had done well, where I had failed, what goals I had achieved or not and what I would do differently in my next set of studies. I then put all my evaluations into a single document, called the semester synthesis. Each semester, I found myself using the synthesis more to define my growth as a self-directed learner. Eventually, I would have to use this road map to make the case that I was sufficiently self-directed to graduate.

I do think, for a student like myself, this process was incredibly helpful. It influenced my own approach even when I entered back into a college system that involves traditional grades. Prior to my entry into the Center my grades were fairly stable. When I got my report card, I knew in advance what grades I would receive. I knew if I worked hard, I would get those grades. Those report cards didn't carry any meaning or any formative value. In contrast, what I discovered was nice about the Center evaluations is that they were filled with pointers, several suggestions embedded in the feedback about where to go next. I remember I was working on my U.S. History requirement. I was doing a crossover study with women in history. I remember putting together some reflections on women's journals, and I remember the evaluation that Mrs. Paul had written. It wasn't about "did I get it right, or did I get it wrong?" She suggested that I was "on the road," and gave me some ideas to follow. Even at the end of that course, the questions and comments focused on where I would go next should I want to take this project further, some areas that I would need to read more about, some places that I had already covered where I might need to go deeper. As a novice in this field, I found her direction to be incredibly helpful. She stretched me like silly putty. Her main evaluation wasn't about whether I got an A or a B or I did or I didn't do x or y, but it was about directionality, about striving, regardless of the grade, to always be on the path to improvement.

Even as I now work at a university that requires grades, I know that the Center evaluation system influenced me in at least two ways. First, I know that what helps students most is my willingness to give them the feedback that points them in new directions. Yes, they will get their grades, but I don't assume the grades help them be better learners. That is left to what I ask or tell them about building on what they have learned about learning in my course.

Second, by experiencing evaluations from different teachers and mentors in the Center, I learned to appreciate how even the best of us need to learn how to give the feedback that is most helpful to learning. In the Center, I will say that some teachers were better at easing us into what we needed to improve than others. I would say the key faculty, those who had gone through training and from the get-go had given a lot of thought to this, seemed comfortable with feedback that focused on both strengths and weaknesses. I do remember that some others, usually by the volunteer group facilitators or mentors, were more descriptive. They tended to catalogue what we had done rather than evaluate with constructive advice. Giving helpful feedback, however, is a skill we all can learn to use well with students.

As I look back 35 years, I am so thankful for the foundations that the Center built for me in my brief three years there. It is with more gratitude and appreciation than they will ever realize that I think back on the amazing teachers who fostered my development across those years. That experience left me deeply passionate about education reform and human learning. I am amazed as one part of a group of people here at Clark University who are writing about what we call 21st Century learning skills that so much of what was embodied in the Center is today at the heart of our conversation about higher education reform. The work done by the Center pioneers—students, parents, faculty—presents a historic touchstone that teaches the enduring values of community, inquiry and reflection bound together to create a singular force facilitating deep learning. That is the test of time.

Nancy earned her B.A. from Vassar College before earning a Ph.D. in Developmental Psychology at the University of California, Berkeley. She and her husband hold faculty positions at Clark University (Mass.) where she is Associate Provost and Dean of Research. Nancy and her husband have carried on their field-based research on human learning and development in the Netherlands, China, Germany, and New Zealand.

Short Takes

Margie became Margaret and moved to the desert.

She finished a master's degree, built a family, a home, a career, a community. When her husband left, she reinvented herself as a single mom doctoral student. Now she's a professor of public administration in West Virginia.

She's a mountain mama but still lives in the desert in the winter!

~Margie Stout, 1978

You Can Never Take Away the Center from a Draftee

Blair Miller, 1975

I think I was drafted into the Center. I was having a high school experience that really wasn't grabbing me. My sister, Tish, was a member of the inaugural Center class. She was so excited and involved that talking with her about the Center was like talking to her about her favorite movie. I just had to see that movie. It wasn't long before I started getting pulled into the Center events, parties, dances and the meetings that would be at our house. And I felt like I was a part of this Center even before I signed on, even though I wasn't sure what I was getting into.

So, I agreed like a good draftee to follow her. By the time I graduated, I not only learned a lot; I had formed a new mindset. My folks were supportive of my draft status. They were excited about my sister...I think because Tish, who had never been an enthusiastic student, lit up in the Center. They hoped I could have a similar experience. When I got up the nerve to ask, they were all for it, although they still didn't understand how anybody could have an education with no classes and lectures. But they were a fairly progressive couple. They were willing to give the Center a flyer for me, hoping I too would get the spark.

At first, Center learning was a real challenge. It was like boot camp. When I joined, I didn't know what I was doing. That first couple of weeks I was absolutely befuddled. I was having a great time. It was interesting. It was exciting. But I didn't really know what was going on. When the whole Center gathered in Town Hall to create what we called "the learning experiences" (Small group classes were just one option under the more generic heading of "learning experiences."), I started hearing what other people were planning. I had never seen such enthusiasm, especially in school. There was a dynamism that drew me in. It attached me to the learning experiences that other, more seasoned Centerites, were planning. As befuddled as I was, I was loving the adventure. I think this was because I loved strategy games. I was a big strategy player. I loved playing Risk and Diplomacy, board games in which you have to negotiate. And forming classes, picking internships, or doing projects was a lot like that. You would get together. You found some people who were interested in learning something that interested you. Then the push-and-pull. "What are we going to learn?" "What's going to be our focus?" "How are we going to go about doing it" "Where?" "When?" It was one big negotiation.

I think, in retrospective, some of my favorite days were in those semester starts when 100 plus people were figuring out what they are going to learn in the next several months. How are they going to learn it? Where are the resources? It certainly wasn't much like standing in line at McDonald's waiting for a pre-packed burger on a plastic tray. Out of this chaos, order somehow emerged. It wasn't the order for organizing the masses. It was the order that each of us made for ourselves. I loved it and hated it at the same time.

Today, when I look back, my takeaways are easy to pick and to classify. There were those structures that helped each of us set up our personal schedules. Then there was the atmosphere, the people, and most especially the many intangibles I learned. The Center had a richness about it. That richness was grounded in its variety—the variety of students, the variety of adults, and the variety of opportunities.

Almost anytime, I could just sit around and end up in a discussion about a piece of poetry or something that somebody was writing or just hang out and hear what people were doing with their lives…or not doing. I found lots to be learned by both doing and not doing. It's sometimes good to hear about what people are doing or not doing. I don't know how many teenagers would admit to it but there is a little bit of learning going on by watching what's working for other people and what's not. You remember picking something up by watching other people. When I watched, I remember there were good examples and there were bad examples. Both ended up helping me understand what the Center was about. It wasn't about the real artsy folks, the drama kids, the people who had a more scientific bent or any of the other ways high school students create stereotypes. It was about noticing which people seemed to be getting the most out of their experiences, the doers, versus those who were passive, allowing things to happen to them or just sitting and waiting and getting much in return.

For the most part, my pick for bad examples were those kids who came into the Center as passive, unlit candles and couldn't figure out how to get active. They had gotten As in how to be passive and Ds in their courses, letting teachers and their parents run their lives or just turning off all pressures and ignoring the adult world.

When I was new to the Center, I remember how important it was for me to see both good and bad examples. Remember, I said I was confused. I wasn't much different from the other Center newbies. We were just starting to learn what self-direction was about. My first self-directed choice, I think, was deciding between taking charge of my learning and saying "no way" to just sitting around and waiting. I was glad I made that choice early on. Each of us new to the Center had timelines for that decision. I wasn't going to wait. A few others did for varying amounts of time.

It is easy to recall the structures and events that helped the Center work for me. Unlike the regular school where I wandered through five scheduled classes a day, I had a rich variety of ways to learn in the Center: classes, small groups, tutorials, internships and on and on. Nothing was handed to me. For instance, I can easily remember my favorite "class." We called it a class because we made a fixed schedule and had a fixed facilitator, an adult who would guide us. But it was different than sitting in a "classroom" class right from the start. I remember I was sitting at a table during one of the few opening day quiet moments. David Kudan and Julia Robling, two older Centerites I didn't even know yet, sat down and told me "Blair, we've got this class on comparative religions getting ready to start. Do you want to be a part of it?" I told them that I had no idea what comparative religions were. And they said, "Neither do we." I guess some people would be appalled. We were wide-eyed enough not to know better.

We started talking about the possibilities. Before we knew it, there was this collection of Center people, seasoned veterans and the newbies like me, and we are making a list of all the religions we knew and talking about how this list could help and what the focus of the class would be.

Within an hour or two, we had this really interesting class outlined. The class ended up having two parts. This was my first experience starting a class with a serious negotiation. It was easy to negotiate the list of religions to compare. The harder part was to negotiate how to proceed. We agreed to meet twice a week for several hours. Part of it had to do with reading about different philosophies and religions and actually going and spending time at a temple, a church, an ashram, or a synagogue in the Chicago area where we met the people who ran it. In between, we brought in religious leaders to talk with us. We brought in a rabbi who was David Kudan's father, and a Unitarian minister who was Chris Pera's father. They introduced us to other ministers.

The second part of "Comparative Religions" was about meditation and reflection. Julia was interested in Buddhism and was into meditation. She convinced us that it was important for each of us to reflect on what we were learning and think about what it meant for us. Thus, after the talking about religions and how they were alike and different, we would have a potluck dinner and end with meditation time in a group. We did that for a year and a half.

Group classes were not the only way I went about learning. Another was the internship. Some kids got the chance to work with some really great people such as Chicago artists Edward Paschke, Diane Simpson, and Richard Hunt. Others were mentored in a local vet hospital, the Lambs School, or a flower shop. I did one internship that was really remarkable. It taught me lessons I hadn't planned on learning.

I did this internship at a new forest preserve that Lake County was making from an old farm in Bannockburn. One way or another, David Haas and I found out about this opportunity. We were assigned to work with this guy who had been the farm's groundskeeper. He had a wicked sense of humor. I think he had a much better handle on who we were and who we thought we were. It took both of us some time to discover that this agricultural work was not what we wanted to do with our lives. And this guy had enough pearls of wisdom that he could sprinkle when we got down so that we did the full four-month internship we had committed to do. For me, it was a counter-learning experience.

We had thought we would go and really learn how to be forest workers and environmental educators. It would be a snap. We did come away having learned a lot about animals and the hard physical work involved, but my biggest learning takeaway was "man, I want to really work hard at school; I really want to work hard because I don't want to do this. I don't necessarily want to do this for the rest of my life." However, as my parents pointed out, it was a positive experience. It was my first job. A real job. It was hard work and I learned to be on time every day sticking it out to the very end.

Going places aka travel was a favorite with Center kids. If we didn't have the money, we would figure out a way to raise it so everyone who wanted could go. Over the years, I heard that groups even planned for Europe, with one group making it to Paris. The best my class could do was Springfield, Illinois and Wisconsin's North Woods. The North Woods trip earned its way into Center travel lore. The trip took place during the Winter Interim after the winter holidays. We put together a plan to go to Mr. Johnson's family cottage in Eagle River. I don't remember what the official learning objectives were. But the experience I do.

We were up there five days not counting the day trip each way. I recall how we shared cooking duties, eating the meals together, cleaning up and long, long conversations. Mr. Johnson was really good at tossing out provocative questions and leaving us to carry on different conversations. I am not sure how much we slept, but we would talk late into the night.

On the long drive north, we decided we needed to have some artifact for this trip. We wanted to do something that would show what we had learned. We were hoping to avoid the required written evaluations. We settled on building a big igloo out on the lake. Mr. J. had a book about making igloos in his library. We cut a hole in the ice and built the igloo around it. With Mr. J's expert mathematical advice, we did the geometry and then we cut and fitted blocks of ice and water sealed together. After we had our igloo, little crawl door and all, someone suggested that we top it with a Center flag.

In Center fashion, this started a big debate. We retired to the warmth of the cabin and carried our discussion on and on. We prototyped different flags and different things we could have on it such as the Center's favorite motto, "illegitimi non carborundum." In the midst of this brainstorming, someone said, "But wait, why not a 'there is no center' flag?" We cut out the sheet into a piece of fabric the size of a flag and then we cut out the center of it. Along the edges, we wrote "illegitimi non carborundum." Soon, waving in the breeze was this center-less flag. With our adolescent humor, we thought it was perfect.

Ironically, our best-laid plans went a little bad. Mr. Johnson would not accept our arguments about "there is no evaluation." We had to write what we had learned. That's when I first thought about how much we were learning from each other, how the group had bonded and how much the late night conversations, the brainstorming, and the crazy humor meant to me. I wrote those things in my evaluation. Mr. J. was quite pleased.

Of course, everything we did, did not work so well. I remember we had one special event that went awry. Special events were planned on the spur of the moment. They came and went fast. There was a band from Chicago that a group of us liked. The band had a song called "We're going to Gussie's out on Route 41." Gussie's was a diner. We thought, "Wouldn't it be fun to get a group together and go to Gussie's?" And so one Friday evening, three of us planned a special event. So that this was a qualified special event, we had to advertise it and spend time listening to the music and discussing it. To make it really special, we announced that formal wear was required. The guys would wear suits and ties and the girls would go in formal gowns. We thought going to Gussie's dressed formally would be hilarious. Since this was the '70s, formal dress was the opposite way anyone would dress, especially at Gussie's. We ended up having 15 or 20 people join in. We made only one goof, a small tactical error. No one of us had ever actually been to Gussie's. We piled into our cars, got lost and never found Gussie's.

And then there were the Town Halls which met once a week to discuss Center business, make decisions, share ideas, present special projects and so on. Jim Bellanca, the Center's lead facilitator, usually guided the event. It was in a Town Hall that I first learned about computers and got involved in a year-long debate. Ironically, one of our peers with a definite science bent was a guy named Apple...Brian Apple. Ironically, he was the first guy who brought his favorite project to a Town Hall. It was a computer board that he had been secretly putting together in the storage closet. Not even the faculty knew he had copied a key and was working on this computer in secret until he brought it out. After Brian showed us his computer board and cables and told us what it could do, the Center launched into an endless debate, not only for that Town Hall, but also for months to come.

Brian Apple, who just missed the boat at the exact same time they were inventing Apple computers, didn't know it at the time, but he was really close to leading a worldwide technology revolution. Instead, his revolution was in the Center where some people were saying computing was going to be the wave of the future and others saying "no way." But there was Brian Apple's prototype right there in our presence and there it stayed as a scientific sculpture stirring debate and reminding us of the possible future.

I loved to talk, but I hated to sit around. Our big multipurpose room was a magnet for debates. Not just the formal kind as happened in Town Hall, but also twos and threes gathered here and there scattered among formal learning groups and community groups. There was one guy who was of a more conservative bent than I. For days we would go at it for an hour or two and then we would retreat and come back with new facts or new observations. We debated the nature of the war in Vietnam or the nature of economic policy or the best way to organize a group. One of my favorite debates was built on speculating why kids joined the Center. I still debate that with Tish and lifelong Center friends.

I think that the big attractor to the Center was the room itself with its full wall mural and its 100+ mail cans. More importantly, it was a gathering place for people who wanted to be actively involved in learning with others of like mind. I would say many people who wanted to be in the Center were people who really had an active curiosity. They had a motivation to try different things. Risk-takers…and like me, endless debaters.

When I think of the two or three people who did not graduate when their four years were up, I recall they had to put in another semester or another year. I would say those were the folks that sat back for a semester or two and contemplated nothing. Some came in thinking the Center was a lark. Others were dumped in by advisors or teachers who were tired handling the kids' passivity, truancy, failures, ditch slips, or drug problems. Since it only took parent permission to join the Center, this could be a way for parents to put off dropping out or a place of last resort. Whatever, the reason, these kids needed that extra time to get their spark ignited.

Our faculty was really good at clicking the lighter. They never gave up. And sometimes, even the other kids in a community group would pitch in. I think there were kids for whom learning was tough even in a place that was so supportive. They weren't dumb or slow, but like me, they had learning difficulties. I was lucky. I learned to listen to my sister, my advisor, and my parents. I also learned not to excuse myself for my learning disability. I think some of the kids who were lost souls, perhaps had issues that were beyond learning issues and some had just passively accepted labels that encouraged them to stay dependent. In my two years, I can only think of just one person who never found the spark. When he was in the regular program, he had hung out in the smoking area. In the Center, I think that he was looking for a way to drop out of school. I think he thought the Center was a halfway house out the door.

The Center with its emphasis on self-direction was not a place that was a good fit for him. Like I say, I think the people who were the best fit were the people who had that spark, who were willing to engage and were motivated enough to learn how to engage. He never got it and eventually he went back to the regular school. There may have been others, but I didn't know them. The other kids I knew who struggled to find the spark eventually did.

I can attest to what happens with late sparks. I know that over the years, some folks in the regular school didn't like the Center. They didn't think it was what adolescents needed. They would blast off about the passive kids. These critics reacted, I think, to lots of rumors because they never came to check us out, even when invited, or to see a first-hand example of what the Center did for a lot of those kids, the ones who took a while to find the spark. A close friend of mine joined the Center with me in our junior year. Having arrived almost dead (metaphorically speaking), he started off passively. There were some home difficulties. He had been directionless since I knew him in junior high school. Or better yet, I should say he was a guy who thrived on social networking. That's what school was about for him. He had lots of interaction skills. In junior high, it never caught up to him. I think he saw the Center as the ultimate place for his way of school life. He spent lots of time just hanging out, being the do nothing that Center critics idealized as the perfect example of a Center student. What folks not in the Center didn't see were the subtle influences that helped his search for self-direction.

In junior high, I used to think my teachers had eyes in the back of their heads. In the Center, I think the faculty had eyes and ears all over their bodies, with invisible antennae too. From my friend's community group, his advisor, and friends like me, the heavy stuff started at the end of his first semester. For his synthesis, he had nothing to show. Our feedback was that there was nobody to blame beside himself. His lack of movement or progress was really stark. When you have a feedback loop like the Center's, the picture gets pretty clear. It was hard to blame somebody else for not learning when you are the one who is responsible for setting up what you are doing. With nobody to blame, he had to really look at himself. He had to be accountable to himself, to hold the mirror up to see himself. Gradually, the spark came and he did some amazing projects before he earned the right to graduate.

Graduation was a big deal in the Center. For those first-year students, when the Center had no history, it must have been a huge risk to shift from grades and GPAs to a committee that was going to ask you to prove your self-direction. By my time, our evaluations, the semester synthesis, and the grad committee meant a lot. I would often wonder why I gave up getting grades for the challenge of writing my own evaluations. And then the synthesis! Mushing everything into a few pages. You just weren't late with your synthesis. You couldn't even use the excuse that learning facilitators or mentors hadn't returned their portions of an evaluation or that you were a poor writer. Believe me I tried. And when it came to the graduation, you had to give your committee the reasons why you should graduate, use your syntheses, and then make a plan for your final self-directed semester.

Your committee's last meeting was the final decision when they determined your self-direction and your readiness to get an official Center diploma (in addition to the New Trier diploma) at the Center's special graduation celebration in Bumpy Park. Bumpy Park sits next to Lake Michigan three blocks from the school. The Center year ended in a celebration in the Park, open only to the Center's enrollees and faculty. Each graduate received a special diploma from his or her graduation committee and advisor. Undergraduates wrote poems, played and sang songs, and otherwise paid tribute to each graduate. It was a culmination of what I call my last big takeaway, the bonding that forms over the year among the faculty and students.

Even though Centerites scattered every day around the Chicago area and even beyond, the community groups, the debates, the Town Halls, and the many special events had a unique power to bind us together. Thirty years later, I still feel those bonds. As I look back thirty years later, I can note some of my fondest memories, my most important takeaways. When I try to characterize what was going on in the Center, the dynamism that was present, the bonding, the sheer variety of learning experiences from independent studies, internships, people studying at colleges, bringing in parents, college professors, teachers from different parts of the school to guide us, I can track the richness and a vitality present. I don't know how many schools had students hanging around early in the morning and late in the afternoon wanting to stay there, not wanting to go home. But that was going on in the Center.

But of all the takeaways, I think the notion of being responsible for my learning was the most profound. Some of this was clear to me before I graduated. Other parts came later and, in a way, were the most influential contributors. I think most about my learning how to write. The expository skills I should have developed in high school, but never did. That was my doing. I know my advisor and the other facilitators tried, but it never happened. I didn't set it up for myself. Writing was difficult for me and I actively resisted it. When I went to college, I was terrified. It was dawning on me, "Oops I am not good at this." I realized that I had turned down all the chances to learn writing.

In my first year at college, I gave in and took a non-credit college writing course. I worked my butt off, but I learned how to write. I should have done that in high school, but I didn't and it was nobody's fault but my own. I knew that and thanks to what I learned about being in charge of my own learning, I figured out a way to compensate for my prior bad decisions, overcome my fears, and get on with the course.

In hindsight, the self-direction also sent me on my career path. As I remember the brainstorming, the group work, the collaboration, the inherent newness of that experience, the debates, the laughter and tears, the successful navigation of the shoals of self-direction, the tolerance for ambiguity that the Center really engendered in me and in people around me, I don't know if I understood at that time that there was a career path there. But I went from somebody who didn't really have a great education experience in his elementary and early education years. The Center really gave me a very positive experience. It was that positive experience that I think led to my becoming a schoolteacher right out of college with the very explicit goal of making a classroom that was a more humane and dynamic experience for all the students. And when I was in undergraduate school and was exposed to some design of thinking classes and creative thinking classes, I was really attracted to those.

But again, I didn't quite put it together that could lead to a career or to be more deliberate about that right away. It wasn't until I found a graduate course in creativity and change leadership that I started putting it all together discovering that there is a whole field that studies the ways of thinking I first learned in the Center. Remarkably, many years after my high school graduation when I was teaching in graduate school, developing creative thinking and behavior, one of my students told me over coffee "Holy cow, this grad program is really great. I am loving it and it really reminds me of the work of one of my favorite authors, James Bellanca. What you guys are talking about really is in line with what he taught me." I thought "James Bellanca? I wonder if that could be Jim Bellanca?" The next day, she brought me one of his books with his picture on the back. No, I don't remember who she was. I remember there were a lot of IBM people at that particular session and she was not one of the IBMers. I think she was involved in secondary education.

Blair's time in the Center has had a long-lasting influence. Right out of college, he pursued a career in education, and spent seven years in the middle school classroom, where he initiated experiential learning, theater, and multi-disciplinary programs. Then he followed his passion for deliberate creativity. He took a year's sabbatical to travel the world, then entered the graduate program in creativity and change leadership at SUNY Buffalo, and continued as an adjunct professor. Today, Blair pursues his interest in deliberate creativity through the two companies that he runs with his wife, Sarah Thurber: Blair Miller Innovation (a training company) and FourSight (a publishing company).

Short Takes

I found out I can deal with lack of structure, especially unstructured time, but that it is very difficult. Sarah Ball and I created an exhibit in the rotunda of how women were portrayed in the media. It was groundbreaking! Filled with Blondie cartoons and sexist ads. Guess what? I still focus on gender differences in my work! As much as I learned from having to create my own environment, work in groups, and figure out what I wanted to learn, I regret not having a fourth year of NT's academics.

~Paula McCleod. 1974

CENTER MEMORIES DON'T IMPROVE WITH AGE; I KNEW IT WAS AWESOME WHEN IT WAS HAPPENING

A.E. RUBENS, 1975

Although I earned excellent grades my freshman year at New Trier, my parents feared I'd burn out from the intensity by which I undertook my schoolwork. They felt this new program called the Center for Self-Directed Learning would be perfect for me. Although we surmised that big state universities would probably not be interested in applicants without a GPA or class rank, my parents were not averse to my attending a smaller, private school. I also remember thinking how cool it would be not having to study for a biology quiz, and then realized, better yet, I didn't have to study biology!

My three years in the Center provided me an enormously satisfying, successful adventure in learning. That sounds like an advertising copywriter's line, but it's true! Through the Center, I gained the confidence, tools, maturity, independence, and responsibility to earn multiple honors in college, law school, and my career. I graduated from college with honors, and then I went on to law school.

One might think not having the rigors of traditional academic class work would have hampered me. To the contrary, developing a passion for learning far better prepared me for higher education and life, than cramming for a biology quiz. Looking back as an adult, I'm amazed by many of my Center experiences, especially in light of the narrow scope and lack of creativity in my children's high school education.

I remember each semester we had Town Hall brainstorming sessions with sheets of blank newsprint taped to the walls so we could write our ideas for learning groups that energized and motivated a group of otherwise potentially apathetic teens. In designing our studies, we felt empowered and limited only by our creativity, having phenomenal resources within the Center, with facilitators for every basic subject, and often using outside experts, professionals, and Chicago as our classroom. Mrs. Paul was my favorite Center teacher (facilitator). I loved history and her.

The Center was an intense environment for me. I felt I didn't fit in, and that I was a boring traditional guy among all those free spirits. She made me feel I belonged; I connected with her. She was a liberal, intelligent woman who led us on an adventure exploring innovative and unique ways to learn. That was beautiful. With her guidance, studying history represented the greatest highlight of my three-year Center experience. As we began forming our group, she suggested we should take advantage of living in a dynamic city with ample access to original sources.

Our history group traveled two or three times a week to the Chicago History Museum. (formerly the Chicago Historical Society) We had special access to the private archive library on the top floor. Wearing special gloves, we were allowed to pore through original letters and documents. On my very first day at the library, I read actual letters between Mary Todd Lincoln and Abe's former campaign manager who befriended her after she was institutionalized. It was an awesome experience. Mrs. Paul "facilitated" and guided 16- and 17-year-olds "touching" history. That's incredible, and we couldn't do that in the parent school. I spent two years at that private museum library because it was such a great place and we were so welcome that we expanded our learning to include multiple history topics of interest, which the library could facilitate. Consistent with Mrs. Paul's direction, we used Chicago as a backdrop for our learning. I recall first satisfying my U.S. History requirement and then continuing with other studies my senior year.

I remember my research and history papers addressed the U.S. between the wars, and using the Historical Society archives, she suggested I start with first-hand accounts of events as they unfolded, and not as they were ultimately documented in history books. In this vein, I first traditionally studied the Volstead Act, then innovatively learned about the effects of prohibition by poring through Chicago newspaper microfiche reporting on the St. Valentine's Day Massacre starting with the first articles the day it occurred.

When my study enveloped the 1930s and Roosevelt's efforts to end the Depression with various newly created agencies, I recall she suggested, as illustration of Roosevelt's effort to put the unemployed back to work, I study the Skokie Lagoon as representative of the Civilian Conservation Corp. The Historical Society had detailed reports and photos of its development. To trace its history, I met with current administrators responsible for maintaining the lagoon. I lived a couple of miles from the Skokie Lagoon and never knew I lived so close to history. Next, I studied the industrial revolution and the growth of big business. The title of my paper was "The Industrial Revolution in Chicago; The Rise of the Frango Mint." It was a study of Chicago from the great fire of 1871 to the beginning of the twentieth century.

My research focused on Potter Palmer, George Pullman, and the Burnham Plan, but mostly on Marshall Field—"give the lady what she wants"—as representative of how he created a niche in Chicago and a road map for retailing in America. I attached a small box of Frango Mints along with my final report, hoping it would help in my evaluation. And it did! I thought about that report a few years ago when reading *Devil in the White City*. Thirty years later, the author documented much of what I had studied as a kid!

Through it all, Mrs. Paul was there to help me. She struck me as the most grounded Center teacher. Sure, it was "self-directed learning" but she held us accountable. Every Friday she and I had a one-on-one meeting where I shared with her what I had studied that week and she'd ask me specific questions. She helped me establish a thesis and determine how I would tie that information into my research paper. Over the years, I've shared what I did with anyone who would listen. I talked about my research in the Historical Society private archives. People can't believe kids were given that much latitude. In hindsight, I can't believe it either.

I never liked math, but for the first time it didn't scare me when I approached geometry and third-year algebra through independent study augmented with private tutorials a few times a week with Vernoy Johnson, the Center's math teacher-facilitator. Algebra at college was basically a review of what I had covered in the Center and I aced the course. My college professor, however, never excited or motivated me like Mr. Johnson did.

With teacher-facilitator Bill Gregory, our civil rights group approached the topic from social, political, literary, and cinematic perspectives. A group member's housekeeper from Montgomery shared stories concerning her experience during the Montgomery bus boycott. We studied the 1964 Civil Rights Act and the 1965 Voting Right Act, and then met with a legislator who talked about the debates on these landmark laws. We read Susan Gregory's book, (Mr. Gregory's daughter) *Hey White Girl*, the play *Raisin in the Sun*, and watched the movie *In the Heat of the Night*. A relatively unknown young Chicago Tribune film critic (and New Trier alumnus) led our discussion. His name was Gene Siskel.

My art history group, with teacher-facilitator Irene Niebauer, studied Impressionism, Post Impressionism, and Modern Art. We visited the Art Institute and Museum of Contemporary Art to view the works of artists our group studied. Recently, I was at the new Modern Art wing of the Art Institute and I was amazed at how many artists I recognized from 35 years earlier!

The facilitators were a major force in guiding me and others into young adulthood by making us responsible for our education and decisions. They gave me the confidence, tools, and maturity to succeed. I feel privileged to have experienced this innovative form of high school education that laid the groundwork for my successful college and law school careers, and lifelong love of learning. In the Center, in addition to substantive material, we learned how to learn and that, I believe, is one of life's most important lessons.

> *A. E. is a retired attorney and businessman. Following a successful legal career in corporate America, he now advocates for the Illinois Chapter of the National Multiple Sclerosis Society in Springfield, IL and Washington D.C. He has returned to Glencoe where his youngest child attends New Trier.*

Short Takes

For almost twenty years, I've owned and run my ice cream shop and won't get a summer vacation until I retire. The other half of my work is music. I write music and lyrics, and my blues/R&B band is going well.

~Rick Campbell, 1979

The Music Man

David Abell, 1976

I was very much into music when I entered the Center as a sophomore. I knew that was what I wanted to do for a career. So, my curriculum in the Center was heavily steered towards music. I did a couple of courses in the high school all three years, mainly orchestra and opera, but also some dance as well. And I pursued other interests in the Center, like history, literature, and poetry. There was one class called Kids Live that read some cutting edge literature. My mother was really interested and she sat in on the classes that were held at our house in the evenings. Over all, I had a wide-ranging curriculum although it was concentrated on performing arts. I often went outside the high school world, like playing viola in a string quartet at the Music Center of the North Shore.

One of the best things that I did was going down to the American Conservatory in Chicago to study something called Modal Counterpoint— basically 16th century composition and one of the best ways to learn about music—with Stella Rogers, who had been a student of Nadia Boulanger, probably the greatest teacher of musicians and composers in the world. I received high school credit for that through the Center, and I subsequently studied with Boulanger in Paris when she was in her 90s.

Being in the Center didn't cut me off from the music that was available at the parent school, like orchestras and musicals. In fact, being in the Center enabled me to devote a larger amount of time for those classes. The group activities in the parent school, combined with the freedom of the Center to pursue slightly different things like the counterpoint lessons was a good combination. I think one without the other might not have worked so well. Having both available to me was pretty perfect.

I wrote *Lagniappe*, the all-school musical, my senior year. It was always a book musical, a book and a collection of songs that aim to tell a story, just like the classic musicals of Rodgers and Hammerstein. Our faculty sponsor, Mr. Boyle, chose a seventeenth century English play, Ben Jonson's *Volpone*, as the basis for the show. We set the story in the Wild West, so I had to come up with music to match. Volpone was a shyster, a conman, and the story had lots of twists. We called it *How The West Was Taken*. I wrote about two-thirds of the music and most of the orchestrations. Ann Hampton Callaway wrote about a quarter of the music, and one or two other people wrote the rest. I knew nothing about orchestration. It was a huge learning curve, a great experience for me, and it's an important part of my work today.

One of my projects at the moment is to publish the full orchestral score of *Kiss Me Kate*, Cole Porter's great 1948 musical for The Cole Porter Trust. They are paying me to publish what's called the "critical edition" of the score, a scholarly edition that can be used by orchestras and theater companies. People who want to perform *Kiss Me Kate* will soon have at their disposal the full score, orchestral parts, and some background material. This will be the first of the great Broadway classics to be published in this way.

The impetus for it and the beginning of my knowledge of orchestration goes all the way back to *Lagniappe '76*. The first couple of songs I orchestrated as a 16-year-old were terrible. When I heard them in rehearsal I thought, "Oh, I have to change this or that, you know this doesn't sound good." Now I know what I am doing. *Lagniappe* was a laboratory, a living laboratory for a musician learning to write music and orchestrate.

The Center also gave me the time to conduct the production. It was a huge sort of labor and those are jobs that are usually done by three different people. I was doing all of them. That's how I got into Yale with no grades for three years of high school. My SATs were okay but, more importantly; I made the admissions committee a tape of me doing just about everything I could possibly do. I sang and played the viola, including one of my own compositions. I also included some orchestration I had done. I think the Yale music department just said, "We need this guy." Yale put me back in a traditional academic atmosphere. In a sense, it wasn't that different from the Center because we had a lot of choice and we didn't have to decide our major until junior year. I just took what I wanted—the foods that tasted nice and some that were nutritious.

At Yale, I met a conductor who was very active in opera and later became his assistant at the New York City Opera and at the Washington Opera. Two years later, I went to the Julliard School and earned a Masters in conducting when I was 25. Now I live in London and conduct music theatre, opera, and concerts, such as a Sondheim eightieth birthday concert with the Proms here at the Royal Albert Hall.

The center was good preparation for my career because I have been a freelance conductor for almost 30 years now. In that profession, I have to be very self-directed. I have never had a permanent salaried position. I just go from job to job, setting my own goals, figuring out how to meet them, finding the people who could help me meet them, setting my own schedule, and evaluating whether I had met the goals. The Center started that process early on, the sort of stuff that I do, to this day, every day.

> *David attended Yale, the Julliard School, and the Conservatoire Americain in Fontainebleau, France. His teachers included Nadia Boulanger and Leonard Bernstein. His career has taken him all over the world, conducting major orchestras in Europe, the U.S.A, and the Far East. Although best known for the televised "Les Miserables" 10th and 25th Anniversary concerts, his passion is opera and he also conducts symphonic concerts. In 2012, he conducted "Porgy and Bess" at the Cincinnati Opera. He lives in London with his partner Seann Alderking, a pianist, and musical supervisor.*

Short Takes

The Center gave me a lot of confidence in myself and allowed me to find out who I was. I remember the feeling of being part of something different and important, where learning was fun and relationships developed. Being in the Center was the best part of high school.

~Barb Schwarz, 1974

FROM SMALL SEEDS

CURT MILBURN, 1976

In the days that bridged the 20th and 21st centuries, I toiled in an urban redevelopment project that was a Center grad's dream. In 1995, the Phalen Corridor was 2½ miles of a polluted rail corridor rambling through four low-income communities in St. Paul, Minnesota. Due to industrial flight and job losses, the original redevelopment goal was jobs, jobs, jobs.

Corporations joined with neighborhood groups and government agencies to craft legislation creating the first large-scale pollution remediation grants of their kind. We all pulled together and went to Washington, DC to raise the $21 million for a road linking our sites.

As the project director and first staff member, it soon became clear that in order to keep the focus of all our partners and funders, and to make a strong impact on these deserving communities, we needed to expand to a holistic focus of "new urbanism." We began to incorporate affordable housing, wetland reclamation, multi-model transportation, job training, and education.

I know it must sound like hyperbole, but by 2006, when we voluntarily closed our doors, the project exceeded $600 million in investment; thirty-one businesses had located on the corridor creating 2,500 jobs; eight wetlands had been reclaimed, including the nation's first moribund shopping center being torn down to bring back the lake that had once been there. An inner-city school was opened as well.

Of course, the Phalen Boulevard was open to traffic linking the projects together. As one of the agency representatives once said, as director, I was the United Nations of the initiative, working to keep everyone's focus on the prize of completing the project. However, another colleague also noted I had all the responsibility for the project and none of the authority. It was often a struggle to keep the myriad of elected officials, business people, neighborhood groups, and governmental staff pulling together on one narrow piece of real estate in the entire city of St. Paul, Minnesota. It also must be noted that the initiative did not cure all the ills the communities suffered. Unemployment is still high, the existing housing continues to deteriorate, and the sub-prime lending collapse hit those neighborhoods like a sledgehammer.

However, it was a unique moment in history. The community was ripe for change, government was beginning to focus on collaboration, and corporations could clearly visualize the tangible benefits of redevelopment. We have been studied by experts from around the country, but I'm left to wonder if such a project could ever be replicated. My "I wonder" about the project is a lot like my "I wonder" about the replicability of the Center.

I remember the reaction of my parents to my entering the Center was one of cautious relief. In my sophomore year at New Trier, I had had the distinction of amassing more ditch slips than any student in the history of that venerable institution. I had this verified many a time by the vice-principal. My memory? "Curt, what are we going to do with you?" Well what they did with me is send me to the Center and frankly if they hadn't, I never would have finished high school.

Through all my years of growing up, I harbored a passion to do things my own way and something inside me also contained a drive to make something great happen for others. I don't know if the Center attracted unique individuals who have a sort of fever to do things in alternative ways, or helped them (me especially) form their individualistic lifestyles into something worthwhile. Perhaps it was a bit of both.

Once in the Center, I was even more self-directed than the structure of the Center recommended. I continued my practice of skipping out on organized events, avoiding the Town Halls, and meetings with my advisors. It was in the Center, however that my independent spirit was not quashed, but allowed to breathe. I began to write original songs on the guitar, many of which I still play today.

Also while in the Center, I directed what could be the worst rendition of the play, *Twelve Angry Men*, ever produced and tortured twelve of my fellow Centerites to be in the cast (sorry guys). *Twelve Angry Men*? It was more like 12 befuddled actors. Only a couple of the guys in the cast had experience in acting. That became frighteningly apparent when our dress rehearsal took over four hours because so many of the angry men forgot their lines. On the night of the performance, I stood just off stage, when possible mouthing the script, but quite often whispering the lines when anyone would drop one. I sounded like an incessant snake hissing off stage left. I have heard actors talk about a moment in their careers when their mind goes blank and they have absolutely no idea where they are in a play. We had twelve well-meaning guys have umpteen of those moments throughout the performance.

In the Center, it became my forte to set up intricate projects. This resulted in an 18th Century American dinner party complete with a confidence scheme designed to rob my guest of millions. The dinner party was set in Virginia sometime in the 18th Century and was based on things we learned in the text on the Potomac River. Our menu was well-researched and included what well-to-do landowners of the day would have. (leg of lamb, sweet potatoes, corn, etc.) After dinner, the men retired to the study, (my parent's TV room) to discuss investing in my proposal to build a canal from the Potomac to the fabled Northwest Passage. I showed them a map that proved its existence. (I had planned to take their money and head down to New Orleans and spend it on fast women and liquor.) The women were supposed to retire to the parlor to place cloves in apples (an early air-freshener) and gossip. The problem was the ladies in the Center weren't going to go back a couple of centuries to become second-class citizens and they crashed the meeting of the men. No one, boy or girl, would even invest pretend money in my scheme that night. It taught me that I stink at leading a devious and nefarious life and I had but to arrange my affairs with moral fortitude. (Rats!)

And there was, of course, the Rivers project. It sprang from a seed that Mr. Greg planted. That seed not only resulted in the Rivers project, but in my publishing a book about the History of St. Paul. After high school, I tumbled around backpacking and picking up jobs here or there mostly to pay for my travel habit. I eventually moved to Minnesota and went to college. My fervor for studying history and a love of learning took off. After being a horrible student in high school, I excelled in college. Attending classes helped.

I met a German girl on a park bench in St. Paul and within four days we were in Glacier International Peace Park hanging out in the Rocky Mountains. One thing led to another (actually three others) and we had a son named Paul. He is now 12 years old and he is very willful and challenging. He's also one of my best friends. Our next child was Julia and she died at seven weeks. During that tough time, my wife took the day shift at the intensive care unit and I took the night. I've never sung so many Frank Sinatra songs to anyone. She died in our arms and the grief was horrible. Next came a strapping, smiling Daniel who is now eight and continues to be my angel on earth.

Professionally I shed the handle "Curtis," and started calling myself "Curt." (I thought it had a more manly sound to it.) I worked for eight years "hands on" with neighborhoods, getting rid of crack dealers, prostitutes, and gang members. I then took an amazing job on one of the largest inner-city redevelopment projects in the country. That was the Phalen Corridor.

Finally, my need for independence and my goal of helping to shape a brighter future for people came to the fore. As we began to enjoy the project's success, I made a critical mistake, I was finishing what I started out to do and decided to close down the office. The project, I thought was a success, ready to stand on its own. I got a job in business with a corner office, two secretaries. I was miserable. I resigned from my job and with the economy heading into the toilet, my mortgage, wife, and kids to support, the wife says, "Remember when we married you promised to move to Germany some day?" (I had just said it to get her to marry me.) So, we loaded up the truck and we moved to Germany.

After almost two years, I don't know if it's a temporary deal or permanent yet. Being in Germany has been like being a 16-year-old in the Center all over again. I have finished writing a suspense-thriller novel and I am working as a tour guide with a company that encourages me to dive back into historical research and invites eccentric behavior from their guides. (I fit in quite well.) I have also finished training to be a kindergarten teacher, a job that starts in the fall. I am still exploring music. I know this seems crazy, but when I have time, I perform as a street musician and I play my guitar and sing for the people passing by. Some even drop a few Euros in my guitar case.

All of us might have poignant moments in our lives where we are affirmed, but which might almost be embarrassing to recall to others. However, I think it is important for a book on the Center to relate one such moment here.

A number of years ago when I was back visiting the North Shore, I happened upon Bill Gregory on a small walking path in a garden by the Wilmette Harbor. He seemed happy to see me and I was thrilled to see him again. He asked me what I had done with my life and I told him about some of my work in the inner city. He surprised me as he began to weep. He told me so few of his former students went on to what he felt was important work, work dedicated to helping others. I can only wish that Bill Gregory had lived more years so that he could read in these pages about the high regard in which he was held by so many of us. I have a feeling that his important work as a teacher and that of all of the staff of the Center will be affirmed by the inspirational work that many of my fellow Center graduates performed over the last thirty-plus years.

Currently, Curt is the owner of Big Hat Tours and he is the highest rated tour guide in Munich, Germany.

Short Takes

After graduating from Yale, I worked for the Ford Foundation moving up through the ranks to become the Regional Grants Administrator for Latin America and the Caribbean.

Now at grad school, I am about to finish my M.S. in International Affairs with a concentration in Socioeconomic Development. I've had a great time, doing an internship with the Africa Bureau at the UNDP, and then did a consulting gig with the Earth Institute at Columbia University, evaluating a Millennium Village in Mali for Jeff Sachs.

I became involved in political activism in the 1980s, working to change U.S. foreign policy in Latin America, and have worked as a volunteer for the past 24 years for a nonprofit called Dos Pueblos, of which I am now the board chair. In all, life is good. The Center was a life-changing, life-saving, hugely transformative and formative experience for me.

~Ann Garvin, 1974

The Centerfold Revisited

O ne of the first Center-wide projects was the *Centerfold*, an erstwhile student publication that contained photos, sketches, poems, essays, jokes and a little news. It was published at the whim of its committee members and sardonically titled after the centerpiece of a then popular magazine. The Center's *Centerfold* is revived here one last time to create a few thousands words in a few surviving photos.

Starting the year; brainstorming in action.

Memories From the Center's Archives

Jim Bellanca, Center's first coordinator, facilitates Town Hall schedule making.

Student presents team study results.

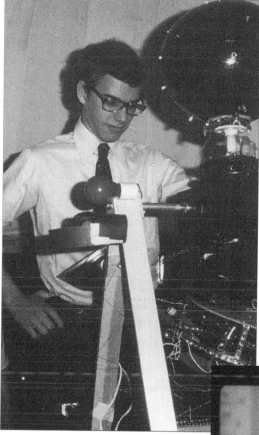

Eliot Neel and his projector mechanism for the Center planetarium.

Vernoy "V.J." Johnson

A World Without Bells and Grades

Bill "Mr. Greg" Gregory

Arline Paul holds the paddle in town hall discussion.

Beverly Miller Kirk

New Trier East Principal Ralph McGee

AN INTROVERT'S EVOLUTION

DOUG GREGORY, 1977

The academic knowledge I gained while in the Center was paltry compared to my first three years at New Trier. It also never gave me an epiphany that would shape the rest of my life. I say these things because I want to highlight what the Center did give me that made my final year a hallmark.

It was in the Center that I was freed to explore facets of my life beyond academics, so that the person I was when I left the Center was far more prepared for life and complete as a human being than the person who entered. It took quite a while for me to realize that the Center was what I needed. I had been one of those well-behaved "gifted" children who routinely earned straight As, and was "straight" in just about every other possible way.

I had no interest in experimenting with alcohol or drugs, didn't disobey my parents, attended the Wilmette Presbyterian Church every Sunday, and did all my homework without supervision. At New Trier, my schedule was full of four-level classes and my report card remained perfect. Dave Simpson, a classmate and later a fellow Centerite, used to call me "Dudley Do Right" in reference to my straight-laced demeanor (at least that's what I hope he meant).

But by the time I was a junior, it started to dawn on me that I was no longer getting what I needed out of high school. I was intensely introverted; my favorite activities, such as reading magazines and building model aircraft, usually were solo. I did take part in activities such as New Trier's boys' choruses as well as the choir and youth group at church, but my ability to interact with my peers, especially girls, was still terrible. I had just a few close guy friends and, by the end of my junior year, had never even asked a girl out on a date.

My goal after high school gave me another worry. I had passionate interests in aviation and military history. My dream was to go to the Air Force Academy and become a fighter pilot. Attending the Academy was going to be as stressful an experience as I could imagine, and it would be an environment where free time, social events, and women would all be in very short supply. Although not as intense as the Academy, New Trier was demanding and competitive, a school proud of its reputation for sending graduates to college. Because I did not play on any of New Trier's athletic teams (I was a late bloomer physically), I knew my only chance of gaining acceptance to the Academy was to excel academically. I therefore worked hard to keep my grades superb, but as I looked ahead, I began to see that I was about to move from one challenging institution into an even more challenging one.

It was not clear to me that I could sustain my motivation (or my sanity) through eight solid years of grinding study. Even then, it may never have occurred to me to try the Center without one quirk of fate: My dad was Bill Gregory, one of the Center's founding fathers. Dad came to New Trier as an English teacher in 1957 and adored his interactions with students. He hated grading papers, embraced the social movements of the 1960s, and knew there were kids who were just not suited to New Trier's structure and singular focus on college prep. I don't know exactly what role he played in the Center's genesis, but he was in it from the start, and it was probably the most perfect environment he could have imagined, allowing him to be far more than a mere "teacher."

Dad did not, however, try to sell the Center to me. In fact, I recall no times when he pushed me in that direction whatsoever. He was just part of the Center, and I learned about it through his conversations at home, or when driving with him to school (one of the perks of being a teacher's kid is never having to ride the bus).

Had I not been aware of the Center through my father, and in so doing come to believe that it was a perfectly legitimate and acceptable alternative to the parent school, I may never have considered it as a viable option. So as a senior in 1976, finally aware that I needed an escape from terminal studiousness, I became a Centerite.

The Center's environment was the antithesis of the parent school, and it was precisely what I needed, which is to say unstructured, social, and completely lacking in externally-applied pressure. Arline Paul was my advisor, and she was simply perfect, giving me just enough direction and supervision to keep me active but letting me have the freedom to find myself.

Although the academic aspect of the Center was the least of my concerns, I wasn't completely idle about academia. Some other brilliant Centerites, including Preston Kavanagh and Jeff Levin, teamed up with me and we tried to teach ourselves calculus—with little discernible success. We also read *The First Circle* by Alexander Solzhenitsyn. I started writing a novel that I had wanted to write for several years but never had time. It was sort of a sci-fi-meets-third-world-war story; I didn't finish, but did produce 134 pages by year's end. And I continued taking some parent school classes, including physics, boys' chorus, and chorus-opera which staged *Kismet* in the spring. Had I wanted to, I could have taken one or two summer school courses and graduated a year early. Spending that year in the Center instead was, for me, about developing as a human being. Change, as my first selection of what to do in the Center shows, was not easy.

The one activity I remember most from my year in the Center is playing cards. Various groups of us would play Hearts or Bridge on a regular basis, and doing so gave me long stretches of social interplay with fellow students. The Center provided a very safe environment; only there could playing games be considered a legitimate way to spend time in school. And as a group activity, card playing had none of the pressures or expectations of one-on-one interactions, like dating. There were plenty of other ways the Center brought students together, from Town Halls to support groups, but to me it was the card playing that helped break me out of my shell. Maybe that's because it was one of my regular card-playing partners who became my first serious girlfriend.

Teri Lindley was a regular participant at the card table, and over the months, I spent time teaching her how to play Bridge. She became a good friend and, in fact, she was the first person I got to know really well as a friend who also happened to be a girl. Eventually, it dawned on me that I was feeling more than friendship for her, and we started dating over the final two months before graduation (our first date was to see "Star Wars"). The latter sentence sounds ordinary enough, but for me having a girlfriend was a revelation that may not have happened if I had not been a Centerite. Teri and I stayed together for two years before we decided to move on. Teri exemplified perhaps the one characteristic that the vast majority of Centerites had in common—being non-judgmental and accepting of others.

The Center gathered students who were incredibly diverse intellectually, socially, and emotionally, and it mixed students of different year groups. It eliminated the structures and competitions that stratified other New Trier students. Instead, it made everyone equal in importance, gave us all a chance at self-expression, valued anyone's input, and focused on being inclusive rather than exclusive. Centerites, who all were there because they wanted to be there, were consequently open to new ideas, different people, and all sorts of explorations of the human condition. In that environment, I didn't have to worry about what people would think of me. I could just be. So, as perhaps it inevitably would have been for an introvert, most of my self-directed learning that year was about myself.

It was the Centerites around me who taught the lessons, and some of them made lasting impressions on me. Although I knew Preston and Jeff from the parent school, we became much closer friends, and getting to know Teri, Creon Leavitt, Julie Dusablon, Nancy Holloway, Mark Kirk, and a host of others made the year even more special. I must also thank Scott Cooper for teaming up with me on a Monty Python sketch we performed at the Center's talent show (completely expunging my nerdiness wasn't in my study plan).

When I graduated in 1977 I was more confident, happier, and more prepared for my future than ever. I may not have improved my academic self-direction (the Center was, after all, a school), but I did accomplish my all-important social networking goals. I became an Air Force Academy cadet, graduated with honors, and earned a Master's Degree from Harvard University before becoming a pilot. I met my future wife on the first day of pilot training; we have been married 25 years and have two adult children. My Air Force career lasted 26 years and took me and my family all over the world; from Alaska to Germany, including three tours flying the F-16 fighter. I retired as a Colonel in 2007 and am currently working for a defense contractor in northern Virginia.

Looking back at my time in the Center more than 30 years hence, I am sure of one thing: the Center was exactly what I needed at the time. It was a place where I could stop honing skills I already had and focus instead on what I lacked. It adapted to my needs rather than shaping me to meet an institution's needs. It helped me learn about people through interaction instead of books. And it helped make me a whole person. I was incredibly fortunate to have had the chance to be part of the Center, and I am forever grateful to the Center faculty, fellow Centerites, and of course my father, for making it possible.

Besides flying state of the art fighter jets, Doug's Air Force career included teaching political science at the Air Force Academy and managing international security assistance programs in the Middle East, Africa, and Europe.

Short Takes

In the Center, I began to learn how to:

- Take responsibility for my own life

- Piece together the mysteries myself

- Keep creativity in the forefront, not the background

- Appreciate how special people can be, and how our faults are badges of distinction and beautiful in their own right.

~David Spier, 1976

Doing the Right Thing
and Feeling Like a Jerk

Joyce Hanson, 1977

Graduation time was always a supportive time in the Center—for most of us. This was the time when we completed the work of our learning groups and independent studies, evaluated ourselves and asked others to evaluate us, and decided with the help of our self-selected graduation committees whether we were indeed ready to graduate. It was a supportive time because the Center operated on a very personal level.

Because we were in the habit of rooting for one another, you might think that high school students would find it difficult to review their friends' work. But because we were all in this strange educational experience together and wanted to see everybody succeed, we learned the value of true support. You might also think that given the power to select our own graduation committees, we might take advantage of the situation and pack the court with friendly judges guaranteed to make our graduations a shoo-in. But that was the trick of the Center's structure: what looked on the surface to be easy opportunities often became the toughest challenges.

Although students selected their own graduation committees comprised of four members, at least two of those four had to be grown-ups, and at least one of them had to be a Center facilitator. I don't remember much about my own graduation, except that my dad was on my graduation committee and I graduated on time with the rest of my New Trier high school class. What I remember better—and it's a cringe-making memory that I've carried into my adult life—is how I refused to help a fellow student graduate early.

I'll call her "Lucy." Lucy and I had signed up for the same learning group at the start of a semester, and while I attended the group regularly, I don't recall ever seeing Lucy there. One day toward the end of the semester, I was hanging out at a table in Phil Hall when Lucy approached me with an insincere smile and brazenly asked me to evaluate her work in our group. I said no. Feeling like a self-righteous jerk, I mumbled something sheepishly to Lucy about how I really couldn't give her the student-to-student evaluation that she needed to show her graduation committee. She had never really participated in our group. How could I assess her performance?

Yes, I said "no!" This wasn't an easy thing for people-pleasing me to do. But I knew that in refusing Lucy I was supporting the idea of what made the Center work. It was an educational ideal made real, and if we didn't play along with the structure things would fall apart.

For those of us who hung out a lot in Phil Hall, Center life was lived publicly. When I said no to Lucy, I had witnesses, including a couple of facilitators. It was a shining Center moment for me when, after a now-frowning Lucy walked away, they thanked me for doing the right thing and told me I had "done good." Although it didn't feel that way at the time, I was glad for their support.

That memory has stuck with me all these years because it was one of those moments in the Center, and there were many, when I had a glimpse into what adult life would be like. Simply by sitting at a table in Phil Hall, I had made myself available for a learning experience in situational ethics, mixed feelings and standing by a decision I thought was right. A self-directed, self-teachable moment.

Joyce has been a writer and reporter for a number of magazines and newspapers She is now a Web editor at www.AdvisorOne. com. *After receiving a bachelor's in French from the University of Minnesota, Joyce earned her master's in journalism from the Medill School at Northwestern University.*

Short Takes

Going to Italy during the school year was a really special opportunity to learn by seeing. What I also learned in the Center was that everyone is an important part of community and has something to contribute.

~Jane McMurray Coppola, 1979

RIPPLES

CHRIS IDZIK, 1977

First, there's a regret to be shared before filling in the details of my experience at the Center for Self-Directed Learning. I came into the Center my sophomore year and left before starting my senior year. Thus, I did *not* graduate from the Center, and indeed, I never did graduate from high school. Now I am in prison and…Oops, no. Just joking! (If the whole truth be told, I did spend ten years teaching history in prison part-time and I still don't have a high school diploma—but more on this later.)

I have to admit that I have always wished that I had become a Center graduate. Alas! My freshman advisor tried to dissuade my parents from letting me go "there." (I did not like my advisor or the advisory system at New Trier: it was sex-segregated with thirty boys per advisory room.)

As a freshman at New Trier, I had not had much academic success. I enjoyed one class with an English teacher, Mrs. Kemp, who made Homer's Iliad come alive, and I liked another teacher, Mr. McCrae, who taught me Biology. He played his guitar and gave me a D minus so that I didn't have to repeat the year. I also partook in the Saturday social service programs that took me to a library on the periphery of Humboldt Park in Chicago to tutor middle school kids. But that was not on my report card. I had flunked Math, got a D in World History, and knocked heads with my art teacher who said I couldn't use jeans as a subject for my still life. My few glimmers of hope and interest in learning were overshadowed by the mounting negatives and by the end of that year; the only salvation I could see was the Center where some of my friend's brothers and sisters were thriving.

When I conjure up my first impressions of entering the Center, I recall a core value: the genuine commitment to and pursuit of a learning community. The most elemental evidence of it took place on our opening day with the creation of our metal can-based, mailbox system that was along one wall of the largest room. We affixed our name to a one-gallon can and then they were stacked in an orderly way and, voila, we had our communication system established. This was followed by an all-school meeting and breaking into our community groups.

The first year, my advisor was "VJ" (aka Vernoy Johnson), a Renaissance man, great scholar, teacher, and friend of youth. I don't think it was even the first holiday before you felt you were part of his extended family. He was humored by my total lack of mathematical abilities and said to me, "We each have our strengths."

My second year, I was in Bev Miller's community group and she was another warm and dynamic adult who helped to guide us. For me, the community group and the Town Hall meetings were central strengths of the Center. By dedicating that time together, we made the community.

Our Center-wide meetings were our *polis*; those who entered saw how students and teachers talked and argued and cried and celebrated as equals. Within a couple of meetings we, the new students, took to standing and making an announcement about a camping trip, an endorsement of a course offering, an author to study or, later in the year on a parent's night for interested students and families, a description of why the Center was different from the other school.

I remember too, that we talked about politics, how we all were boycotting grapes and knew when Caesar Chavez was coming to Chicago and that some of us would march with him. I know that many of us gained a voice in the Center that was not found elsewhere in our young lives, and especially not in that "other" school. I think many of us became empowered and connected to our learning because we stood and delivered, we asked questions and we defended our alternative educational island.

For me, entering the Center marked the beginning of knowing myself as a lifelong learner. Key to this, I think, was that the teachers of the Center modeled it, they all were scholars, enthusiastic about learning, and committed to equal and respectful relationships with each student. How lucky we were to have such committed and smart teachers who exemplified life-long learning. We knew that they cared about us and we loved them as all fortunate students have admired their teachers for all human time. It was that deep. It was that special. In the two years that I was at the Center, every class and internship was a positive leaning experience.

I have selected a few of the most memorable ones, which demonstrate the expansive nature of the Center's offerings. It is worth noting that several of the teachers I had were not of the core staff, but interning college students and on two occasions, parents of students in the Center with me. This use of the greater community made a strong impression on me; I brought this idea to my classrooms when I became a teacher.

DREAM ANALYSES

Once a week, we would walk or bike or hitch or skitch a ride to our teacher, Mrs. Lee Pieper, who was a true seer, poet, and mystic (as well as parent of a Center student). She opened up her brightly lit living room to about ten of us and we would spend the next two hours sharing our dreams while she analyzed them from the paradigms of Jung, Gestalt therapy, and her eclectic, Celtic wisdom. She encouraged us to explore our subconscious and make meaning of our lives in a deeper way. She appreciated and expounded upon the supernatural and the phenomenon of ESP. She referenced symbolism often and blended in different religious points of view such as karma, reincarnation, and yin & yang. Our sessions with Mrs. Pieper enriched our understanding of the world around us and we always left in "heavy" conversation.

ARTIST INTERNSHIP

The Center enabled me to have a semester long internship with Diane Simpson, the artist mother of two Center graduates, David and Julie. I was a close friend of David's since fourth grade and had spent years admiring Diane's work. Once in the Center, I was thrilled to get the chance to work with her closely as an interning art student and to use her printing press. Over the course of a semester, I helped her print her own work, and created and printed my own etchings.

ABNORMAL PSYCHOLOGY

This was a class that was taught by an interning college student. I remember how we all really dug the fact that we were bypassing the "normal stuff" and diving right into all the "twisted stuff." Before class met, we would read about a particular diagnosis, schizophrenia for example, and then we would discuss the symptoms and the possible cures and how it was abnormal. The teacher knew the material, but also was effective in letting us talk and find meaning for ourselves.

WINTER BACKPACKING

The Center also incorporated outdoor adventure. There was one trip to the Upper Peninsula of Michigan that was led by one of the college interns who had some knowledge of wilderness camping. We planned the trip as a class; drove up to the Porcupine Mountains during winter vacation and, with cross-county skis and backpacks, went deep into the park for a week. The highlight? We spent one day building a snow cave that we all slept in. This trip spawned other expeditions that deepened my appreciation and knowledge of the wilderness.

CO-CONTRACTOR

I had started out as a carpenter's helper in the summer of eighth grade and every summer since, I had worked in construction. When a neighbor wanted to remodel her kitchen, a fellow student, Bob Sobel, who was then learning the electrical trade, and I came up with the idea of making the project into an internship. We tore out the outer wall and put in huge glass panes and, after gutting the rest of the kitchen, we put in cabinets and did all of the electrical. I can still recall driving to school in Bob's electrical company box truck—the coolest ride to class, hands down!

THE BEACH SEMINAR

The longest running class that I had while at the Center was my time spent on the coast of Lake Michigan. We went to the beach almost every day and often for several hours, before classes and afterwards. In the winter it was cold as we climbed about the beached ice floes and in the spring and early summer it was hard to leave and go to school—*very* hard. We spent a lot of time finding fossils and I also found a stone bird effigy carved by Native Americans hundreds of years past. On the beach, we also dreamed and schemed about our future plans (buying a government surplus Jeep and heading off to Alaska was a popular one) and we smoked and we loved and we lit fires at night. Lake Michigan was our ocean and Bumpy Park was our portal to the sea.

I also recollect other classes such as Mr. Gregory's "Famous Rivers of America" seminar and VJ's math sessions. I remember writing evaluations and reading evaluations for everything that I had done. It was very different from getting a report card that I wanted to shred. By this process, I was introduced to assuming responsibility for my learning and in evaluating what I thought I had accomplished. It was an important part of the learning process for both the teacher and the learner.

When, later as a classroom teacher, I had my own students before me, and there were traditional grading systems, I still had students evaluate their effort and the class itself. The lasting impact of all of the above was that the experience in the Center put a democratic and Socratic keel into my life that nourished a life-long learning pursuit.

When, in my senior year, my parents moved to New York, I balked at going back to a traditional high school. Instead, I enrolled in the Trailside School, a program that became affiliated with the National Audubon Society. Its maxim was "Our Classroom is Wild America," and we lived on a bus and traveled to forty-three states, making an education out of the natural world, the great rangers in America's National and State Parks and other community resources. (It was the Center on wheels!) Concluding what would be my senior year, I did not receive a diploma. Moreover, I had not taken the SAT test, but I did apply to Hampshire College, in Western Massachusetts, one of the alternative colleges such as Evergreen and Goddard, and I was accepted.

At Hampshire I constructed my curriculum in many of the same ways that I did at the Center. It was there that I became more interested in education. My junior year was spent student teaching with a progressive history teacher in New York City (who was a boyhood friend of Howard Zinn, the author of *A People's History of the United States* and one of my long-time heroes).

After Hampshire, I taught high school for a semester and spent a year in a carpentry cooperative. I then worked organizing with multiple Central American Solidarity organizations, enrolled at Teacher's College, Columbia University and received my Master's degree in the teaching of History prior to working in various fields of education for almost 30 years.

In the high schools that I taught in, I created new, innovative curriculum with a natural ease—no doubt, in large thanks to the Center. In the daunting years of the AIDS epidemic, I helped to create a class titled, "Senior Seminar in Public Policy: the AIDS Crisis," that brought the AIDS experts and activists of the Boston area into the classroom. I took the class to AIDS wards, hospices, and medical schools.

Later, I created a year-long interdisciplinary program at the oldest high school in America, The Boston Latin School, which examined the history of the rise of the Nazi party and the genocide of other peoples in history. (It was expanded from the core curriculum of the organization Facing History and Ourselves where I was a Program Associate for two years.)

Avoiding the burnout of a high school teacher, and tiring of teaching about genocide, I took a job as the Director of Education for a Heritage area north of Boston where I got in trouble for making the connections between New England and the history of American slavery. More recently, I worked as a mentor teacher and site director with the Boston Teacher Residency Program, a work/study program that awards a Masters of Education, free, for three years of service in the Boston Public Schools. This year I decided to change things up a bit and I taught in the public school system of New Orleans.

As I developed as a pedagogue, the experience of the Center was a touchstone. From the onset as a teacher, I had a deep, heart-felt, as well as cognitively recognized respect for the student as a learner. I also taught for a critical consciousness and to make history a life-changing experience. In the classroom, I validated community history and oral histories, and incorporated labor, gender, and peace studies into the class work. I encouraged students' voices and required student-based projects and teaching in the classroom. This made me a popular and largely successful educator, although it also created friction. In one school, since I did not write up school-wide detention forms or teach for the test, I was dismissed from a teaching position.

Besides teaching adolescents, as I have mentioned, I also taught adults— and not only those who were incarcerated. For several semesters I joined the staff at Lesley University as an adjunct professor in an alternative learning community that developed individual learning plans for adults returning to college. In this position, I again tapped into those years of creating a learning plan for myself as a 15- and 16-year-old. And, just as important as honing my academic skills, I have also continued my trade. I still use my hands to build, to fix, to form, and to make money. (This last part is very important.)

Every summer, as a teacher, I built an addition or took on a major carpentry project. Five years ago I joined a mason as an apprentice and have continued to learn that trade as well. I have had great satisfaction in balancing the work of the mind with the hand. It is this triad: investment in community, alternative/experiential learning, and manual and craft training that I can trace back to my years at the Center. I hope to take these three elements—to build, to think, and to learn—into the very last days of my self-directed-learning life.

That is the micro account, for although this reflection is about what the Center did for me, the ripple effects—the macro—is much larger and important. The largest wave for me personally is that my three children are all active learners. They are curious, they are self-motivated and, unfortunately for them, often bored by the typical classroom teaching. (When a parent is a self-directed learner, how could his or her children not be?) This, along with the influence I hope to have had with some of the over the two thousand students that I have had the honor of teaching, is perhaps is the greatest spin-off of those pivotal years. Thanks to the Center, I was able to add a little more to passing the generational torch of self-directed learning and it will roll on with my children and, hopefully many of my former students.

After spending the last two years as a labor organizer in Southern Louisiana, Chris continues his travels, his teaching, and his search for adventure.

Short Takes

I joined the Center to create my own class schedule around an internship with a prominent jewelry designer which enabled me to succeed as a nationally recognized jeweler.

As gratifying as this experience was, I was often frustrated by students who slid by. I wish the screening process had been stiffer.

~Polly Susan Hart, 1978

Learning Faster, Thinking Deeper

Mark Kirk, 1977

I *did* have an intellectual life before the Center, but the Center catapulted me into the major leagues. It was in the Center that I built lifelong habits that showed me how to solve really hard problems. There I learned to apply my intellect in a self-directed, disciplined way. The Center utterly changed how I went about learning and my commitment to academia. I don't think I ever got a particularly high grade before the Center. I never received less than an A after the Center.

Throughout my career—in the Navy, at the State Department, the World Bank, the House International Relations Committee, and as a U.S Congressman—and now a United States Senator from the Land of Lincoln, I have relied on my Center experience. It provided a key set of tools and life experiences that have enabled me at significant moments of my life and career to work hard with a clear focus on learning difficult subjects.

It was 1976 when I decided to join the Center. I wanted to study something unusual, current, and not from a canned textbook. The Soweto parent-teacher strike was going on. We formed a class on apartheid that I ran during my first semester. We studied the strike, the Mbeki struggle, and we learned a lot about a man named Nelson Mandela, considerably before everybody else knew who he was. We learned about the history of South Africa from the Boer War up through what the apartheid regime was doing to everyone.

Ten years later, when I traveled to South Africa, the first thing I did was go to Soweto and see all the places I had studied as a high school senior. In my second semester, Jeff Levin, Preston Kavanagh, and I teamed up to create a class we named "African Leadership," so as to be politically correct. Privately, we weren't. We called it "Kings of the Jungle." We studied Haile Selassie, Mobutu Sese Seko, Kwame Nkrumah, and Idi Amin Dada. We even phoned Idi Amin. The call started because Bob Green, a reporter at the Chicago Sun-Times, had called Amin and published his phone number. We called Uganda on the Center phone. I still remember the number—2241. I can't imagine what his switchboard operator thought, but we did get through and talked to a cabinet secretary. We wanted to interview Amin because he had said some crazy things—he thought he would marry Jimmy Carter if not for Carter's grey hair, and that he, Idi Amin, was coming to liberate Hawaii. So we wanted to interview him. We said we were from the Center magazine, Off Center. His cabinet secretary didn't buy it. We later made a fake tape with Jeff Levin pretending to be Idi Amin Dada that we played at Town Hall. We "fessed up" to the adolescent gag only when the New Trier News called and asked to publish it.

When I signed up for the Center, I hoped to accelerate my studies, especially in science. I started toward my goal with an independent study on missiles and the rocket race, building gyroscopes and learning how to guide missiles. I studied taxonomy at the Chicago Botanic Garden with the Director of the National Arboretum who was on a visiting fellowship. The Botanic Garden experience was fascinating, an intense look into the biology of plants and classifications from the earliest classifiers to the most advanced. DNA and genetics were barely understood back in the mid 1970s and I was studying them. By decades, I was the youngest student in the garden labs. I could keep up with the others and I still recall how important I felt as I learned in those labs and classrooms.

My science education continued outside the school walls. I learned the physics of flight, navigation, and FAA rules at the Palwaukee Airport flight school where I did some flying with my dad after I passed the FAA pilot's written exam. When I went on to Cornell University, I continued my love of science and was a Physics major until my junior year when I developed a strong interest in foreign affairs and shifted to being a European History major.

I never worked harder than I did at Cornell as I tried to find ways to study 16 hours a day, seven days a week for months; then continued the pace at the London School of Economics, where I earned a master's degree. It takes hours and days of thoughtful, isolated intellectual work to, "develop information dominance over a subject," as the military would describe it. When I do that now as a Senator, I can leave my favorite room, the Members Room at the Library of Congress, and know that when I walk into a meeting I own a really complicated subject better than anyone else in the room. I can boil it all down, explain it to others, and drive a solution.

For example, at the time I was serving as a Congressman, we had a problem bringing pressure on the Iranian government to stop making nuclear weapons. It is a really complicated problem with a variety of potential solutions. After a long weekend of delving into it, I said, "Oh, my God, I can't believe these guys are totally dependent on foreign gasoline, and if we cut off their fuel supply we generate enormous pressure on them to stop their nuclear weapons." After five years of work, I introduced a resolution and developed a bipartisan coalition with 412 Democrats and Republicans in the House voting for it. The Senate also voted in favor and President Obama signed the legislation last summer.

Somali piracy has become a really complicated problem. To get on top of the issues, I returned to the Reading Room where I could learn about each clan, each clan's leaders, and their backgrounds. It was important to know why the pirates are at sea, and what roles the Chinese, Russians, Europeans, and Americans are playing. Dedicated, focused intellectual activity on a complicated subject will often yield a nuanced and effective approach. That enabled me to become the chief advocate and rally Republican and Democratic backers to forge an effective solution. I do all of this intense reading and then try to make sense of all the material because when there is a problem on Capitol Hill, many folks play politics like seventh graders play soccer. Basically, too many repeat the partisan viewpoints they hear on TV. If you're a Democrat, you say what you hear from other Democrats. That is true of Republicans as well. Many times, I have to vote on standard issues and I simply go ahead and vote. But on emerging issues, I really believe it's better to find a new view and then drive a solution that's not partisan.

Early in my career, I was in the military in a position where I received the president's daily schedule. I was astounded by how much China dominated his daily life. That triggered me to do a three-week long "dive" on China. That led to an article I wrote for Foreign Policy magazine, followed by a series of speeches on the formation of the U.S.-China Working Group with 70 Democrats and Republicans that became the lead group on China.

All of these habits derived from my Center years where I learned that once I could say, "I'm interested in this topic and I am going to do a deep dive," there is nothing to stop me and no teacher to tell me to move on. The best thing about Arline, VJ, Bev, and Bill was that they were facilitators in the true sense of the word. They were there to help and encourage us. "Go, man, go!" One of the things that I regret is how more traditional "inside the box" thinking led to the death of the Center. I felt many teachers and administrators in the parent school didn't approve of the Center and were hoping to kill it off. Some even used the Center as a dumping ground for kids with problems in their classes. These teachers would say, "Oh, don't drop out of school, just go into the Center." These students were really unfocused, had problems at home or an alcohol or drug problem, but they were certainly colorful. It's hard to blow up your life at age 16, so they weren't in full destruct mode yet, but they were heading in that direction.

After I talked with my peers during the Center's reunion, I learned I had to change my ideas. I learned that the Center had played a significant role in changing their direction, just as it had helped me change mine. Like me, they learned to love the fast learning opportunities of the Center and how to become a self-directed learner.

Today, I am concerned that there are many students who don't have the option to advance faster or dig deeper as I was able to do. As a Congressman, I began and hope to continue as a Senator, a program called the Tenth District Laureates Program. Every year, for the 10 years I was in the House, I wrote a letter to all the junior highs in the district asking for the name of the top student in seventh grade who would be invited to participate in the Program. Every year we had a different theme such as Astrophysics, Mini-Medical School, Combat Medicine, and we would take them to the appropriate top institutions.

One year, a highlight of that program's Mini-Medical School was to observe an open-heart surgery at Rush Hospital. I thought, "Wow, this involves a lot of blood. How will they handle it?" The doctor came in and talked down to the students as he explained the opening of the chest and showed a model of the heart asking, "Does anyone know what the structure is?" And like a good seventh grader, one of the girls just rolled her eyes and told him, "That's the vena cava. Everybody knows that!"

> *Mark completed his service years in Naval Intelligence before election to the U.S. House of Representatives from the Tenth Illinois District and then the U.S. Senate as the Junior Senator from Illinois. Mark is noted for his intense commitment to his Illinois constituents and his attempts to bring collaborative bipartisan agreements between Democrats and Republicans in the House and Senate. Since suffering a serious stroke, Mark has displayed the same intense commitment to drive his recovery and return to the Senate chambers.*

Short Takes

Learning at the Center gave me hope and confidence in my ability to achieve, and the knowledge that my inquiring mind could find answers—sometimes on my own and sometimes with the help of others.

My favorite class was "Chicago Neighborhoods." We learned about changes in urban life and didn't stop there—we visited the communities and the people there. I suppose, looking back, the bottom line of all my learning experiences was about the people—both those in the Center and those I learned about.

~Karen Bowers Thompson, 1980

AKIN TO COUSINS

JEFF LEVIN, 1977

More than any other impact that it had on my life, the Center brought me out of my shell. In the parent school, I was pretty much a nerdy brain (or a brainy nerd, perhaps), with a small group of close friends. Once I got to the Center, things were a lot different for me, socially. I had lots of good friends and I enjoyed going to school every day. Not to utter a cliché, but learning became fun, a true adventure.

The Center encouraged me to think outside the box, to go against the grain, to not be afraid to be a lone wolf, and in general, to stand up for what I believe in even if everyone else thinks I'm misguided or off-track. Anyone familiar with my scientific work would recognize the indelible mark left on me by this set of values nurtured in all of us through our time in the Center. The courage to be oneself, in full flower, whomever that might be, with all the uniqueness and baggage that might entail, and despite the resistance of the world around us—that is a great virtue, a character-building trait whose affirmation was subtly and not so subtly communicated to us as Centerites.

Concepts like fostering diversity, tolerance, self-esteem, and a focus on the whole person have become lampooned buzzwords in secondary education in recent years, and perhaps for good reason, but I've always felt that the Center was way ahead of the curve on this, decades before these ideas became fashionable and trivialized. I believe that our facilitators truly loved us and wished for each one of us to flourish as strong, self-motivated human beings, as we moved into adulthood. No matter the content of our respective beliefs, attitudes, transcendent values, life goals—our facilitators were a constant voice telling us to embrace life, not to cower from life's challenges, and to go for it, whatever "it" might be. I still hear that voice.

Without question, what I remember most about the Center are the rich friendships, many of which have remained until the present day. These include the best man at my wedding, an old girlfriend, and a few other lifelong buddies—we are all still very much in touch almost 35 years downstream. Some of those buddies and I still recall a learning group we had that focused on the leadership of African dictators and was facilitated by Vernoy Johnson. At the end, we tracked down the phone number of President Idi Amin, the dictator of Uganda and placed a call to his office. We didn't reach him, but did talk to someone in his office. It seemed like a fitting capstone experience for the group.

I've always thought of the Center as a kind of special fraternity/sorority, and I think of us all as akin to cousins. When a Centerite does something significant in life, I feel a personal connection to it: that "one of us" did something special to impact the world. I've never felt the same attachment or sense of ownership to New Trier in general, or to my college, or hometown, or to any other social group, besides my religion. I am a religious scholar as well as an epidemiologist.

We were all blessed to be a part of a very extraordinary social experiment, and I will always feel a kinship to other Centerites that is kind of like extended family. I feel privileged to have been a part of a program that was at the vanguard of progressive, experimental, humanistic, student-centered education. We had the great good fortune to be taught and nurtured by a remarkable team of facilitators who were genuinely committed to our growth as individuals. I appreciate my Center experience more and more with the passing of time. I wish there were still places like the Center.

Jeff holds a distinguished chair at Baylor University, where he is University Professor of Epidemiology and Population Health, Professor of Medical Humanities, and Director of the Program on Religion and Population Health at the Institute for Studies of Religion. He also serves as Adjunct Professor of Psychiatry and Behavioral Sciences at Duke University Medical Center.

Short Takes

In the Center I realized my dreams could become realities. I was able to create some very strange music and actually perform it with a group of Center musicians who worked harder on music than any I have worked with since. It was the best two years of school I ever had.

After the Center I was a mover, attended a technical college for a pilot's license and avionics technology, followed up by running my vintage amp repair shop while playing in several different bands. I've helped run a recording studio and recorded two of my own albums. Now I am an electronics technician specializing in motor coach conversions.

~Jim Butler, 1974

Right Place, Right Time

David Simpson, 1977

I know three things the Center gave me. Each was unusual. There is my thirst for alternative education, followed by a suspicion of authority, and finally, confidence in doing what I need to do for myself.

By indulging my creative urges, the Center probably cemented my fate as a film artist, a career/life path that I mostly don't regret. I consider myself lucky to have had the opportunity to reject the top-rated high school in the country at that time in favor of a little, bold experiment in a corner of the school, inhabited by a strong group of individualists who many thought did nothing more than pluck cotton from their navels.

My primary activity during those years was filmmaking. My work was grounded in the parent school filmmaking courses. I lived in the film department for four years. The Center gave me the freedom to get utterly lost in my art. The film courses were taught by Kevin Dole, and then Peter Kingsbury. They exposed my impressionable brain to the canon of avant-garde cinema (Stan Brakhage, Bruce Connor, George Landow, and Michael Snow)— influences that are with me today.

In the Center, I built a homemade optical printer from a broken Super-8 projector and frosted glass. All my spare time was spent in the alchemical laboratory of my bedroom, cooking up allegorical visions in the crucible of the film canister. Years later my focus shifted from experimental to documentary work. To this day, my career and identity are bound up with filmmaking: I produce, direct, and edit social-issue documentaries, many of them with Kartemquin Films in Chicago.

Film is not my complete life. That's because the Center provided me with some stretching experiences that encouraged me to see the world from different viewpoints. What else stands out? Buckminster Fuller studies, "The Adams

161

Chronicles," expository writing, winter camping, and Soviet studies shaped me in different ways.

The Bucky Fuller studies were a highlight of my Center non-film experience. The span of Bucky's work defied categorization back then, and still does. It spawned in me a love for crossing academic borders, for "comprehensiveness" and synergy. It fueled my undergraduate studies in design, environmentalism, and philosophy. A small group of us undertook an investigation of Bucky's philosophy, inventions, and designs. We went to hear him lecture at the University of Illinois at Chicago and built a geodesic dome for the Bumpy Baccalaureate (our graduation ceremony). I was taken by Bucky's theory of Dymaxion sleeping, which posits that if you take short naps at regular intervals, you can get by with way less than eight hours of sleep. I arranged my schedule to take a nap every six hours. This included getting the school nurse to let me conk out in a bed every day at noon. What other school program would've tolerated this experiment? It worked really well for several weeks (I can't remember why I ended it). I've since used the technique during crunch times in college and afterwards.

Another key opportunity for me was studying writing with Jim Bellanca. To this day, I try to apply an approach I feel I learned from him: "Break your idea down to the simplest possible expression." This reminder shows me how little I have actually been saying and how much room remains for more. Other specific "JB" decrees (borrowed and modified by Strunk & White) that have stood the test of time (and I now teach to my kids): "Kill the adverbs and question the adjectives," "*Have* and *to be* are weak verbs; replace 'em," "Speak in the active voice." I also remember doing a writing exercise that might have occurred under JB's tutelage (one of my fuzzy memories). I sat in front of an exterior brick wall with a chalk line enclosing a square foot or so. The assignment was to fill two pages with what you see inside the square. The connection between that assignment and my subsequent life cannot be overstated. I went on to write my undergraduate philosophy dissertation on the psychological/aesthetic phenomenon of beauty. I can summarize my artistic and spiritual aspirations (they're one and the same) as an attempt to perceive and articulate the complexity and beauty in random samples. It may not have all started with the brick wall, but that moment tapped into something essential for me.

The Center was not for everyone. I think it functioned better for some kids than others. It worked well for me because I knew what I wanted to do and it gave me the freedom and support to do it. I did feel self-directed—a product of my upbringing and temperament. I'm unsure how well the Center was able to induce self-direction in those not already so-inclined. I'm sure there were kids who mainly smoked dope and slid by, but they probably would have done so in the parent school.

The Center felt like an experiment in Utopia. Even at that young age, many of us were aware that its underpinnings, its very existence, were part of a national Zeitgeist of innovation and reframing. We felt we were tapping into something on the cutting edge: The chance to take the reins of our learning, and to question the very modes of learning. The open architecture of the Center room, and the open minds of the people in it, gave the sense of limitless possibility. You felt as if anything could happen there and did—as if on any given day you could encounter someone or something that might alter the game plan for your day or your life. It was pretty vibrant.

It strikes me as tragic that the Center was relatively short-lived. The ideas at its core seem solid and universal. Was it ahead of its time? Was it too rooted in its time? Did the educational climate turn too conservative and timid to countenance such an experiment? What a loss. How fortunate I was to be part of it. We were in the right place at the right time.

After his undergraduate years at Evergreen State College and St. John's College in Santa Fe, David earned his MFA at Chicago's School of the Art Institute. He has produced a number of documentaries including the PBS production "Refrigerator Mothers." He is the father of two boys.

Short Takes

I don't think, without the Center, I would have finished high school! I felt a lot of validation, and learned what was not in any existing discipline's course of study, American Sign Language, and I've been an interpreter for many years.

~Jiraph Wirpel, 1974

BEHIND THE GATES,
I FOUND MY ROSE GARDEN

LARRY DIAMOND, 1978

My son, Mikey, had just started fourth grade when he and his good friend, Chris, were hanging out in our den after school…just watching TV. The kids liked to talk to me about politics. I was impressed Chris watched the news and read the paper. We started talking about how newspapers operate. I explained how I helped start two newspapers when I was in high school and later in college.

Mikey said, "That sounds so cool to be on a newspaper."

Chris added, "Yeah, that would be awesome."

I asked if their school had a newspaper and they said, "nope." I responded, "Well, why don't you guys start one? If you want, I can help you."

This led to a conversation about how I knew so much about newspapers and how my friend and I started a newspaper in a unique program in my high school called the Center For Self-Directed Learning. (I really got their attention when I told them the name of the newspaper was called "Centerfold!")

These two curious kids began to ask me many questions about the Center. This was the first time I ever explained my Center experience to kids, so I decided to use a visual to help me convey the unique character and idealistic mission of the Center. I brought out a card table from the storage room and grabbed a pen along with some yellow sticky notes.

I placed the card table upside down on the floor with the four foldable legs still tucked into the backside of the table. I then explained how there were basically four principles at work in the Center and when these four forces were working in harmony with each other almost any goal could be accomplished. I wrote, "DESIRE" on the first piece of paper and stuck it to the first leg as I unfolded and snapped the first table leg in place.

164

I explained that in the Center you could brainstorm and dream up any topic to study depending on one's passions and interests. The sky was the limit in terms of what you could study. There was no one forcing you to learn about a topic you were not interested in and this opened up a whole new way of thinking about school. Next, I wrote, "INITIATIVE" and stuck the yellow sticky note to the second leg as I unfolded and snapped the second leg in place.

In the Center, nothing happened unless you were proactive and took action to turn your ideas into reality. I explained in the regular high school, kids typically go from class to class with a more passive mindset as if they were "buckets" trying to capture all the information being sprayed at them by the teachers. In the Center, the academic tool of choice was a "shovel" where kids were more like prospectors searching for gold. In the Center, students were encouraged to dig deep into the topics they were passionate about. The goal was to seek knowledge not for a good grade but rather for the intrinsic fulfillment a student gets when one digs for information and discovers golden nuggets of knowledge on their own.

With desire and initiative in place, I wrote out the third tenet, which made the Center such a realistic microcosm of the world. The third leg of accomplishing any goal was "COMPROMISE." I explained how each student would write out their ideas for classes and post them on a giant wall in the Center where 150 other kids would post their ideas for possible classes. If you were interested in any of the classes posted on the big wall, you would simply sign your name below the course description. Sometimes, kids would write notes, "I'm interested in this class but only if you focus more on a different aspect," and then this potential class member would detail what their preferences were for the class. This was how the Center's registration for classes took place. Sounds simple enough, but on a deeper level that big wall of suggested classes represented the free market of ideas. You could propose any class you wanted, but the catch was you had to generate enough interest from other kids and you had to get at least one teacher to sign up and be a sponsor for the class being offered. This way, there wasn't total chaos since gaining a teacher sponsor allowed for a system of "checks and balances." Stubbornness had to give way to negotiation in order to attract other kids and a teacher sponsor. Just like the politics of Washington, DC, this democratic process of creating a curriculum could be "messy" business at times.

As deals and compromises were hashed out, the magic of the process was evident later in the week when "your" idea for a class soon became "our" idea for a class. After a few days, the best ideas tended to generate the most support from other students and teachers and that's how the curriculum was established each semester. In today's world, such a system would sound revolutionary but back in the good old days of the Center, such a process was routine and business as usual.

Mikey and Chris could not believe the story I was telling them and they sat on the couch mesmerized as I went on to explain there were no grades and state graduation requirements could be fulfilled in a self-determined, self-directed way. I explained how the Center had Town Hall meetings, which took place to determine Center policies.

They were amazed that the Center operated on such democratic principles where students had real "power" to determine their academic destiny. With three table legs locked into position, I turned the table over and it stood precariously in place. I asked them if they thought a good foundation had been established. Of course, they agreed a fourth leg was needed to make the table more stable before we could formulate a plan to start their school newspaper.

I took another yellow sticky and wrote, "PERSISTENCE," and placed it on the fourth leg as I unfolded this final pillar of the Center's success formula. I explained how the Center was a safe place to think out of the box and aim high. The Center was an educational utopia where one's reach often exceeded one's grasp.

Aiming high also meant missing the mark sometimes. Mistakes would be made but there were no grades so you couldn't really "fail" at anything. It was the "process" of learning that mattered most. In this process, with the guidance of amazing teachers, students were encouraged to be persistent and not give up. Mistakes would lead to adjustments, improvements, and new results. In the Center, kids didn't just try to memorize a bunch of facts to do well on a test. The mission was to embrace the process of learning and, in that process, we all "learned how to learn." This process could be frustrating at times, which is why it was important to stay focused and not give up on accomplishing the unique goals each student had created.

I explained to Mikey and Chris that if they started their own school newspaper, it was likely that many mistakes would be made, but the goal would be to use desire, initiative, compromise, and persistence to make the second issue better than the first one and so on. If they embraced this process, then each issue would get better and better.

After my little seminar on the Center, I took out a pad of paper and we sat around the card table now secure with four locked legs and principles in place. Just as I learned to do in the Center, we wrote out a game plan for what was needed to make their newspaper "desire" a reality.

The next day, Mikey and Chris took the "initiative" to go into the principal's office and asked her if she would support a new school newspaper. She said "yes," but that a parent sponsor was needed. I, of course, volunteered.

Forms were sent out to all the fourth and fifth grade classes. I was told by the principal that usually one or two dozen kids sign up for such "clubs," but a few days later I learned 62 kids had signed up! I had no choice but to organize the kids like a real newspaper. The kids who demonstrated the most interest became editors and the rest were divided up into separate departments (features, sports, news, photo, art, etc.). Mikey and Chris were the two managing editors and I had a blast with all these kids.

The paper was a great success and all 62 kids contributed articles, pictures, jokes, poems, etc. During one of the newspaper meetings after school, a couple of kids came up to me very frustrated that they could not think of any topics to write about. Like a true Center facilitator, my immediate response was, "Why don't you write an article about how hard it is to think of topics to write about." They ended up interviewing teachers getting their advice how to brainstorm topics and it ended up being a great article about how to approach writing and how to find interesting topics to write about. After our first issue came out, I set up a press conference between the school superintendent and all the student editors. I took pictures, recording the entire press conference.

Another way in which the Center impacted my life was in the area of politics. I've always had a deep interest in politics. For instance, I worked closely with our school superintendent to pass a referendum a few years ago that prevented teacher layoffs and cutbacks in our school district.

My interest in politics can be traced back to the Center. In a meeting with Arline Paul when I was a senior. I remember mentioning to her an interest in politics and she suggested I simply call our congressman's office and see if they needed any help. Secretly using the phone in the Center, I called Congressman Abner Mikva's local office and asked if they needed any assistance. After a brief interview, they accepted my offer and I became an intern answering phones and helping the local staff assist constituents who were having problems dealing with the federal bureaucracy. The highlight of my high school internship with Congressman Mikva was being his chauffeur when he returned to Chicago on weekends.

Later, I became a political science major in college and went on to the University of Chicago where I received a full fellowship in their Ph.D. program in international diplomacy. The roots of the ivy towers where I studied could be traced back to the Center. It was the Center which facilitated my internship with Congressman Mikva and this internship exposed me to the nuts and bolts of local and national politics, and further ignited my interest in politics and international affairs.

On Fridays, Congressman Mikva would often come from the airport to his local office in Skokie but after work, he would need a ride home. I volunteered my services and the congressman and I spent many car rides talking politics in my little two-door blue Camaro. He was a wonderful human and always made me feel comfortable. The only time I would get stressed during our drives was a difficult left hand turn across a major four lane street which was a bit nerve wracking during rush hour traffic. I remember thinking that the fate of the country, or at least the next big vote in congress, depended on my ability to get the congressman safely home.

Congressman Mikva later became a federal appeals court judge and also became an important mentor to a local politician named Barak Obama. I kept the congressman in one piece thanks to my skillful driving so I guess I get some credit (or blame depending on one's political views) for Barak Obama's rise to power.

Later in college, my connection with Congressman Mikva helped me become a White House intern where I worked for one of President Carter's top senior advisors, Anne Wexler. Working in the White House was one of the most extraordinary experiences I've ever had in my life. My connection with Congressman Mikva helped me become a candidate for the job, but the "Centerite" attributes of desire and persistence helped me get the job as I competed with many other highly qualified candidates. By taking some personal initiative, I was able to contact an intern from the previous year who worked in the White House. This former intern and I hit it off on the phone as we spoke for almost an hour. He said to me at the end of our chat, "Larry, I can tell you would be a great White House intern, so I'll put in a good word for you and I'll give you the direct phone number of a guy named Charles who is the person in charge of hiring interns." I persistently (and politely) called Charles' office one or two times per week and eventually charmed my way past his secretaries who finally allowed me to talk directly with Charles. Charles was very busy, but he was nice enough to take a few minutes each week to talk to me during the months of waiting to find out if I'd be hired as a White House intern. We would talk about what I was studying in college and, of course, I'd be on top of the news since we would discuss current events as well. I emphasized how I was willing to work night and day for the President if they gave me a chance for one of their coveted internship positions. Finally, after perhaps a dozen calls, Charles said to me, and I'll always remember his exact words, "Larry, if I hire you will you agree to stop calling me!" I said yes and thus began an amazing experience, which I'll always treasure.

The lessons I learned in the Center such as the importance of desire, initiative, and persistence also helped me maximize my experience in the White House. For example, most interns were given a blue badge, which limited their access to the Old Executive Office Building (a giant office building where most of the White House staff works next door to the White House). Due to the enthusiastic initiative I demonstrated, I was given one of the coveted green passes which allowed me access to the West Wing and most parts of the White House anytime 24/7 (excluding the top floor of the White House which is the personal residence of the President and his family). Every day, I would walk by the Oval Office in awe of the majesty of the office. Next to the entrance to the Oval Office is a scene I'll always remember. Every day, I would walk past the special military attaché who sat outside the Oval Office with the briefcase of nuclear war codes handcuffed to his wrist. Quite a powerful scene for a college kid to witness every morning.

I briefly met President Carter six or seven times. The first time was when I saw a couple of Secret Service men walking in front of the President as he approached one of the White House entrances. It was just pure coincidence that I was opening the door as the Secret Service men approached me. I wasn't sure what to do so I just held the door open and the Secret Service guys walked through the door and then the President walked right past me and said "Good Morning" to me and I said, "Good Morning Mr. President," as my 21-year-old heart almost jumped out of my chest from excitement.

Then I remember thinking it was odd that the President was about my 5'8" height. The President seemed like a larger than life figure on TV but in that brief moment when we were eyeball to eyeball, he wasn't much taller than me and that has always made me have a more realistic impression that national leaders are not superhuman but are similar to the rest of us.

Another time I crossed paths with the President was late one Friday evening around 10:30 pm. as I walked past the Rose Garden. It was a cool clear night with lots of shining stars. I heard a funny puffing sound like someone short of breath. There weren't really lights on in the Rose Garden, so I couldn't really see where the unusual noise was coming from. I slowed my pace and squint my eyes toward the direction where the sound was coming from. Then I saw a figure of a man running straight towards me huffing and puffing as he ran. I didn't know what to do so I just sort of stood frozen in my tracks as the President of the United States jogged right by me and smiled as he was taking a little late night jog. There was no Secret Service around (at least that I could see) and my only regret is I should have asked the President if I could join him on his late night run around the Rose Garden.

I was in the White House during the late months of the 1980 election when Carter lost to Reagan. After the election, the hectic pace of activity in the White House slowed down quite a bit since Carter was now a lame duck president. There were still several weeks remaining before my internship ended so instead of sitting around doing nothing, I "Centerized" my last weeks by setting up interviews with many of Carter's top advisors. I realized these advisors were less busy now, and I had a unique opportunity to use my access to meet them.

Earlier in college, I had used some of my Centerite attributes to help launch a new college newspaper (which still exists today). I decided I would try to set up a series of interviews for my college newspaper, which later ran as a series called, "Behind the White House Gates." I set up several interviews including an hour-long visit with Carter's right hand man, Press Secretary Jody Powell.

Mr. Powell welcomed me into his beautiful West Wing office, which was quite cozy with the sounds of a blazing fireplace off to the side. The right hand man to the president put his feet up on his desk while cupping both his hands behind his head and said, "Larry, fire away—what do you want to know?" In the middle of our interview, his phone rang and I remember thinking it could be the President calling him and here I was, a lowly college intern who may be witnessing some important historic event. Powell picked up the phone and said to his secretary, "I thought I said no calls…Oh, ok, that's important I'll take the call. Hold on a moment Larry." He took his pen and was taking notes.

Was there some international crisis brewing, I thought to myself? As he was writing, he was saying, "Yes, ok, yes, right." I wondered whether another Cuban Missile Crisis was unfolding or perhaps a new headache in the Iranian hostage crisis was developing and Jody Powell would confide in me about the nuances of what was taking place. Then he put down his pen and said, "Ok, I'll make sure to pick up the lean corn beef—not the fatty kind and rye bread, ok see ya later." I guess it was his wife or kid calling. He never did need me to help resolve any international crises, but we went on for some time talking about the presidency, the election, and the future of the country.

I left the Center in 1978, but the Center never left me. In my life, the Center has not been a place or a memory. The Center is really a verb since the process of learning has never stopped for me as evidenced by the 25 books about Kabbalah I just received from Amazon.com. If one of the goals of the Center was to produce lifelong learners, then I am a walking testimony to what the Center represented.

My friends in the regular school used to tease me for being in the Center. Of course, they were jealous that I could basically do whatever I wanted to do. I used to go to the racetrack every week or two with a Center buddy and we used to tell our regular school friends we were getting math credit by analyzing the racing form. Or I'd make up stories that we got gym credit by riding our bikes to school just to get a rise out of my non-Center friends.

On the other hand, I understood where they were coming from. When my regular school friends would walk into the Center to visit me, any number of bizarre scenes could be taking place. Sometimes, there were small clusters of kids just hanging out—not a book or piece of paper in sight. Sometimes you could walk past a student taking a nap or someone could be playing a guitar. Of course, there were times you had to step over the couple making out on the floor in the middle of the room.

Many days, the Center could be very chaotic filled with lots of students and you could hardly hear the person talking next to you. To an outsider, the Center may have appeared on some days like it was a miniature Woodstock and on other days it may have seemed like, as my grandfather would say, an organized mess. I was never defensive when my regular school buddies teased me about the Center. I would simply ask them, "Do you love school? Are you excited to get to school when you wake up in the morning? How often do you have lunch with your congressman?" Usually, questions like that quickly changed the conversation.

I'll always remember the Center as an intersection of idealistic students and supportive faculty. It was an amazing place where students were encouraged to grab a shovel and start digging into their passions in order to extract knowledge for the sake of learning. One time after telling Center stories, my son summed up the Center best when he asked, "Isn't that what education should be about?" Since there were no grades to be earned, knowledge was the currency exchanged and accumulated during those idealistic years in the Center.

Later in life, I have come to appreciate the magic of the Center even more as I see how this currency of knowledge has grown exponentially into a wealth of wisdom allowing me to navigate successfully through life and, in the process, create my own destiny.

Larry attended Pitzer College, started a college newspaper, worked in the White House and majored in political science. After Pitzer, he was awarded a fellowship to the University of Chicago where he studied international relations and diplomatic history. Returning to Chicago, he joined the business world, became a parent and began a writing career.

Short Takes

The Center made me more open to creative thinking, the necessity of self-reliance, the beauty of group support, and the efficiency of collective problem solving. Memorable highlights were the incredible Italy trip with Mrs. Paul and the group of eight, as well as a trip to VJ's cabin mapping and canoeing the headwaters of the Wisconsin River. I still remember looking at stars and planets with Elliot Neel in his planetarium and studying avant-garde filmmaking with two parent school teachers.

~Michael Rosenzweig, 1979

MY MISERABLE YEAR UNDER THE SKIN

SUZANNE ELDER (NÉE LAGERSHAUSEN), 1978

My Center year was a *miserable* year! As far as I can remember, I drifted. I floated. I was no longer sure of anything. It was chaotic and unpleasant to be so young, rudderless, and unable to navigate. I accomplished very little. I have no work product, nothing from that time that I can point to and say, "See!"

What did happen for me that year was quiet, under the skin. In that year, I found an emerging sense of self and the beginnings of my adult life. It was the time when I began to learn how to think. My Center year was the year that saved my life.

Before that year, my family was unwinding. In September, I transferred from Regina Dominican, an all-girls school, where the sisters' structure and the students' backlash was suffocating and disorienting. The Center was an open environment, flexible and welcoming. With nothing to rebel against and nothing to react to, I reset my internal compass, and began to recognize what I needed and where to get it. The Center enabled those changes.

I remember struggling with mathematics and geometry. I knew I was missing basic knowledge and I was frustrated, insecure, and afraid to ask for help. Peter Kidd and I had become friends that year and one day, off-handedly, he offered to help me. We would meet at the House of Pancakes to do our work and dine on Dutch babies. We were incorrigibly silly and we laughed all of the time. "Funny" became our most prized currency, not answers. Eventually with Peter's help, I forgot to be afraid and I learned how to find answers on my own.

Histories get fuzzy with time. It surprises me how people think it was the 1960s that were notorious. It wasn't until the 1970s that familiar spaces and identities were transformed and new untethered, free-form genres were bubbling up. Were there sex, drugs, and rock and roll? Oh, yes (and at frequencies, quantities, and volumes that both amuse and horrify my middle-aged self!), but there was much more. Computing, biomedicine, and all the technologies that have reinvented everything from music to mass transit were brewed in that soup.

It is no coincidence that the Center produced as many of the leaders that have advanced those genres as it did. The Center fit. The Center worked because it felt and facilitated its time, it embraced the students it attracted, and it cultivated a sort of genius in its soil. Since leaving the Center after but one year, I have lived. I have traveled, settled in different countries, built two businesses, found love, and started a family. I finished graduate school and set out in a different direction. I ran for public office and lost—but found a calling. I picked myself up, fought again for something even bigger, and won.

> *Suzanne holds a Master's degree in Public Policy from The Harris School of Public Policy Studies at the University of Chicago. This led to her leadership role in the Illinois' initiative for The Care of Students with Diabetes Act in Illinois, conducting a utilization study of select state health policies for the Center for Human Potential and Public Policy at the University of Chicago and her advocacy in Illinois and other states for the advancement of progressive health care policy and evidence-based solutions for the care of students with chronic health conditions.*

Short Takes

My career in special education grew out of internships I did while in the Center. My deepest memory is of Vernoy Johnson's insightful comments in my graduation committee. I found it many years later and was surprised by how well he knew me and predicted my future.

~Nancy Stewart, 1976

THE POWER OF COMMUNITY

BILL HUGHES, 1978

I have fond memories of the Center for Self-Directed Learning. The academic diversity helped me transition from a more regimented school environment to the greater freedom associated with college. More importantly, there are three lessons I learned in the Center that I have carried with me since:

- I work best in a community
- Everyone has something to contribute
- I hate chaos

First, a little background; I blame everything on Preston Kavanagh. In my junior year, he and I were in Boys Ensemble together. He introduced me to the idea of the Center. At first, I was politely curious. When I began to build my schedule for my senior year in the parent school, I was very disappointed in what lay ahead for me. I had transferred to NTE for my sophomore year. The result was that I had to take a number of freshman classes when I was a senior. I was not happy about this.

The ability to create your own curriculum within guidelines captured my imagination. My original motivation for joining the Center for Self-Directed Learning was for the challenging academics. This is ironic, given its reputation among some in the parent school as a "sheltered village" for those who otherwise would have dropped out of New Trier.

In contrast, I was impressed by the range of colleges that earlier Centerites were attending: Yale, Evergreen State, Wisconsin, Antioch. The truth is that, although I was in upper level classes, I was not studying hard. I wanted more of a challenge. It struck me that the Center was comprised of those with excessive enthusiasm that the parent school struggled to harness and those with insufficient enthusiasm for whom the parent school was drudgery. The Center worked because it drew the two groups together in one room. This was hard to see from the outside and virtually impossible to quantify.

After the initial organizational period (more on that later), I dove into the Center. I was taking too many classes. In addition to AP Chemistry and Cho-Opera, I took nine center classes. If a class was vaguely interesting, I took it. I overdid it, but that was OK with me. (I showed a little more discretion the second semester, but not much.)

DISCOVERING COMMUNITY

For the purposes of this book, I first thought it would be most appropriate to describe the internship I set up at Northwestern University with the Chemical Engineering Department or the English course on American Classics. However, today I carry the most enthusiasm we leveraged with the Wafucowie Canoers as the sign of what the Center meant for me.

It was *community* that best captures what meant the most in the Center. First, there were the Center's Community Groups. In contrast to Advisories in the parent school or homerooms in most schools, which were about taking attendance and making announcements, the Community Group was more about building mutually supportive relationships.

Within the 12-person Community Group, there was also the practice of formal support groups to help us evaluate our Center performances. These structures were in stark contrast to the regular school. Here, there was no competition among students with overly-competitive individuals sabotaging each other. In contrast to evaluation in the parent school, which was entirely about individual performance, the support groups prized collaboration and encouragement.

Our invented courses flowered from this spirit. Wafucowie Canoers was a group experience that hit at the core of what the Center meant in my life. Wafucowie Canoers sounded like one of those phony classes about which the parent school kids use to tease Centerites. We met early mornings and weekends to plan group outings and travel to different locations to practice our sport. This group attracted a broad cross-section of Centerites, all of whom had skills to contribute.

What I most learned in these unique Center groups came as a later aha in my life. After my classes in college were done, I learned that there are very few other times in life where individual achievement is so important. After college, most of our lives are spent making teams, groups, families, and companies more successful. The Center gave all of us the tools to begin working more effectively in the communities that make up our adult lives.

For me personally, the power of community and what I had gained in the Center impacted my college life in a strong way. Only after I joined a professional fraternity, did my college grades soar. I was in a community with other engineers where I could find support. I wanted the group to succeed and the group wanted me to succeed. I gave where I had skills and benefited from where others had skills that complemented my deficiencies.

I find it amusing that I joined a fraternity at an Ivy League university because of my experience in the Center. Kappa Delta Rho was not a stereotypical fraternity as found in "Animal House." It was much more like Lamda-Lamda-Lamda in the "Revenge of the Nerds." Neither was the Center a group of counter-culture misfits. It is hard to shake stereotypes, no matter who holds them.

My Center community experiences also affected the next stage of my life. Engineering was an excellent undergraduate degree for me. However, it held little for me as a profession. I wanted to become a product manager in high technology. This meant attending business school. At the time, the only M.B.A. programs that accepted newly minted college graduates were the University of Chicago and Kellogg at Northwestern. Back in 1982, most did not even know that Northwestern had a business school. At the same time, Milton Friedman's free market prescriptions were beginning to work for the U.S. economy and taking us out of the stagflation for the late '60s and '70s. As a University of Chicago professor of economics, his star brightened the business school.

I was accepted into both programs. After soul searching, I decided that I preferred the team-oriented approach of Kellogg classes, even though there was little prestige with the Kellogg name. I engaged in dozens of team projects at Kellogg, using the techniques I first learned in the Center.

This team approach truly does differentiate Kellogg from the other business schools. I am a founding member of the Seattle Business School Alliance. We regularly meet to promote different business events in the Seattle area. You always find a Kellogg alum building bridges with the alumni from other schools. For me, this habit started with lessons in the Center.

CONTRIBUTIONS FROM EVERYONE

One of New Trier's greatest strengths, its "level system," is also one of its weaknesses. The higher-level classes selectively include only those students thought to have the capacity to learn the most advanced work. The downside of this approach is that four level students (New Trier numbers its tracks) become isolated from those students who are motivated in other areas or not motivated at all. This may be a good practice to improve the *academic* performance for those that are scholastically oriented and motivated. The downside is that it insulates this group of students from the real world. We are all bound, sooner or later, to leave academics and deal with different skilled or different motivated people.

In the Center, I learned that everyone has something different to contribute. In the Center, I learned from people smarter than me. More importantly, I learned from peers whom I first thought were not academically as smart as I. In one instance, I recall a discussion with a fellow Centerite who reeked of pot smoke and didn't dress like me. We were talking about the characters in a book we were reading in a class we had formed. (Like me, he was there by his choice, not by a test placement score). I cannot remember who he was or the book's name, but I remember being impressed on his insight and seeing my prejudices about smartness being challenged.

Later, in my Organizational Behavior class at Kellogg, I learned that there had been numerous experiments with groups that had found that none of us are as smart as all of us together. When a team is given the opportunity to contribute, even in a very hierarchical setting, the outcome is always superior to any one individual's setting the direction. The takeaway is that superior leaders listen. Less skilled leaders believe that they have to act like they know it all.

When I learned that, my mind immediately flashed back to my experience in the Center. Unlike some Centerites, I appreciate the parent school. However, by my senior year, I had gleaned about all that I was going to get from regular classes. Because the Center was set up to encourage individual, self-directed learning, I learned life lessons that I would not have learned elsewhere, at least not for several years. For instance, today when I face a group, I am very careful to watch the dynamics of the group, and target the outlier to seek their opinion. Sometimes, there is nothing gained, but more often than not, there are useful contributions that come from individuals who may have looked like they had nothing to add.

THE EXPERIENCE OF TRUE CHAOS

There was one lesson that I learned in the Center that I have never truly experienced elsewhere, and never hope to experience again. That was the chaos associated with starting the 1977-1978 academic year. My lesson: chaos and I are oil and water.

I was very excited for the new academic year to start some classes, not in the traditional sense but in the sense that I would be involved in creating the class. Nothing could have prepared me for the chaos that came during the first few days of the Center. The lack of direction and ambiguity, which was intentional on the part of the facilitators, tested the patience of everyone involved. It was very shocking for me not to have the teachers direct each class on what we were going to learn. I knew that classes were to be invented each semester. I had no idea that the entire process would start from scratch each year. I do not think that I knew how to express the confusion I felt, but in retrospect, it made quite an impression on me and planted the seeds of self-direction in the soil of a supportive community.

The longer-term result was that I took classes on leadership and organizational behavior in college and graduate school. Outside of school, I have studied rules of leadership. As an adult and parent, I teach leadership skills to Boys Scouts in my troop as a part of their Eagle project. (Contrary to popular myth, an Eagle Project is not about doing a big, good deed. It is about learning how to manage a project. It just happens to be for a good cause.) In each case, the example of what I want to avoid is the experience of the first few days in the Center. Having gone through this experience makes that lesson more poignant for me.

Bill, a marketing strategy executive and father of three, now lives in Seattle. Bill has taught at Kellogg School of Management and led initiatives with Microsoft, IBM, GE, Motorola, Nextel, Tyco Electronics, and Xerox. He is the author of articles covering innovations in the wireless industry; his writing has appeared in Forbes, U.S. Today, *and* Wireless.

Short Takes

During most of the Center's existence my father-in-law was dean of students of the "parent school." For many years he tried to bait me into arguments, usually by calling the Center a haven for slow learners and delinquents. Early on that might have been the most generous thing he had to say. He finally settled down after I put his son through graduate school at Northwestern and earned my second postgraduate degree.

~Lisa Clark, 1977

REFLECTIONS ON BUILDING
THE CENTER PLANETARIUM

ELIOT NEEL, 1978

When I first proposed building a planetarium in the Center, very few understood its value to the Center. The very idea of a planetarium seemed too esoteric. Many issues worked against its completion, not the least of which was the cost. Although I knew the concept would work, and most of the components could be cobbled together from readily available but re-purposed and modestly priced parts, as the designer and fabricator I had never built anything of this scope and complexity. Failure would always be just around the corner.

The first big problem was selling the idea to Centerites, both students and faculty. I recall making a presentation board to display, at the right moment during a lull at a typical Town Hall meeting when nearly the entire gang of students and faculty were assembled. I made casual mention of it and the initial response, after a bit of a delay, was something like "What was that you said?" "You want to build what?" "Why?" I knew the concept was feeble, somewhat incomprehensible, and therefore suspect. It could easily be dismissed as mere enthusiasm from a kid with an imagination, but no sense of reality. So I let it simmer for a while and eventually, after some subtle marketing, I let it slowly gain acceptance until Town Hall reached consensus and gave me a share of the $500 donated by a parent to underwrite student projects. One student even offered money of her own to support the project.

Once the steel wire dome structure was finished (sans cloth) and temporarily set up in the main room of the Center, people began to understand the scale of the project. Students would fold back the flexible wires and move furniture within the hemisphere. I saw faculty having after-school meetings inside the structure. For a while, it functioned as a figurative zone of sanctuary, as if some sort of force field was efficiently channeling disruptive energy away from its footprint. I figured if the project only went that far, then it could have been considered "tensile art" and perhaps it would be best to leave it at that.

The good news was that this giant dome did get finished. It actually functioned. People saw it and they were astonished. I was too. Actually. In retrospect, it was truly a piece of work, one that renewed, if not permanently secured, my membership in the "Society of Junior Mad-Scientists."

The best part of the story was that since there was an alternative educational environment available within the school, one that accepted the notions of students to outline their interests and complement their education beyond the typically structured high school curriculum, the project was potentially feasible. I doubt it could ever have been a reality without the existence of the Center for Self-Directed Learning. Initial skepticism turned to enthusiastic support over the 16 months it took to complete the project.

Vernoy Johnson thought the project might be too ambitious for a high school kid (he was right), but he pitched in with a full box of power tools as we crashed to complete the carpentry work before the end of the project's first school year. Two fellow Centerites, Mike Rosenzweig and Bill Nugent, provided countless hours of assistance, and a neighbor, Robert Brandon, supplied me with the wire rods that formed the dome's frame. When it was finished, a reporter from a local TV news program asked me what the difference was between the Adler Planetarium and my Cub Scout version. "About nine million dollars," I replied.

The Adler had used a projector built by Carl Zeiss, the renowned German optics manufacturer, which had two "star-balls," each contained 1300-watt incandescent lamps that projected light through perforated copper plates. The star images were represented by the holes in the plates and 32 lenses focused the star patterns onto the domed screen overhead. The whole contraption looked like a couple of deep-sea diver helmets connected by a cylindrical steel cage. The projectors that displayed the sun, moon, and planets were housed within this cage. They could be moved in accordance with their respective orbits. The entire machine could be swiveled and rotated by remote control from a console located inside the dome. It was a pretty marvelous piece of engineering; especially considering that it was designed prior to the age of digital projection.

And all by itself, it cost $250,000 in 1970.

I figured I could raise only a few hundred dollars.

Nonetheless, I wanted my design to show the visible planets, sun, and moon. I also wanted to have a projector move the sun's image to illustrate the sun's apparent motion against the stars, to show the effect of the earth's orbit around the sun. On demand, I would be able to demonstrate the change of the sun's elevation in the sky due to the seasons—high sun in summer, low sun in winter. I had seen a toy planetarium that could show about 300 star images on the walls and ceiling of a small, darkened room. It could recreate the rising and setting motion of the stars by hand-turning a perforated black globe mounted to a latitude-adjustable "polar axis" or hollow metal shaft on the bottom of the unit. The star images were created by allowing minute amounts of light to pass through pinhole-sized apertures pre-drilled into the surface of the plastic sphere.

This, I thought, could be the basis for my design. I originally dreamed about showing at least 3000 stars on the globe, but I wanted to be a high school senior for only one year and on a dark, clear night away from city lights, one can probably see not more than about 1000 stars in the sky. Each star to be projected—the built version had roughly 1500 stars—would have to be located on a suitable opaque sphere, plotting their positions from a star atlas I often used when observing the sky with my telescope. Each star then was assigned a brightness code, according to a six-step scale.

Using tiny drill bits obtained from a hobby shop, I drilled holes up to 1/16-inch for the brightest stars and less than 1/64-inch for the faintest ones. I fashioned the sphere by combining the rims of two identical 12 inch diameter clear-acrylic hemispheres sold as terrarium covers.

In addition to individual stars, I also figured out a way to show the faint band of light we see as the Milky Way. It arcs across the sky when viewed from a dark place; it's really quite beautiful. Since it is rather fuzzy, it was actually fairly easy to reproduce. I had intended to paint the interior side of the globe flat black but before I did, I masked a portion of the interior with tape such that the outline of Milky Way was correctly proportioned on the surface of the sphere. I then painted the interior of the sphere with black spray paint. After it dried and cured, I removed the masking tape and painted over the clear area that remained with a very light coat of paint such that some light would pass through the masked zone. The result was a pretty realistic rendition of the Milky Way. It added much to the experience of the night sky.

Instead of a hand crank to demonstrate the change of the sun's elevation in the sky as the earth moved through the seasons, I used a six-volt electric motor and a chain and sprocket drive cannibalized from a toy-building kit. The sun's image was projected by a metal drain tube that had a lens on one end, an aperture stop in the middle (representing the disk of the sun) and a high-intensity bulb from a desk lamp. The image was quite bright and could be seen even with all of the dome lights turned on. The motor turned the tube so you could essentially speed up the annual motion of the sun from one year's time to about three minutes. I was successful in getting the solar image to move independently of the star projector even though they were fastened together on the same support structure. I also added a calendar projector that displayed the name of the months upon the screen. It was preset so that I could align the solar image with a particular month and then be able to establish a viewing date for the stars after a "sunset."

That little device was homemade, too. I just photocopied some text printed on white cards and mounted the film negatives around a 360° drum positioned close to the sun projector. Technically speaking, it was projecting "The Ecliptic," i.e., the apparent path of the sun, moon, and planets in the sky. The names were projected on to the dome via a flashlight bulb with a tiny filament (like the star projector). After many weeks, (months, actually) of work on the "Star-Ball," sun and planetary projectors, I finally was able to assemble the individual components and see the machine in its entirety. It deviated somewhat from the original sketch that I had envisioned almost a year before. It was heavier than expected and slightly out of balance.

The final version could be operated to show the sky from the Equator to the North Pole any time of the year. About a dozen tiny lenses were added to the star-ball to enhance and sharpen the images of the brightest stars (otherwise they looked like little "full moons"). Some testing was done and only a few adjustments were necessary. It worked fairly well on the first try. I had the apparatus mounted on a horizontal shaft that rotated between two A-frame supports that were fastened to a portable control box underneath the planetarium projector. An electric synchronous motor turned the entire projector once in two minutes. I used this motion to mimic the earth's spin and you could look up and see the stars rise and set.

Many of the controls used transformers and selected components cannibalized from toy train sets. Other components were purchased from hobby stores and scientific supply warehouses. The domed screen was fabricated from thick, triple-layered, photo blackout cloth. I cut triangular sections and sewed them together on sewing machines donated for use by various faculty members at the Center. (I very well may have accelerated the demise of one of them in trying to get the needles to run through six layers of cloth at one time.)

The cloth dome was draped over a steel wire structure and later the interior surface was painted with artist's white gesso. The dome was 12 feet in diameter and rested on a wood base that was attached to twelve short wall panels. Entry was from one side that had a slightly elevated header, so a person would not have to crawl inside—just a minor genuflect and quickstep was needed to gain access. When the house lights were off, the room was totally dark; pitch black. This allowed the stars to shine with fairly decent realism.

The dynamic range from the brightest celestial objects to the faintest ones (like the Milky Way) seemed to be pretty close to the real thing. The long time it took to plot the stars also paid off since the constellations looked reasonably accurate. The planetarium had its own set of interior lights mounted beside the star projector, light blue for daylight and dark blue for the deep blue sky seen after sunset, both controlled by dimmers. I also had a pair of twilight projectors that housed orange-colored seven-watt Christmas tree lamps. Each had curved, black shields and they directed a soft, warm glow to the east and west horizons, recreating the evening and morning twilight scenes.

Other ports were made in the planetarium wall to allow external slide projectors to be used in conjunction with the main planetarium. Some homemade loudspeakers could blast sound into the little room as desired. Still, there were failures and disappointments along the way. I tried very hard to get the planets to move in their respective orbits. At the very least, I wanted to get one planet projector to move on command so a typical planetary motion could be demonstrated, especially the so-called "retrograde" motion seen when the earth seems to whiz by a planet at a close approach. Ancient astronomers were very aware of this strange, backward movement, and some thought only gods could move like that, which is why the planets were named after the Roman gods.

I built a working prototype model using disks and pins that were needed to approximate the planetary motion. One disk about six inches diameter represented the orbit of an outer planet such as Mars, with a "pin" stuck near its outer edge where the planet would be. The center of the disk contained another pin, or bearing, where the sun would be. This disk rotated at a certain speed. Another disk, smaller in diameter, was also placed directly above the first one, and it had a "planet pin" representing the position of the earth placed on it. The earth pin was closer to the center of the two disks than the Mars pin. The two disks could move independently, but the Mars disk was supposed to take almost twice as long to spin as the Earth disk. I put a sliding bar through slots in the pins and mounted a planet projector on the bar.

When the two disks moved according to their appropriate relative motions, simulating the real planet's motions, the planet projector did a fair job of tracking the actual path of the planet on the screen. I knew I could not account for the speed variation that occurs when planets travel in elliptical orbits—I had to let that slide; it was too hard, mechanically, to reproduce. Unfortunately, I could not get the basic apparatus to work reliably; it kept getting hung-up and eventually I decided to abandon it.

The moon projector, once envisioned as a complicated projector that would change the moon's apparent phase or shape as we see it from earth while it moved in its orbit, was also simplified to an optical tube that had preset phase images built-in to the projector. I had illustrated about 12 different moon-phase aspects and set microscopic images of them in a rotatable disk. You spun the disk to get the phase you wanted. Although the simple version worked all right, it wasn't used much in the final version.

A Visitor Asks for a Demo

All systems were operating nominally that day, or at least they seemed to be. I had made several tests and demonstrations by then and those were all more or less successful. I was at the control console, a hastily built plywood box with its top surface exposing an array of switches, dials, and receptacles. Above it were struts that supported the planetarium and allowed the movement required for it to perform its essential purpose: to replicate the appearance and motion of the heavens in a simulated nighttime environment. Below the console, the box concealed a disorderly arrangement of wires and transformers cannibalized from toy train sets.

The gadget was centered under a tent-sized hemispherical screen, large enough to hold about eight people. Old desk lamps were retrofitted into the machine and featured theater-style light bulbs to illuminate the interior and display the changing color of the sky as the sun's image descended below the horizon. As I slowly rotated the dimmer switch, the lights descended from a deep blue to a dark indigo, eventually fading to black. We awaited the appearance of the first stars—but nothing was happening. There were two people in the audience that morning. One was Vernoy, a teacher in the Center, who was initially skeptical about the project, but nevertheless brought in his power tools and helped assemble the theater structure. The other was a gentleman who somehow had learned about the gadget and was evidently very eager to meet me.

An elderly fellow outfitted in a well-pressed suit, he appeared as though he was about to attend a quarterly meeting of the Federal Reserve. Vernoy was assisting me as we led our visitor into the little chamber made of thick white cloth, two-by-fours, and wood paneling. When the gentleman introduced himself as Robert Adler I realized the stakes were high—whatever the stakes were. I only knew I had to make a good impression.

Why didn't the stars come out, though? Here I was, fumbling with the knobs, trying to work the problem and maintaining my cool. You don't want to admit failure in front of the guy whose father's philanthropy made possible the founding of the first astronomical museum in the United States, The Adler Planetarium. Since I did not have a direct link to Mission Control, I felt desperate. I sensed my audition was faltering and I was about to sink below the waterline. It was Vernoy who suggested the obvious: a burned out light bulb. His diagnosis was correct and the Maglite-sized bulb was quickly replaced with a spare on hand. Cost: one dollar.

Mr. Adler was familiar with malfunctioning planetariums. Once I had things back under control, Mr. Adler told a story about how the Douglas Aircraft Corporation had been contracted in the 1950s to design and produce a domed screen made from curved sections of perforated aluminum to replace the flammable and delicate muslin fabric. Douglas had years of experience making curved metal parts for airplanes, and company representatives had visited the Planetarium to make notes and take measurements. The sections were fabricated back in Long Beach, California and transported to Chicago, but not all of the sections fit together properly. Some were just incorrectly sized and they could never be adjusted in the field. Douglas decided to maintain good relations with the museum by offering to remake the faulty sections and install them at their own expense—which they did. Apparently, it was a snafu from which even the professionals could not escape.

My show began as the dome light dimmed to black the stars finally started to show, just a half dozen or so at first, then maybe twenty or thirty, until finally about 800 tiny dots of light were shining overhead.

Mr. Adler, who was familiar with the constellations, was very busy looking around the indoor sky; within seconds, he was already recognizing some star patterns. Vernoy and I both could tell he was enjoying himself, sort of like a boy scout exploring a cave for the first time. Upon seeing the faint band of light arcing across the dome representing the Milky Way, Mr. Adler remarked that he was indeed impressed with what he came to see and thanked me for spending time with him. I, on the other hand, was impressed that he bothered to come at all and today his visit remains one of the highlights of my brief experience with the project after it was finished.

TURN OUT THE LIGHTS, THE PARTY'S JUST BEGINNING

I couldn't remember where I put that lens; maybe I left it inside the house. That's what I thought late one night when I had pointed my six-inch refracting telescope towards the Orion Nebula. I needed more magnification to clearly see the little jewel-like assortment of stars known as the "Trapezium" which was deeply embedded within the nebula—60X just wasn't enough. The eight-foot long telescope and tripod was set up across the street from my house on Winnetka Ave., right across from New Trier's auditorium.

Although I had been stargazing with homemade telescopes since I was in the seventh grade, this particular scope was quite powerful and the proximity of New Trier's vacant parking lots and sidewalks offered me some convenient places to set it up. I found the more powerful eyepiece and while I was in the process of securing it to the telescope tube, I realized I had attracted an unsolicited visitor, a Winnetka police officer, who seemed to be more shocked to see me in lieu of the other way around. I think he was about to take me down to the station until I showed him my I.D. card that contained a "special permit" signed by the Chief of Police; it allowed me to be out past curfew (midnight).

After a few inquiries, he seemed to be convinced that I was not about to fire a cannon and destroy the school building. I also figured that the Orion Nebula was not the best target for a "first-timer" to observe; although bright as nebulas go, it merely appeared as a faint, fuzzy glow because of the interference from the streetlights. That wouldn't leave much of an impression for him, I thought.

Jupiter was visible and so I decided to swing the telescope over and zoom in on it. I had hoped that a view of that planet would satisfy his curiosity. It did, and soon he radioed his buddies away from the doughnut shop (does Winnetka have a doughnut shop?); he wanted them to check out what he discovered by the high school—they weren't going to believe it unless they saw it for themselves.

Within just a few minutes, four cop cars, all with their motors running, were parked along Winnetka Avenue, beside New Trier's auditorium. Five officers were lined up on the sidewalk, all with their hands in their pockets, waiting their turn to peer through the 200-power lens aimed at Jupiter. They could see the atmospheric belts and the four bright moons first seen by Galileo in 1609. The fellows seemed pretty astonished all right; the experience was certainly not something they had expected. One of them wondered aloud if the streetlights bothered me and I affirmed that their presence wasn't exactly desirable. Soon, he returned to his squad car, drove it down the block, and aimed his searchlight at a single photocell that apparently controlled all of the municipal streetlights along Winnetka and Woodland Avenues.

In a split second, the whole street went dark! Now, that was cool! His action didn't harm anything, the re-strike on the mercury light took a few a minutes to figure out that it had been fooled into thinking it was daytime, and slowly they came back on. At least for a few minutes, the local sky was dark. Thank you Mr. Policeman! I found a place to obtain a light like that, one that plugs into your car's cigarette lighter (nowadays, they are available at most any sporting goods shop). It wasn't expensive; it was bright and projected a beam almost a mile away. So, I tried it out and it worked! The street went dark. Ah, it was definitely worth getting.

The stargazing had been pretty lame due to the light pollution from the community and the City of Chicago; even though the skies were fairly dark over Lake Michigan, the glare from local lights was awful. This is when my new light zapper proved to be a useful item. I could control the lights by my street whenever I wanted to observe. I remember one night when I had some friends over to stargaze and one of them said that I certainly picked a terrible place to set up the equipment, right by the high school with too many lights around. "How stupid is that?" I just let the ranting continue for a while until I felt it was time to demonstrate my secret weapon. "Don't like the lights, eh?" I said. "Wait just a minute. OK, now hold my star chart and watch this." I got in the car, activated the light zapper, aimed, then click, and blackout, photon depletion complete. At least 21 streetlights went off in an instant.

At that point, I could just imagine one of those flight controller dudes at NASA saying "Houston to Apollo: Flight confirms streetlight negative function. Do you copy?" My friends were impressed. They never realized that I could be so seemingly clever and diabolical. It was great fun, until the school principal found out what it was I was doing. He made casual mention of it while in a hallway one day at school. He asked me if I knew how to control the lights and I admitted to my treacherous ways. He was actually amused and wanted to know where one could buy a light like that—although I was curious why he needed to know, I figured it would be best not to ask him. I did confirm however, that despite rumors I had heard throughout the school, I was not making contact with space aliens or communists.

When not traveling in a self-renovated vintage Airstream Argosy or building astronomical telescopes, Eliot is an educational and institutional architect in Fayetteville, Arkansas. In his early career, he renovated pre-civil war homes in South Arkansas.

Short Takes

I remember people. How warm and funny Mr. Greg was. How VJ could almost make math interesting, the warmth of Bev and Mrs. Paul. I remember my friends. I remember writing an epic paper about Amelia Earhart and another about the New Deal, where I first learned that narrowing down the subject can save your life.

~Lynn Fitz-Hugh, 1978

An Implausible Ending

Dan Perlman, 1978

I credit and blame my three years in the Center for ending up in a field of work that I would have laughed off as completely implausible when I was a high schooler. Still, at some point I got it in my head that nothing could be more challenging than being an artist and a teacher, especially if there's no one authority and no one community that ever has the last word on what "art" is.

There really aren't any rules to being an artist. The same goes for teaching art. You have to forge your own process and definitions in both the studio and the classroom. Every artwork becomes a unique definition or proposal about what art should be. Every instance of art has the potential to redirect what it is we even call art. If it weren't for my experience in the Center, I would never have come to such naive, wonderful, and open aspirations.

The Center for Self-Directed Learning was my first experience with taking responsibility for the meaning that I make of things. "Self-Directed Learning" meant just that: having a substantial say in what I was going to make learning mean was liberating and puzzling, like a thought-game. I could play with more personally engaging ways of delving into the subject at hand (like learning American History through studying its major rivers, or Architecture through actually re-designing the layout of the very rooms that the Center used at New Trier. To be forthright about my interests and have them validated as legitimate means to serious inquiry was mind-bendingly motivating to me. It was also intimidating in the best possible way.

The challenge of identifying oneself in high school didn't need to be a battle about how I did or didn't fit a standard. It could be an ongoing process. My interests could bear results beyond academics. Every teacher in the Center was a unique example of mindfulness; they each approached their pedagogy (and their very authority) as something always to watch and be present to. Though

I would never have been able to articulate it in high school, I was learning that criticality and responsibility begins with paying attention to process—to the means, never just the ends.

Without knowing it, I was learning from example that teaching was both a challenge to, and a result of, how intellectually open someone can be. To give artists a new road, either into or out of themselves, is about the most I can hope to do as an art teacher. Of course, there are a million ways to do that. Is there any other subject in the humanities that is given such profound freedom and elemental aspirations?

Maybe art has this unique permission because the stakes ultimately aren't all that high, at least not in any direct way. Art is an ongoing discussion about how things mean other things, and there's rarely any hurry, let alone finality, to those always-debatable determinations. Yes, money is exchanged furiously in the art world, but meaning seeps slowly. And making meaning isn't something you can teach, at least not directly.

I especially like to remind students that sitting around for a few hours with no other agenda other than to make meaning of whoever's work we're looking at is a rare occasion, maybe even a privilege. The indulgence of being with your work while others pour their brains into its interpretation isn't likely to happen at all once you are out of school, at least not out loud with a captive audience… unless you teach, that is.

If you told me 35 years ago that the self-directed learning in which I was newly immersed would turn into the self-directed learning I now try to do in the studio (and that I try to facilitate in my students' educations), I would have said, "No way, you are nuts." The studio and classroom are most rewarding when I end up somewhere I couldn't possibly have anticipated when I (or we) started. Landing in unanticipated territory is obviously not something you can force. It takes a certain amount of neutrality, but not too much, a certain amount of patience, but not too much, and even a certain amount of willful naiveté. And it certainly takes trust. I first experienced that alchemy at the Center—I've been practicing it ever since.

Dan, a.k.a. Hirsch Perlman, is an artist, professor, and area head of sculpture at UCLA. He lives in Altadena, CA with his wife, artist Erin Cosgrove.

Short Takes

The Center reinforced my commitment to academic dilettantism, something I have pursued ever since, as a professional cultural anthropologist who teaches college students in London.

I remember an inspiring creative writing class with a former reporter from Rolling Stone, another creative writing tutorial session with Scott Simon in his pre-NPR days.

I also recall an amorphous sense of camaraderie, and a special, pioneering can-do spirit of anything goes, that all intellectual and artistic pursuits should and could be accommodated.

~Ruth Mandel, 1973

My Garnet Earrings

Linda Glass, 1979

I still have my garnet earrings. I bought them in Florence on a Center trip by a group studying the Italian Renaissance. I was so awed by the art and architecture we studied before leaving and what I saw during our big excursion that I majored in art history at Barnard College. Later I earned a Master's in Art History at New York University's Institute of Fine Arts. I specialized in Roman and Modern Art. Those earrings remind me of my life's journey that started in the Center.

My journey began with a small group that studied the Italian Renaissance. With that study, our facilitator, Arline Paul, and I began a tutorial in the Italian language. A Center volunteer, Dr. Girardi, meet with us twice a week at her home. (I loved the sound of Italian and I still do.) At one point, Dan Donohue, a student in our group said, "You know, it's great to look at this art through pictures in books and to talk about the Renaissance, but it would be much, much better if we could see it."

There was an amazed reaction, "What a great idea!"

"Why not organize a trip and go to Italy?"

"How soon can we start?"

After much brainstorming, I became so involved that I created the itinerary. I'd sit in the Center's main room, surrounded by guidebooks, trying to design a trip that would enable us to see the most in the shortest amount of time and require the least amount of money. I'd give my ideas to the group for review. The biggest question was always "will we have enough time?" Then for each city, we made a priority list. I found that itinerary years later. Rereading it, I realized how terrific it was. With our plan made, three hurdles remained.

The first hurdle was to obtain permission from the New Trier Board of Education to embark on a school sanctioned study trip during a school year. Some students and Arline presented the plan. The Board approved a January interim trip. The second hurdle was parent permission and money. Eight students, five boys, and three girls committed to the trip with parental permission. The third and final hurdle was the logistics of travel including lodging and passports.

Fortunately, Marty Heiser's mother was a travel agent. She had a contact with an Italian agent who was able to find us very inexpensive rooms. A month's travel with eight teenagers could sound daunting, but we were agreeable, cooperative, and reliable. When we arrived at a museum or palace, we would put our heads together, estimate the average time needed, and set an exit meeting time and place. Everyone was always on time because it was agreed that if anyone needed more time, they could tell the group they wanted to go back for a bit. That way, we each moved at our own pace. No lockstep for a Centerite! We never lost anyone, nor did we feel rushed. Perhaps part of that was because we had planned so well.

On our itinerary were Rome, Pompeii, Venice, Florence, and Milan. One of my highlights was a day trip from Florence to the town of Urbino, the seat of the Italian Renaissance. In Urbino, there is a palace with wonderful paintings done by my favorite Renaissance artist, Raphael. Using money we raised from a bake sale and spaghetti dinner, we rode a van up the mountain on a foggy morning. On arrival, the fog turned to rain. It was gloomy and wet. We dashed straight to the Urbino's famous Ducal Palace only to see a sign "Closed." There was no place to go, nothing to do. Our van driver took us to a local restaurant for lunch. Everyone was mad at me. So much for the best-laid plans. In spite of the misfortune, I never did forget Urbino. During my college's junior year abroad program, I elected for a month of intensive Italian study in Urbino. I finally achieved two important goals: immersion in Italian and Raphael in Urbino. I added these triumphs to my life altering experience during my first visit to Italy.

In Florence's Uffizi Gallery, I was looking at Gentile da Fabriano's *Adoration of the Magi*. A guide was lecturing about it to her tourist group. She described the symbols and the significance of each worshiper's placement. I don't recall the specifics, but she was telling me how a painting represents much more than what I could see. I was astounded. I didn't know that. I was so intrigued that from then on art history was my passion. As a final project after we returned home, our Renaissance study group organized a Renaissance Day with costumes, food, art posters, and games. This gave us a chance to share what we had learned with the many Center students and others who hadn't gone with us. I know they got the flavor of the trip. But it was only a small taste compared to the life-changing events that later shaped my life.

That Renaissance study may have been my favorite group, but it wasn't the only good one. When I was in the parent school, I had been interested in theater. My attempts to break into the theater world had failed. Peer pressure was strong. I wasn't in the right clique and I felt no one was paying attention to me. That rejection also changed my life's course. Hearing about the Center, I went to talk to Arline. She made the Center sound exciting and welcoming. My parents agreed with my decision.

One of the first things I did in the Center was to take acting classes in a Chicago theater. That required my first daring trip downtown on the El. I followed the classes with an internship at the yet little-known Steppenwolf Theater. At that time, it was performing in a church basement. Amazingly, I worked my way to be the assistant director on an award-winning production with an aspiring cast of John Malkovich, Gary Sinise, William H. Macy, Laurie Metcalf, and Terry Kinney. There I was, a high school kid as assistant director. Unlike the New Trier acting clique, these future stars accepted me as part of their group. The director adopted my suggestion about including an impromptu bit from rehearsal in the actual performances. It was apparent even to the "young me" that these people had something extra. I still recognize the little mannerisms each was developing when I see them perform now.

Life in the Center was not all peaches and cream. Learning to become self-directed was a challenge. On the way, I encountered my share of problems. I recall that I decided to take a safe route with my science requirement and take biology in the parent-school. As I tried to put the class into a Center schedule, it interfered with my Center priorities. That experience was so typical of the scheduling problems I still struggle with. So many choices! Always exciting, never easy.

Although the scheduling process during the first weeks of a semester was exciting, I frequently got frustrated. It was amazing that so many exciting possibilities were being proposed. But then a group couldn't move forward because enough people didn't come to discuss common goals and a process to be used.

For example, I remember proposing a group called "Lenny, Mickey, and Bucky" (aka Leonardo da Vinci, Michelangelo, and Buckminster Fuller). I thought of it as preparatory to going to Italy. Part of it was, but only one other person was interested. He ended up building a large geodesic dome as part of his study of the modernist, Fuller. I was left to either drop my idea or figure out something else for myself.

Another often-frustrating challenge was building our community. That was a tough job. I loved my community group and our community group facilitator, Vernoy Johnson, because he shared with us and inspired us with the things he loved (I still miss him), but I could never decide what made me madder, community group or Town Hall. One day, tired that some kids were not showing up at the Town Halls, our all-Center community, I got a bee in my bonnet. I convinced my friend, Katie, to help me organize a day when we would collect every single person in the Center in the same place at the same time. Remember, this was the Center for Self-Directed Learning! Ironically, we thought that it was really important in terms of community building to get everyone in one place at the same time. It was going to be a two- day experience in a local church. We planned trust and community building exercises, games, and lunch. Everyone did come, even though we were definitely imposing our will, directing the community. With Katie, who is still my best friend today, I love to laugh at the way we "made" everyone belong to the Center community.

After the Center, my first stop was Barnard. It was a Center-like college. I think I was accepted into it because I had this strange self-directed school background that made me interesting. When I arrived, I was ready to go. I had already done the partying and the sloughing off of some responsibilities during my Center days. I was ready to study. It was a perfect match because Barnard was serious from the start. I could handle it because I was self-directed and that self-direction is always with me...even today, right now when as a freelance editor of science books, I work at home, set my goals every day, direct myself, and deal with distractions.

As I have pursued different career paths during my adult life, I have always remembered VJ telling me about how when you walk across the road, some molecules fall off and some grow on even as you cross the street. "You are," he said, "never the same person." Those words really struck me. It was a new scientific outlook for me about the way things are. Ultimately after years as an artist, I began to think of science as a path.

Between VJ's willingness to share his love for math and science with us, and my own love of gardening, I began to think a lot about making science my career. I wasn't 100% sure that I could make it at art. Gardening was something I really liked and wanted to learn more about. I decided the best way to pursue this interest was to take some courses in botany, plant nomenclature, and greenhouse growing. I found a wonderful program that ended years later with an associate's degree in horticulture.

At the end of the program, I got hired as a "consultant" at the Lincoln Park Conservatory in Chicago. What a wonderful job! Basically, I was put in charge of a neglected greenhouse full of orchids and bromeliads. Nothing was blooming and it was in complete disarray. In the two years I was there, I repotted every plant in the greenhouse, learned their special qualities, and arranged them by species. By the time I left, I had them all blooming again. That job came to a sad, Catch 22-type end. The Park District had a hiring freeze on, so I couldn't be hired as a regular employee. Because I was not a regular employee, I couldn't join the union. So, someone reported me to the union, and they made me leave! Ah, well, it was a wonderful two years.

About that time, I found a new avenue for self-directed learning: Northeastern Illinois University, which is near where I live, had a "Community Listener's Program" in which they allowed community members to audit one course a semester—for free! Over a period of about five years, I ran through most of their earth science courses. One of my professors there had a book that needed editing. Lacking the time to do it himself, he asked me if I would work on it. I did, and another chapter in my life opened. Turns out, I'm a pretty good editor. And I liked the work so much, I went out and got a Certificate in Editing at the University of Chicago. After many would-be careers, I finally landed where I'm supposed to be. I've been happily working on environmental science books for about ten years now, and look forward to doing more.

Being Self-Directed—it's a wonderful thing! I have the Center to thank for it. And I still have those garnet earrings.

Linda, a graduate of Barnard (B.A.) and NYU (M.A. in Art History), is now a book editor specializing in the earth/ environmental sciences.

Short Takes

What do I remember most about the Center? My friends, Vernoy Johnson, Bev Kirk, Arline Paul, Mr. Greg. Controlled chaos. Flannel shirts, engrossing classes on Jung and Hermann Hesse, not doing well in geometry.

I have been an office mensch, writer and editor, software technical writer, hospital and hospice chaplain. I am now an Episcopal priest.

~Laura Gottardi-Littell, 1977

Jumping Off the Chair

Carol Lavelle, 1979

My parents say that I left for my first out-of-the-Center trip as an angry, door-slamming brat and came back an angel. I'm still not sure if it was because I felt the world had opened up for me, or if it was just that the teenage hormones had calmed down. Perhaps it was a combination of both.

Whatever the reason, I owe eternal gratitude to my advisor, Bill Gregory, who talked my parents into letting me "jump off the chair," so to speak, and allow me to take a monumental risk. They just wanted to be sure I thought I could handle this big chair jump, and, if I failed, could deal with the consequences of my decision.

This risk started when Mr. Greg told my parents a story. A month later he told the same story to my grandmother. The story was about his daughter wanting to jump off a chair and how the family had handled that. As a result of the story, my grandmother told my parents she thought I could handle this idea that I wanted to travel around by my 16-year-old self with a Eurail pass. That was an unusual request. I bless them both!

One might think that solo travel is not valid coursework, but it was a wonderful "real-life" learning experience to do so, especially alone. My learning came from the little things, like trying to find the train to Munich, and eventually figuring out that Munich was called "München" in Germany! (I didn't know that city names changed depending on what language one speaks.) And when I saw the government buildings in Bonn surrounded by rolls of barbed wire to protect them from terrorists (whose wanted posters were all over the place), I discovered how blessed I was to live in America.

I also learned that the most important thing to learn in a foreign language is numbers, for money, and had the feeling that the world was a much bigger place than I thought, yet a smaller place in that people all over the world are the same. I have felt throughout my life since then that the people I've met who have traveled the most tend to be the calmest and most tolerant of other people and cultures.

My very favorite activity on that trip was exploring old castles; it was like a fantasy world to me, and perhaps pointed to my interest in architecture. The U.S.A is such a young country, it has nothing to compare.

After I returned from that trip, I learned even more about myself. When my sister read my trip diary, she thought I had had a terrible time. I figured out over the years that I tend to write when I'm scared or upset as a way to get it out of my system. I am an artist, and when I'm unhappy or agitated I tend to write to express those feelings, instead of drawing or painting. That diary was full of every moment I felt unsure of myself.

A DIFFERENT WAY

My 1979 New Trier East graduating class had about 1,000 people. It was a place where one could easily get lost in the shuffle or just be a statistic. The Center for Self-Directed Learning, a school-within-a-school at New Trier, was a small community, more like a family than an institution. Our teachers (faculty advisors and facilitators) were much more supportive of our true interests than those in the main school.

The faculty in the Center was quite unique in the ways they worked with us. When I met with my NTE college counselor (a service provided by the main school), she was dead set against my plan to study art at Yale. She didn't like either idea. I could tell her I was interested in art school until I was blue in the face, the same with Yale, and the same with putting the two in one package. "Oh! But Yale has an art department!" She just wouldn't *listen* to me, but Mr. Greg and the other faculty encouraged me to push for my dream. They helped me to look at other alternatives but also to stick to my guns. I did end up going to art school, the Rhode Island School of Design.

I can thank the influence of the Center for giving me the courage to go my own way, my different way, and fight for what I needed for my career. The Center system, where we designed our own classes and course work, was really true to an entrepreneurial spirit. Decide what you want, figure out what you need to learn to get there, and follow through. Make a mistake?

Pick yourself up and start again. It was an ideal program for people who already had an idea of where they wanted their life directions to go.

My parents have told me I was the only child in my family who had that sense of direction in high school; I was, and wanted to pursue being, an artist, even though it's not an easy path. In the Center, I was truly blessed to be surrounded by so many brilliant students who really cared about the learning process, and at the same time knew how to have fun. Half the NTE student council was in the Center when I was there.

I remember a class one day when one of our classmates showed up "high" and was chastised by us, his peers, for not being able to participate in that condition. It didn't happen again! That never would have happened in a normal high school class. The Center system really developed a love for learning, as opposed to learning being something you had to do. Learning is cool! There have been many times that I, as an adult, have told younger folks to take advantage of high school and learn as much as they can, because it will be the last time they'll get a free ride for learning.

After college, I was always taking classes to advance myself: business classes that I didn't get in college and needed to run a business; computer classes I needed when it was obvious in the early '90s that all the old-school design skills were being computerized; taking up French out of the blue because I wanted to take a trip to France (the theory was that if I learned the language, the trip would come). Yes, we eventually made the trip, and I was the interpreter!

Recently, I worked as a tour guide here in Hawaii, a wonderful and fun "job," and was constantly teaching myself new things about Hawaiian and World War II history (I was always being asked if I had been a teacher before!). The more you knew, the more fun stories you could tell. When you have developed a love for learning, it doesn't go away. It enables you to continue learning to achieve any goals your heart desires.

The Center for Self-Directed Learning taught me that. And I'm still learning new things. I've been studying e-commerce business, to open up some online stores in order to support my fine and commercial art goals financially (new world, new skills). I love learning. I love being an artist. I loved the Center for Self-Directed Learning, and all those un-quantifiable skills it taught. Many thanks to Arline, Beverly, Bill, and Vernoy for being there for us, and teaching us how fun and important learning can be.

Learn something new every day! *Aloha*...this literally translates as "breathing good life-spirit on you!"

Carol continues her life as an artist while operating her Oahu tour business.

Short Takes

I continue to be a person who thinks in an interdisciplinary way. In college at the University of Michigan, I graduated from the Residential College, within the Liberal Arts College. This program was similar to the Center in that it encouraged independent thinking. One of my most memorable Center classes was "Moo Cows," a literature class in which we read A Portrait of the Artist as a Young Man, Sons and Lovers, and other novels.

~Maria Tolpin, 1979

Getting Good: My View

Virginia Madsen, 1979

Today, I am a successful actress with an Oscar nomination under my belt. It was in the Center that I started my career path. It was in the Center where I was first challenged to make my dreams become real. It was there that I found the freedom and the tools to express myself and explore my talent.

When I was a freshman at New Trier High School, I was neither successful nor happy. I was a fish out of water, a little bit different from other kids. I was artistic and creative, a person who wanted to learn outside the box. I was not thriving in the regular school. I always had a difficult time just sitting in a class. When my mom and I heard about the Center for Self-Directed Learning, we jumped at it. We knew it would be an excellent learning space for me and I signed up with my mom's permission and encouragement. I remember telling my homeroom teacher (called an advisor at New Trier) that I was enrolling in the Center. Her response was one of strong disapproval. She tried to talk my mom out of approving this move, telling her that the Center was not a good environment and it was a very-undisciplined place. If I wanted to be an actress, I needed discipline she told us. Thankfully, my mom did not listen— and neither did I.

When school opened in September, I walked into this big room filled with people who were so welcoming to me that I could hardly believe it. I had been teased quite a bit in junior high, even bullied, so I was hurting when I got to high school and the teasing continued. But in those first days in the Center, I felt I could be exactly who I was. Nobody made fun of my clothes or the fact that I wanted to be a professional actress. I could tell that I was in a very open learning atmosphere where my ideas mattered and there was close personal contact with the teachers, or facilitators, as we called them. I felt so welcome and able to be myself. Both the students and facilitators listened to me, and my ideas mattered; that immediately allowed me to feel engaged when I went to school. I knew I had found a home!

The open environment was noticeable as soon as I walked into the main Center room. There were no desks, just round tables and chairs separated with movable closets. One wall had large coffee cans, stacked in rows, one for each student to be used as mailboxes. Other walls had artwork, even a huge magic mountain mural. Some students were sitting on the floor and everyone looked happy and excited. Since it was the beginning of a semester, students and facilitators gathered in a Town Hall where we discussed setting goals and what we needed to accomplish for the year, then brainstormed about what we all wanted to study.

The walls were covered with paper on which people would write their ideas for learning groups—Vietnam War, Calculus, Herman Hesse novels and on and on. In the next step, students walked around and wrote their names under the ideas that appealed to them. Time was arranged for those groups to meet and discuss what they hoped to learn and a possible "how-to" structure. Not every idea would survive because of lack of interest, lack of clarity, or because it seemed too daunting an undertaking. The person who proposed the idea could always do an independent study. There just wasn't a cookie cutter or one-size-fits-all kind of class. The facilitators were available to help us breakdown exactly what we wanted to learn and how, as well as the group's final goals.

Facilitators would agree to work with some groups and some found outside facilitators or outside classes. The whole process was so exciting that I couldn't wait to come to school and start my learning. Town Hall and brainstorming were two of my favorite things about the Center. Town Halls were also used to discuss issues that arose or ideas students or facilitators wanted to propose. I loved listening to people concerned about maintaining a sense of community, wanting to start a newspaper or yearbook and asking for some financing from the budget as well as volunteers to help. We also planned special Center graduations. Everyone had a voice and was listened to as we tried to build a consensus. In my three years in the Center, I also received help from my support group in setting goals and designing learning plans to achieve those goals.

Each Centerite picked a support group composed of one adult and some peers. The student could call on them for advice or a member of the support group could call a meeting. We were encouraged to pick at least one student we didn't know too well, rather than all good friends. It was helpful to check in with them and talk about how classes or other learning experiences were going. Sometimes there was a class I was not really studying for or one where nothing was happening because the class ideas didn't really work. We would discuss why the group was not functioning well and perhaps decide that it was important to move on to something that would work for me.

Other times, support group was exciting. Once I brought in a paper I had written or an art project I had done, basically to show my progress. Everyone contributed support in different ways. I really loved that. My support group also helped me by discussing my loudly avowed goal of becoming a professional actress. I was planning to take acting lessons when I finished high school, but they urged me not to wait. They thought if I was so serious about that goal, I should be taking some acting classes or lessons now. We couldn't afford private lessons and I was petrified at the thought of returning to classes in the regular school after my painful experiences freshman year. I was unwilling to chance being mocked or isolated again. Even though the theater students had a reputation for being a clique, my support group assured me that I was now a stronger person than that scared freshman and that I had them behind me— and I could always drop the class. The facilitator of my support group, Arline, said, "Maybe it's time to dip your toes in the water and test it," and volunteered that she knew one specially talented, warm, and caring teacher in theater and would make sure I was in her class.

I did test the water, it was great and then I waded right in. To this day, I am still in touch with Suzanne Adams, that warm and caring drama teacher, now retired, and I have returned to New Trier's theater department to talk to students about acting and my experiences at the start of my professional career.

Another structure to help us feel connected as we went about our independent studies, internships, or classes elsewhere were the community groups. About a dozen students (boys and girls, sophomores, juniors and seniors) met once a week with a facilitator. Often we met at someone's house and it was a big discussion group about any topic someone raised, or we asked each other what we were doing, what's happening in classes. We were expected to show up and if we didn't, there was a lot of explaining to do...to all the members of the group, not just an authority figure. That was very helpful in preventing kids from falling through the cracks.

I recall that toward the end of junior year I seemed to hit a plateau. It might have been hormones, but I felt I didn't want to be self-directed. It was too tiring. Motivation or excitement seemed lacking. School was getting more difficult and I had personal issues as well as serious family issues. In my case the community group was extremely helpful because they noticed and between the community group and support group, I wasn't off alone for long without someone grabbing my hand.

My community group and my support group were available to keep me engaged, to keep me focused. I could tell my story and I had support, non-judgmental support, and when necessary a strong push. I thought I was a very self-sufficient child who tended to withdraw when I had problems and not talk about them. Many people didn't know anything was wrong when I really was depressed because I would act loud and flamboyant, but with the support group and community group, I was urged or permitted to talk about my problems, to open up. I learned not to isolate myself, to talk about issues, and not to keep so many secrets.

This sounds wonderful. It was wonderful. In our affluent school district, I felt like the kid from the wrong side of the tracks. I didn't fit in New Trier's traditional prep school. But this was not so in the Center. There was such tolerance and acceptance in the Center that I could come to school shoeless or bring my dog to school for a class. I also dressed in a very colorful way, wearing long wrap around batik skirts with my hair curly and flowing with bows while most girls wore straight hair, colored shirts and khaki pants. If I walked around the main school, I was teased a lot, but in the Center it didn't matter what I looked like. It didn't matter how smart I was or felt I wasn't. I knew I was loved and heard. Those feelings cleared the way for me to have significant learning experiences during my time in the Center.

When I was a little girl, I loved math and I was always told that "for a girl, you are 'good' at math", whatever that meant. When I got into junior high, I had a terrible problem understanding pre-algebra and algebra and barely got through my math classes. Freshman year in the regular school was not much better. I mentioned this to my support group and one goal for me that we agreed on was that I would try to overcome this block. So it was that I had a rare opportunity to study one-on-one with VJ.

I was a bit scared. He seemed stern and very serious about teaching. We sat down and he began teaching. We went through pre-algebra. In a few days, I was into algebra. I whizzed through the topics at lightning speed. One-on-one helped, but it was more that he taught me in a way that was easy to understand. He used simple language, as I recall, and if I didn't understand it, he would just explain in a different way. Just sitting with him, not lost in a classroom, or intimidated by all those numbers or figures on a blackboard made a difference. When VJ saw I learned in a different way, he would take me step by step. A different way is a wonderful description for the Center…in a nutshell.

Next, I just flew right through geometry because he made it so much fun and I knew that my support group/graduation committee would be pleased and I would graduate. Cautiously, because we didn't get letter grades in the Center, I asked VJ if he would grade me. In the Center, we wrote self- evaluations each semester and received an evaluation in response from someone aware/involved in the learning experience. That was really a daunting thing to ask. VJ said I did A work in Algebra and A+ work in Geometry. Not only did I graduate, but I also felt an incredible sense of accomplishment. That experience healed a bruise I had about not being smart enough, about my failure. It's good, years later, to know that I am really good in mathematics.

BECOMING CAREER READY

Being in the Center, I could spend more time in the theater wing of the school starting my training as an actress. I could spend extra time on a play and the specific scenes I was preparing for theater classes. I also read a lot of Shakespeare, worked on sets, and decided to let the water cover all of me. I spent a lot of time focusing on areas of history that related to a play I was reading or acting in. I remember being in several reading groups. Toward the end of my senior year one group was reading *The Old Man and the Sea* and then *The Great Gatsby*. *The Great Gatsby* really captured me. I loved it as well as our discussions. Then I realized there was a movie of *The Great Gatsby* that would be perfect for me to see because it would connect to my theater journey. Someone, to this day I can't remember who, found a print of the film so I could show it at one of our last meetings. That was such a warm and thoughtful gesture and it touched me deeply. Finally, I wrote a paper on it.

Another reading group of about five students read Bram Stoker's *Dracula*. We decided what our lesson plans would be by agreeing to read so many chapters for the next meeting or to bring in material about Transylvania of that time. We discussed everything: the language, the characters the story, the writing, and the structure of the book itself. I had organized the group and was a leader so I was proud of our success. Almost everything I studied had a history angle to it.

Theater history...the times depicted in plays and novels I read...but especially the '60s. Because I was curious about that tumultuous decade of my childhood, I proposed a '60s class, Arline agreed to help and a number of students signed up. At our first meeting, Arline asked, "What aspect of the '60s do you want to study?" I said everything, and we got specific listing the war, the presidency, the culture, the environment, and the movies, of course. I always had to study the movies. We broke the categories down further by talking about what specific ideas about the presidency did we want to learn about or what specific genre of movie were we interested in. Arline helped us to clarify the process even further with questions like: "What do you want to study week one? How long will that last? What aspects of the Vietnam War are we talking about? Will everyone be responsible for material each session or will a rotating leader be prepared to present and lead a discussion? One major source or a variety of materials?" And so it went until we sculpted a really viable learning experience and it became a successful way for me to learn.

My son, Jack, is a high school student now and from my perspective as a parent, I believe kids have out-grown the educational system of the last century. With the arrival of computers, the world and a world of information were opened to them. It is difficult to engage them by sitting them at desks in a row with a single book and a single viewpoint when, with computers, they can have a tour of an archaeological site or Ancient Rome. I home-schooled Jack for a couple of years when he was in junior high because he was climbing the walls, depressed, and yet clowning around as he was bored with traditional learning. I taught him history, making connections, emphasizing how it relates to us. We also focused on the arts so he could express himself in a variety of ways. He had some online courses and private teachers.

In retrospect, in the Center, I learned self-discipline and self-organization that were so important for me because I was such a passionate young girl who easily could have lacked focus. I learned to hone in on whatever it was I was studying, to finish tasks. I developed a real sense of discipline that I carried into my young adult life because I started my career when I was 18 and I knew how to organize myself. Today, I need to be self-directed because I have my own corporation and in every sense of the word, I am an entrepreneur. I have to generate my own business; I have to sell my own products. The Center gave me the tools and the confidence to be successful.

Virginia was nominated for a Golden Globe and an Academy Award for her performance in Sideways. She has appeared in many films including "Firewall," "The Number 23," "The Haunting in Connecticut," and "The Summer of Monty Wildhorn," as well as several TV dramas.

Short Takes

The Center was a great program in theory but it was easily abused....by me. On the other hand, if I had not had the Center, I probably would have dropped out because I was so unhappy with school. I'm extremely grateful for the Center, I did plenty of "Self-Directed Learning" after I graduated. Maybe the Center helped prepare me for that.

~Janet Neidig Kukec, 1979

THE WORLD FOR MY CLASSROOM

KATHRYN L. WHITE (NÉE FREY), 1979

In the Center for Self-Directed Learning, every person was a student and a teacher. Any appropriate activity was allowed. Every experience was considered academic and appropriate experiences could be counted for credit. Students were given the right to learn or not.

Walking through the classrooms that belonged to the Center for Self-Directed Learning, you might see students studying, sleeping, playing cards, arguing, laughing, reading, having a class or support group, hatching schemes, creating artwork, or playing music. We learned a lot from our peers, who were actually allowed to voice their opinions. We were given the opportunity to talk each other into being sensible and out of some pretty silly stuff. The best part was that we got to decide how, where, and what we studied within the very broad parameters set by the School Board and explained by the facilitators.

The Center was a great place for social interaction. We had students from all social groups and intellects. We had students who were offered a chance to continue their education in the Center or be "kicked out" of public school; students with disabilities; students with health issues who would have been unable to keep up with their studies due to absences; "regular" kids; geniuses; and even foreign exchange students. All groups, classes, and activities were open to all students. Students who never would have interacted with each other were in one place interacting. I once listened as two students discussed how to calculate when they would actually see each other if they passed each other traveling at the speed of light. Another was listening as a student from Israel told about how excited she was to be returning home after the semester and serving her required term in the military.

One reason I joined the Center was that my older brother was already there. The other reason was that I was not happy with the constraints of the traditional classroom. I may not have been the best student, but I was smart and found most of my school classes uninspiring. I was usually finished before the rest of the class. In addition, I was not always sure why I was studying certain ideas within a subject area.

Being in the "Baby Boomer" generation meant that our class sizes were often more than 30 students, making individual attention difficult for teachers. Many times I felt more like a student I.D. number than a student. High school was a little better because our high school classes were "leveled" by student ability, but the large class sizes remained. We also had the "freedom" to choose electives. I was enrolled in the top two levels of classes. This helped somewhat. What appealed to me most about the Center was being able to have more choices. I wasn't sure what to expect, but I was sure that it would be different.

The first day of school in the Center was different from any other I remember except for kindergarten. We spent the first day of kindergarten meeting each other, playing games, and getting oriented. The first day of school in the Center seemed to follow the same pattern. We all met as one large group regardless of grade level. We introduced ourselves and participated in team-building and social mixer activities. Then we were oriented to the procedures and expectations of the Center. Support Groups were explained–each student was required to have at least one student and a facilitator (teacher) who would help guide his or her educational journey.

Community Groups ("homerooms" each consisting of a facilitator and students from all grade levels) were announced and met. They were a time for sharing ideas, needs, student news, school news, and what was exciting or frustrating; and they were for the times when you needed support. And sometimes you supported others.

Next, we brainstormed about what ideas students and facilitators had for classes for the semester. Each idea for a class was posted on a bulletin board that had been divided into short time slots. Students and facilitators had the opportunity to read the wall and choose which classes they might be interested in joining. Each class met briefly during the scheduled time slot to decide when and where the class would be held, how many times the class would meet, what topics would be covered, what materials would be needed to cover the topics, and the expectations for each participant. Every class was required to have a facilitator. The facilitator did not have to attend or teach the class, but did keep tabs on what was going on in the class socially and educationally.

Students created their own schedules of classes. This was not an easy task with so many to choose from. One nice thing was that the classes did not have to be held during the regular school day. This helped students who had trouble attending school during the traditional school day to schedule classes. At first, I didn't know which classes to take. I tried to follow the pattern of traditional education. I kept my Latin language class, dance, and dance composition in the traditional school. For my physical education class, I signed up for canoeing. We learned how to maneuver a canoe, and river safety. Then, we went on a float trip for two days. This meant packing everything we needed in advance and packing our trash out with us. Every day, I showed up at school only to find that no one was waiting there to tell me what to do and where to go. I attended my traditional school classes, ate lunch with my friends, and attended my Center classes. But then what to do? I watched as other Center students came and went, thrilled about what they were doing, excited to be involved, or planning their next endeavors. Some students built a planetarium from canvas and wood. Using a painted light globe, they could make the stars come out. The structure was so well built that you could use it for a whisper chamber. I kept wondering why wasn't any cool stuff happening for me—why wasn't I thrilled, excited, or motivated to learn?

After about two months it dawned on me that I was the reason exciting things weren't happening. There I had sat watching others empower themselves, enhance their education, and expand their horizons. No one was going to tell me what to do or when to do it—I had to do these things for myself. I was in charge of my own education, I could tell myself what to do, and if I needed help, there were other students, facilitators, parents...the world was at my disposal. That was my "Ah-ha" moment. Everything changed. I became my own keeper—responsible for myself. I began to think about what I really wanted to learn—what classes were interesting to me. I could decide how I was going to learn about social studies, science, language arts, music, etc. Since most classes were well underway, I started a couple of independent studies. I thought about things that I would like to study the next semester. Basically, I spent my first semester figuring out how to become "self-directed." The next semester brought a new opportunity to create classes and I was ready.

I continued my Latin, dance, and dance composition classes in the traditional school, but also filled up my schedule with Center classes I was interested in and an independent study. I still had more to learn about being self-directed and about learning. I learned that the best classes were led by passionate people (either facilitators or students). Other classes that seemed like wonderful ideas fizzled because we could not pull together a course outline. Most classes finished with fewer students than they started. So, I finished my first year with great hopes and expectations for the next year. I would look for classes that were led by people who were passionate and dedicated to their ideas.

My junior year fall semester did not go very well. I was worried about what I had been missing in the traditional classes. My friends had all been telling me that I was wasting valuable time in the Center. It was difficult to respond since Center classes were not graded and there were no tests. Each student and the facilitator evaluated classes. These were compiled into a document called a Synthesis by each student at the end of each semester. That was the "report card." I had no GPA or report card to show to my traditional school chums. I also had tried to launch a couple of independent studies and was having trouble getting support materials or a facilitator to help me. I was extremely disappointed in the Center—it wasn't perfect! This combination caused me to re-enter the traditional education track. I thought that I was now motivated to learn and would be able to get the most from the traditional classes without falling into the same old rut of doing the minimum homework, passing tests, and feeling like a sheep being herded from one class to the next.

In the spring semester of my junior year, I re-entered the traditional classroom in the "regular" school. The only subject that I was behind in was mathematics. I was amazed at this. I had not taken a core curriculum of traditional classes, yet I had not lost any ground. I was right on track and still in the upper level classes. So there I was, writing my Junior Year Theme paper, studying second-semester geometry proofs (my Center studies had covered first semester just fine), chemistry, history and of course, Latin.

All went well for the first quarter, but I really began to go downhill after that. I found myself becoming apathetic again. I wasn't paying attention in class, did minimal homework, and even got sent to the office for arguing with my English teacher. (I had forgotten that she was always right.)

In these classes, once again my education had become limited to a textbook, classroom instruction, and opinions of others. I had no input in areas of interest or tangent experiences. Class discussions were directed by the instructor. Any ideas we had were often discounted as incorrect. All around me in the classroom were students who watched the clock, stressed about tests, didn't ask questions, and hoped their answer was the one the teacher was trying to elicit. By the end of the semester, I was back to the day-to-day hum-drum, uninspired, grinding out assignments, and cramming for tests.

So, in my senior year, back into the Center I went. I had taken the ASVAB (Armed Services Vocational Aptitude Battery) test, which indicated that I should enjoy a career in Agriculture or Teaching. I already knew that I liked biology and I had loved planting vegetable gardens with my Mom. I thought that maybe I should explore the teaching idea. The facilitating teachers in the Center were able to find me an opportunity to assist in a classroom at a satellite school that the Native Americans had created to teach their students in the Uptown neighborhood of Chicago. The teachers at the satellite school thought I was nuts to volunteer there. It was a tough neighborhood, in tough times, with tough kids. I felt privileged to get to spend half a day a week at the school working with dedicated teachers and very special students. This experience allowed me to discover that this was definitely an area of interest for me. Since Center classes met during any time of the day that the most students were able to attend, I was able to continue this through the entire year and attend my other classes. The flexible scheduling also allowed me to work at a job to earn money for college so I could get a teaching degree.

That year, one of my Center classes visited the Menominee Indian Reservation in Wisconsin and met with their tribal Chief. We had prepared some questions for him and he gave us some very real answers about indignities visited upon their culture and tribal lands by recent federal government legislation and what they were trying to do about it. This was an experience none who went, including our facilitator, will forget. As part of our United States Government class, we went to the State Capitol and met our representative. We visited the legislature in session. We studied a bill and watched it be voted on and pass.

Center graduation was very personal and special. It was held outside in Bumpy Park. Each student was honored by a facilitator who would speak of all the accomplishments and hopes for the future of the student. The graduates, students, or parents were also permitted to speak, sing, or read a poem if they chose. Then there were hugs all around from facilitators, students, and parents. I remember more about my Center Graduation than the mass graduation held by the traditional school for close to 1,000 students who all dressed basically alike and had their names read off as we were herded across a stage.

I had to delay my college studies a year due to finances. When I was ready, I applied to the National-Louis University teacher education program in Evanston, Illinois. I had taken the SAT and ACT exams and gotten above average scores on both. One of my Center facilitating teachers wrote my letter of recommendation. I was supposed to have turned in two of those, but that one was all I had. I was accepted.

College seemed easy. I had already learned to manage my time. I was working two jobs and attending a full schedule of interesting classes. I got all As or Bs and only one C, graduating in 1984 with a Bachelor of Science in Education with emphasis in Mathematics. Since then, I have earned a Master's Degree in Teaching Mathematics. As an educator, I value what I learned in the Center about the learning process and growing a mind. Students need time to think. They need to be guided, not told. Curriculum needs to be validated with real-life applications. Students should feel respected and comfortable when questioning ideas or stating their opinions. Students need to be responsible for their own learning. Students can learn from sources other than the teacher or the textbook. Sometimes students need to fail so that they can learn how to succeed. A teacher needs to be supportive throughout the process.

These are all things that I try to bring to my classroom every day in spite of the constraints of the textbook-based curriculum. I also co-teach summer workshops for math teachers and host workshops for teachers through the school year. I have been voted best teacher in my building by my peers three times in the past eight years.

As a parent raising a family in a rural area, I used what I learned in the Center about doing things that you are passionate about, being self-directed, finding help, and identifying a need and filling it. I became active in many facets of our community. For example, we started a recreational soccer program for the town, which meant finding volunteers, a league to play in, funding, and building a field so that the children would have something to do after school. Sixteen years later, it is still functioning.

As Parent Teacher Organization president, we funded and built a playground for the elementary school. We were also active in scouting with our children. We were den leaders and hosted several badge earning activities.

People tell me that I do too much, but not doing these things didn't seem right. I learned in the Center that these things are not impossible. Anything can be done, even though it may take more than one attempt. The Center served students by opening up the world to them. It served the student who had mental or physical challenges by allowing learning to occur in many settings at any time. It served students who needed time to "recover" from emotional trauma by allowing peers and teachers to interact in non-threatening environments to build healthy relationships and support student needs.

Students interacted with other students across grade levels, social strata, and cultural differences. There was laughter, anger, tears, drama, music, hugs, and most of all community. Here was a place where student voices could be heard. Everyone had a turn to speak. Everyone was heard. Anyone who could create a valid argument and convince enough students about an idea could make it happen. We had a say in everything, and support was everywhere. Ideas were expressed, complaints were heard, grand discussions happened, feelings got hurt, apologies were made, rules were evaluated, and revisions were made. There was problem solving in action and democracy at every level.

I feel that this created people who were able to think about situations, listen to (and hear) others, and do something sensible in response. I am aware of the many paths that Center graduates have taken: Editors, lawyers, scientists, musicians, actors, artists, business owners, and entrepreneurs. We learned that we were all special people who had been given the right to develop our special talents. We went on to become creative people who contribute to their communities.

Kathryn attended National-Louis University where she earned a Bachelor of Science in Education. She is currently employed as a full time middle school teacher and curriculum specialist. After earning a Masters of Science in Teaching Mathematics, she also teaches the mathematics portion of a workshop for middle school teachers at Missouri University of Science & Technology. Other interests have been organic gardening, catering, Labrador Retrievers, and dance.

Parts and Other Matters

Maren Brown, 1980

"What is the most important part of a car?" I wondered as I drove to the airport today. "And who can help me to answer this question?" I called my mechanic, John. "John? Maren Brown here. I have a question. What is the most important part of a car?"

John paused, reflecting. "Well, I think it would be the engine, because the car wouldn't start without one. But then again, the brakes are important too, because once you start, you have to be able to stop."

I thank John and hang up. John is what Malcolm Gladwell calls an expert. He has over 20 years of experience working on cars. He should know. But John's response, as expert as it is, reveals a whole set of assumptions that we all make when we answer any question. What is the context of the question, and what is our ultimate goal? Do we want to go somewhere? (In this case, the body and wheels would be important.) Do we just want to start the thing? (Brakes aren't important, but the engine sure is.) Or is it simply looking at the car that matters? (Here the body would be an essential item.)

So, you ask, what does all of this have to do with the Center for Self-Directed Learning? At the Center, I had many opportunities to follow my curiosity, to explore the questions that stretched the limits of my adolescent mind. Now, as an educator myself, I understand the significance of this experience in shaping the way I approach my teaching today. To say it had a profound effect on me is an understatement. Which leads me to ask: Was the Center the most important part of my education? To answer that, two of my Center experiences hold some clues.

The first was a course of study where I investigated the impact of a very new technology—audio tours—on the visitor experience of the Toulouse Lautrec exhibit at the Art Institute of Chicago. I remember observing how visitors on the audio tour chose a very different path from those who did not utilize the recorded tour, and they appeared to experience the work more superficially, taking less time with the work, viewing it from a single vantage point, and not interacting with others.

At a very young age, I was allowed to investigate a field that I now have worked in for over 25 years: Arts Management. Immediately after graduating from college, I started work in the field as a museum educator, one of the folks who provide you with audio tours. I wrote a few audio tours myself and led many tours of different museum collections. I think it was this memory that led me to find different ways to interpret the collections, interpretation that encouraged individual ideas and engagement, such as working with a local disc jockey to create a pop music tour of the collection for kids, and inviting art-making into the galleries.

The second experience took place when my Center study group and I delved deeply into the study of nuclear power. To examine this subject, we talked to a variety of experts: legislators, nuclear power representatives, regulators, anti-nuke activists, and others. One indelible impression was when we visited a nuclear power plant, and after going on a tour of the plant with a very perky power company representative, we were invited to visit the plant's library. There we found primary documents detailing the history of the plant, as well as a wall of binders marked "unexplained occurrences." The binders described small incidents at the plant, such as equipment failures or unplanned emissions. It gave me the creeps. Another memory: after researching how to properly format and address letters, I wrote to one activist organization with the greeting "Dear Gentlemen." The representative of the anti-nuke organization gave me a firm scolding in a page-long letter. But the most significant part of this entire learning experience was that, at the end of this journey, all three of us who were in the class came to different conclusions as to whether or not we supported nuclear power. The fact that we all came to different conclusions, given the same set of information, helped me to understand the value of a real, unbiased education.

As an educator, I strive to create an atmosphere where students can investigate ideas without prescriptive ideology. For a time, many cars in my adopted town in Massachusetts sported a popular bumper sticker, "Question Authority." In many ways, this is what we were encouraged to do in the Center, but with respect and civility. Passing around the talking paddle during Center meetings helped me to realize the need for each voice to be heard. Allowing for collective decision-making and consensus were equally as impactful. Having teachers who enabled ideas to emerge in young minds without imposing their opinions was a revelation. It was significantly different from virtually any educational experience I had had prior to the Center. Today, as an educator, I rejoice when people disagree with my ideas or ask penetrating questions. I know they are engaged and curious and there is nothing more gratifying.

Maren, M.B.A., formerly the Director of the Arts Extension Service (AES) at the University of Massachusetts-Amherst, recently established an arts management consulting practice. She is co-editor and contributor to the fifth edition of Fundamentals of Arts Management, *which is utilized as a foundational text by 45% of the arts management degree programs in the nation.*

Short Takes

The Center gave us choice over what we learned. I believe that high school students need a more hands on approach to learning. I've co-created a non-profit in Arizona called "Kids Who Care" that promotes service learning tied to curricula. Students apply what they are learning in the classroom to community projects with local charities.

~Jana Sample Wilcke, 1982

LEAD AND LET LEAD

MARY FLYNN, 1980

I'll never forget the day. Mrs. Paul pulled me aside after a marathon Town Hall. I don't remember what we were trying to decide at the meeting, but I do recall that I had put a lot of energy into trying to bring it to some kind of closure. Instead, we collectively ran out of steam and left everything unsolved, or so I felt at the time.

The whole experience raised doubts in my head about the value of decision-making by consensus. Hierarchy was anathema at the Center, but that day I longed for a benevolent dictator. Instead, I got Mrs. Paul. She quietly led me to a table and invited me to sit down with her. "I want you to think about something, Mary," she said, looking at me with piercing eyes that showed signs she, too, had lost a little patience in the last few hours of communal arguing. "What would happen if you didn't lead?" I looked at her blankly. "Picture it," she insisted quietly. "What do you think would happen if, at the next Town Hall, you sat back and listened, instead of talking?" She paused while I looked puzzled. "Do you think nobody would say anything?" she asked. The question made me uncomfortable. "Do you think nobody would have responded? Do you think no decisions would get made?" she pressed, as I squirmed. She paused to let her words sink in. I started to blush as I realized how arrogant my behavior had been. I had thought I was working for the common good by pushing us to get issues resolved, but instead, my anxiety-driven impatience with the process had actually polarized people and hindered us from achieving closure that day. Mrs. Paul began to get up from the table. "Try it next time. Think of it as an experiment. Just watch what happens."

I took her words to heart. At the next Town Hall, I forced myself to be quiet, practically sitting on my hands so I wouldn't raise them in an attempt to speak. To my pleasant surprise, the very issues that had seemed so divisive in the previous meeting turned out to have more consensus behind them than any of us had thought, and by the end of the session, the group had made decisions on all the key points—with little or no assistance from me. It was a humbling experience. And it's one I'm reminded of often in my professional life as a reporter and producer, where my work relies on collaborating with others. In my otherwise stellar liberal arts college experience at Vassar where I majored in English, there were no opportunities to work in groups in the classroom. Fortunately, there were plenty of extracurricular activities that gave me opportunities to hone my team skills, such as playing squash, living in a townhouse with other students and working on a magazine that, like the Center, operated by consensus with nobody named Editor in Chief.

Knowing when to lead and when to let others lead remains a challenge for me, but whenever I find myself talking too much in a meeting, I hear Mrs. Paul's voice saying, "What would happen if you didn't lead?" My first job after college was in book publishing in the paperback division of Random House, fulfilling my childhood dream of living in New York. I found book publishing too slow and too insular so I moved into journalism, covering technology at magazines (*PC Magazine* and *U.S. News & World Report*). As a magazine writer, I did a lot of TV appearances and went on TV full-time as a broadcast reporter, with the Internet as my beat, when MSNBC launched in 1996. I regularly appeared on NBC and CNBC programs, including "Today" and "The News with Brian Williams." Then later I worked as a reporter and anchor at CNN and its sister business network, CNNfn. When the dot com bubble burst, CNN laid off about 400 people, and I was one of them. I freelanced for five years and had my daughter. About five years ago, I began a full-time job at The Deal, a financial news organization where I cover technology as well as financial reform and the housing crisis. I also anchor an award-winning online video show and I think about the Center all the time.

Mary still lives in New York with her husband, John Quain, a fellow tech reporter who writes frequently for The New York Times *and others. Her daughter is a third grader at Hunter College Elementary School, a public school for gifted children in New York City. It is Center-like in some ways! The parents all remind her of Center students.*

Short Takes

I think the Center saved my life. I enjoyed having such a diversity of friends. I learned so much about different styles of learning, and that learning doesn't just happen in school, how to work in a team environment, how to facilitate groups of people. Every school kid should have relationships with their teachers like I did with Mr. Greg, VJ and Arline. What amazing people!

~Ellen Spier Trotochaud, 1981

Turns Out, I'm Smart...

Melissa Perrin (Britt), 1980

I didn't know it until my twenties. I still didn't really believe it until a few years after receiving my doctorate. Now, I do believe I am smart. I don't remember anything of the first semester of my junior year at New Trier except the day Mr. Greg and VJ came into my history class. They spoke of a "school-within-a-school" for kids who wanted to learn and were self-directed. In truth, I may have only started to listen when I heard the words "No papers, tests or grades." What kept me listening was how they responded to the questions of my fellow students. They answered each question as if it was important and as if they had time to actually discuss the student's points. They knew that most of the kids thought it was a "blow-off school" but even answered those questions and comments with respect and clarity.

Mr. Greg looked directly at me, while he gave the closing part of the presentation, saying: "This is a school for kids who think differently and aren't satisfied parroting back information. This is for kids who want to go deeper into subjects and kids who learn differently." Then he winked at me. I asked him later why he did that. He told me that he could tell I was a Centerite whether I chose to join or not. Until that time, I only knew that I was either stupid or lazy, depending on the subject and the teacher. My grades were low to acceptable in most subjects. I could not wrap my mind around most math concepts. School was agony for me. Multiple-choice tests were difficult; science was intriguing, but I didn't test well in it; math was impossible. Kids would groan when I raised my hand. Some teachers would too. I learned not to ask questions or express my thoughts. My peers were beginning to think about college in junior year. I was not. High school was compulsory; college was not. As far as I was concerned, I was done with education when I graduated.

224

By junior year in high school, I had struggled with major depression and suicidal ideation for four years. My job, as I saw it, was to muscle through high school, getting the best grades I could (spitting back to the teachers what they wanted to hear or see in order to move me along the conveyor belt to graduation), and not kill myself. My best working hypothesis at the time was that when high school ended, my depression would ease since I would no longer have to wrestle with whether or not I was stupid, whether or not I was "trying," and whether or not people would tolerate listening to the thoughts that I had. My mother understood my need for the Center. My father, on the other hand, required persuasion. The only time my father ever turned red and spluttered with helpless anger toward me was when we were having conversations about whether or not the Center was a good choice for me. When he realized that I truly was not considering college, that school was an agonizing experience for me, he gave his permission. I was in.

It seems to me that within a week or two of that decision I was tooling down Lake Shore Drive toward the Field Museum in my yellow VW Beatle. The most important "class" for me in that semester was an independent study with Dr. Ben Bronson, director of the Indonesian Studies, at the museum. I worked on transliterating two Batak Divination Books that I had bought in France for $500.00 two years before. The time of study included learning all I could about their culture, tools, myths, and history. I got to explore the warehouse! I mean, I was asked to catalogue the material (spears, masks, statues, etc.) in the warehouse. Bliss. When I wasn't doing that I was scouring the books I had, looking for patterns of letters that formed words. (Footnote: I didn't know I was studying pattern recognition, sequencing, cataloguing, study skills, social studies, living history, note taking, transcribing, and keyboard skills.) I was very anxious in the beginning, that although I had begged for the opportunity to do this work, I was, in truth, too stupid, slow or inept. After all, whenever I tried to complete a project for the parent school it was inane. Whenever, I tried to discuss my thoughts in social studies, I slowed the class down. There was a schedule to keep. I remember asking my parents if perhaps everyone had made a mistake letting me do something so incredible and exciting. Surely, someone else was better prepared and would do a better job. All of the adults around me urged me forward: Mom, Dad, VJ (my community group leader), Mrs. Paul, and Ben. All of them believed that I could "do it" and if I couldn't "do it" to my satisfaction, I was still learning. Perhaps perfectionism was an issue too.

The Field Museum, transliterating the Batak divination book, is my best and most thrilling memory of high school. I could do it. I did belong as a researcher there. Best of all, I was learning something that was interesting to me. The material mattered so much to me. It was also the first time that I felt the world might have a place for me.

Dreams class at Mrs. Pieper's house introduced me to psychological theory but it also created a sense of intimacy and security. There was acceptance in her house. I came to understand that classrooms are a concept; learning is a minute-to-minute thing, can happen anywhere, anytime, and isn't always externally imposed. This freed me up to be open to anything and everything. Still does.

In my senior year Bev and I spent an intensive two weeks at the Newberry Library in Chicago, focusing on treaties between the Sioux and the U.S. as well as cultural and sociological information. Other classes that thrilled me included Great Big Books (reading and discussing the classics), Copy Cats (reading certain authors then writing material in their style to be reviewed by our peers), and helping M.K. (Marcus) build a yurt. The yurt was Geometry lived out. I did not and do not understand the math of geometry. M.K. worked out the space requirements, the length of wood needed, and the fabric measurements needed. I couldn't wrap my mind around that. However, putting the materials together and listening to him talk out the rough spots helped me experience it physically, spatially. While I could not verbalize it, and am having trouble verbalizing it now, I have a visceral sense of the space, the roundness, of the yurt as well as how the parts came together. I was also amazed that when Marcus measured and cut something it always worked out. Somehow, when I measure something, measurements are fluid and unreliable. M.K.'s measurements were always specific and concrete.

The Synthesis was another gift. It was all well and good to have no papers, tests or grades…however we were still accountable for our behavior, learning, and effort. We didn't ever want to fail to turn it in on time because one never really wanted to experience the wrath of The Paul…we worried that she might kick us out! That was the very worst thing that could happen. As she said often, we had so few deadlines that there was really no excuse for turning it in late. A dear friend and I wrote our syntheses lying on our stomachs with our typewriters back to back, listening to Traffic's "Low Spark of High Heel Boys" each semester. I learned how to concisely describe a series of work efforts, honestly evaluate my choices and behaviors, and to seek (and give) productive feedback from (and to) peers. I was asked to serve on the (Peer Group? Jury?) in my senior year. This surprised me. My personal evaluation of myself was that I was not someone whose opinion should be respected. However, with VJ's and Mrs. Paul's urging, I did join.

Those sessions, listening to choices my peers made, the thought process used to make the choice, and discussion of consequences or lack thereof, were mind blowing. I learned about the power of a healthy group and the importance of community. I realized in these sessions that philosophy and ethics are not just in books; they apply to every situation. Philosophers have verbalized thought processes and examined human behavior; application is a powerful thing.

Another powerful group experience occurred in the first semester that I was in the Center. It was time for Community Group and VJ rounded us up telling us that one of our peers hadn't come to school or any of his classes/meetings for over a week. We talked, as a group, about how to reach out to him. VJ reminded us of our commitment, not only to learning what we could learn, but to helping each other as well. We decided to have the Community Group at our classmate's house. VJ called his mother for permission and we caravanned over. We sat down in the living room and his mom went to get him. When she told VJ that he wouldn't come down we talked about what to do. VJ's point was that a commitment was a commitment even when one was depressed or didn't feel well. As someone struggling with depression, this resonated for me profoundly. We went upstairs, filed into his room, and sat down, each of us explaining that we cared for him and if he couldn't come to us, we would come to him. I'm sure it didn't feel terrific for him but he joined us and his attendance improved at school for a while. VJ's lesson was a strong one for me. (I certainly didn't want them showing up at my house when I was in my pajamas!)

In my senior year, a group of us were told that we needed to fulfill a state requirement for a math class. So, we took Basic Math Concepts with VJ, math genius. When it came to math, VJ's mind amazed me. He didn't "dumb it down" for me per se. But he was surprised by my limitations. After the third meeting, VJ ran me through a few problems at various levels and asked me some questions that made little sense to me. I did my best not to be defensive and brittle in response. I knew that he was trustworthy and was respecting me while seeing the depth of my vulnerability in the subject. VJ told me I learn differently and that someday there would be a language to discuss it and learning styles that would work better with the configurations of my brain. He was right.

I graduated with my class at New Trier. I could not help but raise a victory fist as I crossed the stage to receive my diploma. Graduation had been an iffy proposition in my mind and I was thrilled. The Center's graduation ceremony at Bumpy Park was a much more intimate affair. I felt as though a mantle was passed, that I was strongly charged to learn, teach and to do it at my full capacity. VJ, Mr. Greg, Bev, and Mrs. Paul had all told me that I was much more capable than I believed myself to be. I had been taught to seek information in libraries, from people, books, experience, and detective work. Besides, I love to pass it on.

The Center prepared me beautifully for college. My college peers were faced with learning, quickly, how to manage their time, prioritize their work, and how to find the information needed to learn the material and complete projects. I had been doing that, with guidance and instruction, for a year and a half. I was an old hand at it. College was a wonderful experience except where math was concerned. I took a basic math course, which my classmates and I dubbed "Math for Morons," twice, barely passing it the second time. This was problematic. I was majoring in Psychology with an undeclared minor in English Literature. I had full plans to continue on into a degree in Psychology. However, if I couldn't pass Math for Morons, I couldn't get into the statistics class necessary to graduate with a B.A. in Psychology. My advisor called me into her office in the fall of my senior year to tell me that I needed to change my major to English Literature in order to graduate with a degree. I explained my goal of achieving a doctorate in psychology. My memory is that she grimaced and said: "Melissa, you aren't doctor material. You'll never be a doctor. You'll have to do something else." I then asked what I could do with a liberal arts degree in English Literature. She responded that what she could imagine for me was to be a cashier in a small store. I was flabbergasted and said: "But I can't do Math! How could I be a cashier?" She then told me that she had seen that cash registers were becoming computerized and I wouldn't need to have skills in math. I don't think I spoke with her again until we reviewed my graduation requirements. I graduated with a B.A. in English Literature and moved home to find a job. Following college, I worked part time in a small bookstore and part time at Lutheran General Hospital as a Psych Tech on the Psych units.

As I grew into that job, the psychiatrists and residents often commented that I had a gift when it came to psychology and should really consider going to school. I was too embarrassed to explain that I struggled so profoundly with math. I love psychology and working with clients. Around that time a couple of teens were admitted to our unit with testing reports from the One To One Learning Center, a center that offered IQ and learning disability testing. I read the reports with great interest and thought of VJ's observations about my math abilities. I called and made an appointment. When asked what my goals were in being tested I replied that I needed to know if I was really lazy and stupid or if I had a learning problem because I needed to go to grad school and get a doctorate in psychology.

Turns out I have a learning problem. Three of them. For the next year and a half, I met with a tutor three times a week at the One to One Learning Center and learned math from first grade through college. I thought of VJ almost every day. When learning and engaged in discovery, I carried VJ, Mrs. Paul, Mr. Greg, and Bev with me. They had believed in me. All of them may have wearied of my verbosity but never, ever, let me know that. This feels melodramatic to write but I felt that I owed them my energy and depth of learning. They had seen something in me worth attending to. I had been charged to learn what I could, what I wanted and that there were no limitations for me other than those that were self-imposed.

There are many letters that I wrote to VJ in my mind that I never sent. The one that told him that he was right: I did, indeed, have learning disabilities. The one in which I told him that I was accepted into graduate school, afraid that I may have fooled everyone again, but was going to do my best and learn everything even if I didn't get a degree. The one in which I told him I was a doctor.

So. I'm smart. I'm a doctor and I love to learn. I also love to teach. I taught as an adjunct professor at a small university and made some of my peers and my students a bit uncomfortable with my teaching style. I encouraged my pre-doctoral students to be self-directed in their projects. Many of them expressed great anxiety when faced with less structure than they were accustomed to. One student burst into tears in class when she realized that I was looking for what she learned, not what I taught her. I realized that this was much too nebulous a concept for her and the peers that she spoke for when she said: "How can we give you what you want when it's going to be different for everyone? How will we get As?" The vastness and scope of all of the things people are interested in cannot be covered in school.

I have taught my two children how to use the library, and now the World Wide Web, to learn what is important to them. When they were younger, we talked about exploring and discovering rather than learning. This was a necessary divide when my son was eight, and he told me that learning was boring because the material was never what he wanted to know about. It was based on someone else's interest. Discovering and exploring, on the other hand, sounded pretty exciting and free. Indeed. Off we went to the libraries and museums then home to invent and explore.

The Center saved my life. This is not a melodramatic statement. It is fact. I was burned out and empty by the age of 16, waiting for something better; full of bitterness and self-hate. It took many years for me to believe, on a cellular level, what I was told in the Center: that I am smart, interesting, and capable of so very much. The less tangible lesson, however, the one I feel weaving around this essay that I cannot seem to verbalize, is that learning is everywhere, happens in so many ways, and isn't measurable. Acquisition of repeatable facts is measurable by multiple-choice tests, ISATS, MAP tests, and other forms of assessment. Learning is something that is pervasive, permeable, and can primarily be lived out. There is reporting and then there is knowledge. If my educational career had continued to focus on reporting and assessments it would have ended by the time I was 18. I simply know that the Center gave me so very many options and the facilitators gave me enough encouragement, love, and acceptance that I took a risk and was successful enough to risk again. Bliss.

Talking with my cohorts from the Center and communicating with Arline has been a remarkable experience. After years of silent belonging, I have experienced a grounding sense of realness. The metaphor of a spy coming in from deep cover is one full of resonance for me as we mutually enjoy our experiences of such a wonderful place.

> *Melissa is a licensed clinical psychologist in suburban Chicago. Still curious and a self-directed student, she is often found in a library or perusing the internet for research when she is not providing therapy, giving a workshop, traveling, or offering consultation.*

My Launching Pad

Stuard Detmer, 1981

It was a grand experience full of excitement, discovery, failures, and frustration. In short, it was an ideal launching pad for the great game of life. I shudder to think where my life and legs may have traveled without the Center opportunity. Certainly not to Moscow, Paris, Geneva, or the many other cities in which I have entered.

I entered the Center in my sophomore year. It was the program's waning years. I knew a number of upperclassmen who were in the Center and held them in high regard. To me they were smart, cool, and always up to something exciting, such as building a planetarium or programming computers at Northwestern. As a freshman bored out of my wits in the "parent school," I had no doubt that I wanted to go to the Center, but to my parents the whole proposition seemed fraught with risk. The common wisdom was that the Center complicated the college admissions process, and asking a 15-year-old boy to manage the apparent lack of structure looked like a tall order. However, after talking with parents of other Center students and attending a Center orientation night where the students impressed with their tales of adventure, my parents finally relented and I was in.

My memories of the Center from that point on are a bit dim, but a few things stand out: first there were the Town Hall meetings where we seemed to endlessly hash out community issues and search for that elusive consensus (we even debated what consensus meant). Then, there were the projects and classes outside the bounds of the New Trier campus, which vaulted me into the wider world. The Town Hall meetings were great training grounds for learning how to influence debate. I remember having strong opinions about the subjects at hand and I enjoyed trying to affect the outcome of the discussions. With the rose-colored glasses of hindsight, I imagine that I positively influenced many of these debates. I know I took up more than my fair share of airtime.

Beyond learning how to debate constructively with my fellow students, I also eventually learned about listening. In these open discussions, the more outspoken students generally had the upper hand. I was often surprised when one of the quieter students would say something that laid to waste my carefully argued points, and I was forced to beat a tactical retreat grudgingly acknowledging that the other person had a point. This process taught me several things: Just because someone is quiet does not mean he or she does not have something to say; if you browbeat someone into accepting your position, you will still have to get on with that person and your "victory" may be fleeting; consensus is really the goal, not winning the argument; and, by participating in the life of the community, you can make a difference with words.

Off the Center campus, I enjoyed a wide range of opportunities. I took two years of physics in the parent school, including the Advanced Placement (AP) course. I studied astronomy at the Adler Planetarium in Chicago. I took math courses one-on-one from a graduate student at Northwestern and learned to program computers at the Vogelback Computer Center at the same institution. I ran on the beach at 6 a.m. with the "Assault Team" to fulfill my physical education requirement. I learned about how Chicago politics works by studying the workings of the Chicago Housing Authority. I learned about solar energy, visiting installations at Argonne National Laboratory and conducting a feasibility study to install solar panels at New Trier. I backpacked in the San Juan Mountains of Colorado and learned how *not* to descend a snow-covered mountain by the light of a full moon. I learned about dream analysis and about the works of Joseph Campbell and James Joyce from a poet named Mrs. Pieper. And I traveled to an education conference with a group of students led by Bill Gregory, where we awed the attending educators with our tales of Center derring-do.

One of those experiences stands out above all. A group of five of us chose to launch a full-year study of the Chicago Housing Authority (CHA) to fulfill our government requirement. The institutionalization of Chicago slums in the famous Robert Taylor Homes and Cabrini-Green projects was clearly a failure, and the CHA—a creation of federal, state and local politics—was regularly pilloried in the local media. The actual housing projects were close by in Chicago yet a world away from the cozy confines of the North Shore.

This project was a real eye-opener for our group of suburban kids. As part of our study, we toured many of the CHA housing projects, mostly from the safe confines of a car. We wanted to know how poverty had resisted the best intentions to eradicate it. We attended the bi-weekly meetings of the CHA Board of Directors and learned about the political struggles amongst the board members and I interviewed one CHA Board member, the Chief of the Chicago Afro-American Fraternal Order of Police who had been appointed by Mayor Jane Byrne. Our up close and personal interview allowed us to hear him grouse that he found himself outflanked by the old-time Chairman, Charles Swibel, and his allies and we learned directly from him about corruption in the CHA and how certain board members benefited directly from CHA contracts.

We also had the good fortune to study the CHA as it was experimenting with new approaches to public housing, such as building three family units in middle class neighborhoods. Since then, both Cabrini-Green and Robert Taylor Homes have been razed and many of the then-experimental programs have taken their place. For our study group the experience was energizing. We found ourselves immersed in real-world issues and were surprised that adults were willing to talk to us and help explain these issues to us, or at least give us their side of the story. The CHA was filled with compromise and corruption, but it did provide housing for tens of thousands of people. Despite the difficulties, the residents, the board members, and the government agencies soldiered on, understanding that through their efforts change would come, if only slowly.

What else stands out from my Center experience? I enjoyed the fact that I was treated like an adult and that the faculty did not condescend to me. This helped breed confidence. If faculty members thought I should be doing something differently, they let me know through patient suggestion and at times even let me fail to make the experience more memorable. I was also allowed to go where my interests (or my classmates' interests) took me, and projects like the CHA project allowed me to learn about government, social issues, and politics in an integrated way, which was more practical and engaging than sitting and doing course work.

The Center was the greatest thing that could have happened to me in high school, and my parents now agree, which is gratifying given their initial skepticism. So, what lessons have stayed with me from my Center experience?

I am in charge of my education—now and forever. Look for consensus, not victory. I can make a difference. Don't listen to people who tell you to take the conventional route. The scenic route is always, well…more scenic. Sometimes it's bumpy. Most people are improvising as they go along—I can too. People are motivated by different things, and some just don't care about the things that I care about. If they're in my community, I have to learn to work with them anyway. All those lessons came in pretty handy as I moved on from the Center.

After my Bumpy Park graduation, I went to Vanderbilt University, where I studied Economics and Russian. I spent two summers at Indiana University in a total-immersion program for Russian that led to a semester study at Leningrad State University in the U.S.S.R. Russia became a passion for me and led to a series of adventures that traced the fall of the Soviet Union and the rise of a new Russia and a long list of colorful experiences when I:

- Worked as a company representative aboard Soviet fishing trawlers in the Bering Sea and Pacific Ocean

- Managed the New York SoHo studio of exiled Russian painter Mihail Chemiakin

- Taught English in Hamburg, Germany while studying German

- Organized a U.S.S.R. cultural exchange program for the Smithsonian Institution

- Lived in Moscow during the last two years of the Soviet Union, securing the first FM radio broadcasting license in the U.S.S.R. and hosting a nationwide broadcast of the Russian-language show "U.S.A Top 20," which was written by the producers of Casey Kasem's "American Top 40"

- Earned an M.B.A. with honors at the University of Virginia

- Lived in Peru, Columbia, England, Russia, and the United States while working for Mobil Oil Corporation

- Established the first western-branded service station network in Moscow

- Rode the Internet boom in a dot.com company (stock options worthless)

- Helped build the largest independent western oil company in Russia, eventually becoming CEO and selling the company to Gazprom

Now living with my family in Geneva, Switzerland, I am deciding what to do next.

Stu lives in Geneva, Switzerland with his wife of 20 years, Olga, and teenage son, Austin. A daughter, Angela, is a student at DePaul University in Chicago. Yes, he is still deciding.

Short Takes

I'm in my eighth year as a high school teacher of Foods classes in Maywood, IL.

I also do professional embroidery, t-shirt printing, and quilting. Prior to teaching, I worked out of the Merchandise Mart in Chicago and had a home decorating business.

~Karen Golin, 1975

Ahh, Newton!

Mary Josephine Bellanca, 1983

When I was little, I remember going to this big, big room with my dad. It was called "The Center." I played on the desks and under the tables all about the room, because Center people were always moving them around. Years later, it was amazing to be in learning groups, as a student, in the same big room with the same moveable blackboards and often moved chairs and tables.

As a sophomore in high school, I entered the Center because of my dad. He was the creative force behind the Center so I was raised with his ideas about self-directed learning. I was interested in education and it was exciting to be able to try out self-directed learning. It was good for me because I was always curious about many things and I wanted the opportunity to explore new ideas myself. It would, I thought, be more stimulating and less madly competitive than the regular school.

At the very beginning of my sophomore year, doing calculus in French with Vernoy Johnson and three other students was a stimulating exploration. Vernoy taught us math in French. He learned French when he taught in Africa and I had been studying French since seventh grade. Also, I really liked a lot of mathematics and wanted to learn more. I loved reading this big, big book called *Fundamentals of Calculus* that was my first real introduction to mathematical language and to Newton's profound mathematical ideas. We organized the class so that we would read independently and then meet with Vernoy to discuss the ideas.

At each meeting, one student was in charge of presenting the ideas to the group. This required that the presenter would have to learn the material well enough to be able to explain it to the others. When we proved the fundamental theorem of calculus, Vernoy had exclaimed, "This is one of the most exciting theorems in mathematics."

Now that I have my Ph.D. in physics, I appreciate that he was totally right. I read a biography of Newton several years ago and still like these fundamental ideas of calculus that are vital to the physics I studied. The theorems we studied were some of the most amazing intellectual accomplishments I have experienced. When my dad, an elementary school teacher, and I put together a book for elementary teachers of science that shows how to use project-based learning with the Next Generation Science standards, I made sure that Newton and his ideas were included.

To celebrate the group's success Vernoy played his favorite recording, the *1812 Overture*. He was very good at getting us to realize how important intellectual ideas can be. Not only was that class good for my French, but also I can do mathematics now in a lot of languages I don't even understand. The other important lesson learned was that in order to explain the material to fellow students, my knowledge had to be solid. I studied the material. If confused, I consulted Vernoy, my expert, and then I proceeded to work out the problems myself. That was a valuable skill that I used in college and later in life. That class was my first exposure to it.

A lot of my love for mathematics comes from Vernoy. He encouraged me, thought I was really good at it, and told me so in a supportive way. In the Center, I was able to use more time to explore mathematics at a deeper level with him than would have been possible in a regular school. Also, as a girl at that age, there were the classic social pressures about math. I knew I was good at math, but his telling me I was really great at it was key to my love for the field. None of my regular schoolteachers did what he was able to do. Vernoy also taught me how important it was to inspire students, to get students excited and involved in what they are doing.

What I learned about teaching math really worked for me when I was teaching in Loughborough, England several years back. I read parts of Newton's biography to my calculus class and also in the calculus class for physics students. I would present different parts of new research that I would find in the lab such as the search for new planets that are similar to Earth. We talked about the planet search when we studied certain aspects of calculus that involved gravity because the search for planets is based on gravitational expectations. Also, from a historical view, we could look at what was occurring in Newton's day and what is going on today. I taught them a little about my own research when it was relevant to the calculus we were learning and they asked good questions.

The feedback was rewarding. Showing one's own enthusiasm, as I learned in the Center from Vernoy and other good teachers, including my dad who read poetry books with me when I was a little girl, captures students' attention and starts the love of learning.

I didn't spend all of my time in the Center doing math. I also had an internship in a pathology lab at Evanston Hospital and I had an opportunity to see an autopsy, something high school students don't normally get to view. There was all the fat in one man's body and it was apparent he was a heavy drinker because the effect on his body was visible. The colorfulness of the human body was impressive, too. I was very interested in all science at that time, but in medicine in particular.

Physics was another academic area that I studied using two different learning techniques. I did an independent study, a tutorial, with a graduate student at Northwestern who had been a Center student. Then with Vernoy as facilitator, three or four other students and I studied basic physics and optics. Vernoy had taught physics in a traditional program and we used a traditional textbook and did many of the standard experiments in the text. I wasn't very good at physics (even though my doctoral degree would say "Not so!") Experimental physics is still the hardest for me, as for many people. We did experiments with waves and then tried to do deductive reasoning from them. That was my first introduction to waves in optics, actually my specialty now, but quite challenging for a high school student.

Optics was probably my least successful project in the Center. Self-study to learn introductory physics is especially challenging because physics presents a new way of thinking about things. There's a great amount of material and it is very different from any of the other sciences or mathematics that I was studying. I got a basic introduction, but I didn't achieve the deep conceptual understanding of the field until I was well into graduate school. When I went to graduate school, I became a physicist even though I wasn't automatically good at it. I really had to work at it by calling on my Center experiences to understand challenging ideas. However, in college I really fell in love with the idea of the atom that was introduced to me in a chemistry class when the professor first started talking about the quantum mechanical picture of the atom based on the orbital theory where you think of an analogy to Earth circling the sun. This weird idea was based on a differential equation and I knew what that was, but not how to solve one. That's when I decided I wanted to learn this in physics because that's where I could learn the mathematical connection and description of the atom. So, I fell in love with quantum mechanics, a beautiful theory with a beautiful philosophy behind it.

I became an atomic physicist and am still fascinated by that field. At the same time, I still loved literature and writing. In the Center I joined a Great Books class led by Jack Mattox. He was a facilitator from New Trier West High School's alternative program that was combined with the Center when both high schools re-merged. We picked books from the Great Books list and read one every two or three weeks. We would have a group discussion led by two student facilitators. We were introduced to Tolstoy and Dostoyevsky and then to a class later on of just Russian authors. I really enjoyed actually thinking about this kind of philosophical exposition in literature for the first time. For a young person that was really exciting. We also did some writing in these groups, but the robust writing of self-evaluations was a memorable experience.

Each semester, the self-evaluations from our various studies were combined with the feedback from facilitators into a two-page summary called a synthesis that was sent to the Records Office in place of a report card. I put much effort into the evaluations and the syntheses, revising them and rewriting them in a meeting with my support group. It was a tense time, not only because what I developed was a permanent record, but also because attached to the task was the firmest deadline ever in the Center. I still have a memory of one Centerite typing madly with two minutes to go.

Because I wasn't interested in history, I gave it my least attention. I joined a group called "Why War?" to study some of the major wars, using philosophical and historical writings. My senior year I was back in the regular school because the Center had closed down. I enrolled in an American History class, but I never became interested in history again until I went to Germany as a post-doctoral fellow. I was 29 or 30 and began to travel all over the world. Monuments, castles, forts, battlefields, ruins, and evidence of prehistoric man whetted my interest in history when I had matured.

The sense of belonging to a community and the development of social skills were a basic part of my Center experience. In Town Halls, we worked together to solve problems. We had to interact with many other people and arrive at a consensus that provided a great sense of accomplishment for the group. This was really good for me because I was a quiet, nerdy kid at the time and that was the first time I could interact and learn how to speak up in Town Hall, actually speak in front of a group, saying what I thought. It's scary when you start learning those skills, realizing that you could influence people and make decisions. Community groups were small groups of students and one faculty person that met once a week to touch base, talk about anything at all, support each other, and have fun.

A boy in my community group was a talented artist who apparently had a difficult family life and was having problems in the Center. Our advisor was Arline, who worked with him in a compassionate way, but also was a bit tough with him. At the same time, she tried to get the rest of the community group involved, telling us it was our responsibility, as well as hers, to figure out how to deal with him. There was a lot of struggle to get him to stop being rebellious and angry, to learn that he could focus on his art, but he also had academic and personal responsibilities that needed to be taken seriously. In the Center there was compassion for people who were having difficulty in the program, viewing them not as bad kids, but as kids with issues to deal with and who needed help to find new ways to get something accomplished. It was important they knew that people cared about them and that was transmitted through the community groups and Town Hall meetings.

My values about education are influenced by that, and of course, by growing up in a family that espoused independent learning as well as teamwork. As a teacher, I want to involve students in their learning, help them think for themselves, and help them do problem solving while also being productive members of their learning community.

With a scholarship to Williams College, Jo journeyed East to earn a B.A., M.S. (Harvard), and Ph.D. (SUNY Stony Brook) in nuclear physics. Post-docs followed in Konstanz (Germany), North Carolina, and San Diego before she settled in Boulder as a laser physics project manager for Lockheed Martin and marriage to theoretical mathematician, Holger, whom she met and married on a Colorado high peak. They live, work, travel, and raise their son, Elias, in Sydney, AU, where both parents teach at the University of Sydney and camp in the Blue Mountains.

Out of Commitment, Curiosity, and Innovation

Chris Brandt, 1983

It was my friend Kyle who first introduced me to the Center. His descriptions struck a chord with me, but I will admit I did not have a full understanding as to what I was looking to undertake. My parents were concerned, but I think it was a combination of frustration with me, frustration with the traditional high school, generally being overwhelmed by my insistence, and at some level, an appreciation for a better, more personal education that had them put up little resistance to my request. And so, I joined the Center.

Although my time in the Center was brief, its impact was significant. It was wonderful to discover that there was an alternative to what I felt was a terribly flawed traditional education system. What I experienced in the program has deeply influenced how I approach my personal and professional life. High school for me, like I'm sure it was for many people, was a tumultuous time. I recall feeling very disconnected and frustrated with the system that I was in. While I recognized that I was going to one of the finest schools in the country, I always felt that I was being taught at, that I was there to check a box on an attendance sheet and I was just a number.

My main interest in school at the time was playing guitar in an empty stairwell. When I look back, I have very little recollection of my many years in school. The two periods that stand out distinctly for me are my years from three to six at Ronald Knox Montessori and my time in the Center. I think the reason for that is that those were the periods where I was engaged and felt I had ownership of what I was doing. As I found out later, my friend Kyle who recommended the program to me, had also been a good friend of mine in the same Montessori class.

Between these two standout periods, what I do recollect is the rigid structure at the public school with the "speed tests" for math and the large amount of busywork that consumed the day and my time at home. This came after the days of inquiry and investigation I had enjoyed in the early years. Only when I finally ended up in the Center did I realize that I had been looking for the kind of environment that the Montessori classroom had provided. It is the environment that I am still seeking for my children.

After the in between years of public school indoctrination and boredom, the biggest adjustment in the Center was that the adults running the programs were co-learners rather than teachers. Now that I look back, I can't imagine how much effort the faculty must have put into guiding a program that ran night and day without a lesson plan I could see.

The first days of the semester were always fun. It was one massive brainstorming effort by the whole program to imagine the full range of subjects to study. Some were bizarre, some wonderful, some beyond the reach of a high school. There were the improbable and the impractical, but somehow from this process exceptional ideas rose to the top.

I recall classes comparing the lives and works of Darwin, Marx, and Freud, the mechanics of synthesizers, the physics of light. I recall taking an oceanography course at the house of a Northwestern professor who was a bit of a bird aficionado. Learning about the ocean while always on the lookout for dive-bombing birds, one had to be prepared for the unusual to break out at any moment. This is what gave it character. I was even given the opportunity to lead a class on computer programming. My style was loud, complex, and impatient. Within a short time everyone was gone. It was an epic failure. I learned that just because you can do something, it doesn't mean you can teach it. I also found that trying to teach something really challenges your understanding of the subject. I also realized that you can't force your passion on someone else.

It was this willingness to tolerate failure that was an important characteristic of the community. I have also found that failure is a key component of growth and success. Throughout my life this lesson has become more meaningful. It is important to accept both my own failures and failures of others, because failure is a product of experimentation and challenging oneself. If I am not occasionally failing and learning from that experience, then growth is stymied.

When I look back on the Center's Town Halls, I have a hard time believing they worked, but they always did. Everyone came together to make decisions, work through problems interpersonal and otherwise, handle the business of the program, and at the end enjoy a song or two from some people in the community. What was exceptional about it was the group's ability to always come to consensus. The willingness of people to put aside their own desires for the good of the whole is something you rarely see. In times when I feel the need to muster up some optimism for humanity, I look back on that example.

What the Town Halls did teach me was the importance of common vision. With common vision, a group of people can accomplish almost anything. It allows people to focus on the day-to-day, while making sure they stay true to the end goal. In the business world, this translates into the difference between leading and managing. If one can continually share the vision of a company one doesn't have to manage the tasks, the unexpected situations, because everyone knows where they are going and what the common goal is they are trying to achieve. When the vision is poorly communicated, organizations become absorbed with micro management, inefficiency, and conflict.

The important things that I learned in the Center didn't come from the classes as much as from the approach. I learned that learning comes from a personal effort. It doesn't come from being told something, or being lectured to. I learned the difference between data, information, and knowledge. The Center didn't rely on standardized testing to evaluate performance. The emphasis was on the value of what we were learning; the focus was on processing the information into understanding rather than facts that could be regurgitated. When comparing the lives and works of Charles Darwin, Karl Marx, and Sigmund Freud there were no simple or right answers. There were insights that I related to my own life and that were impossible to summarize in a letter grade. I learned to follow my interests, develop questions and to seek my own answers. I learned how to learn.

In the Center, the faculty was often learning along with us. They were not there to give us answers and there were no answers in the back of the book because most of the time we didn't use textbooks. Materials were often original sources. If I floundered, I was directed to the library and had a lesson in research or perhaps directed to a person who might be a good resource.

I have been fortunate enough to be able to follow my interests and to work in various fields: educational publishing, marketing, advertising, and technology. With every career change, I had the confidence that I could figure it out and learn as I went. I have repeatedly used the skills and approaches I learned in the

Center in my own businesses. I have found that the best way to get the most out of people is to get out of their way and give them the freedom to work.

Knowing that there are better approaches to education has led me to enroll my children in a Montessori school that provides a wonderful, nurturing, self-directed, child focused environment. We feel part of a really wonderful and engaged community of parents, teachers, and children. This school will carry them through to the eighth grade, but I worry about where they will go after that. It makes me very sad to think of their progressing into the high school meat grinder. In anticipation, I have begun working with other parents towards developing an alternative high school for our kids to matriculate to. The experiences that I had in the Center form a great base upon which to build. The artifacts of the program will serve as a roadmap towards what we want to build.

I am glad that there were educators as committed, curious, and innovative as those that built the Center. Now that I am an adult, I have an appreciation for the time, effort, and dedication that went into the program; and I am grateful for it. The program instilled in me a love of learning that I am thankful for every day. I really hope that my daughter and son can enjoy the richness of experience that I saw in the Center when they get to high school.

Chris is currently CTO for a company that builds data center facilities and is active on his children's school board of trustees. To assuage his concern about their high school education, he initiated the start of a Montessori high school and is creating it with other parents.

Short Takes

The Center changed my expectations for my relationship with education and created a different network of friends. With one friend, Linda, we planned "Centerstock", an all-Center activity over several days that was designed to recreate a sense of community because we thought it was slipping.

~Kate Judge, 1979

Vernoy Johnson's Bumpy Baccalaureate Address, 1977

Words are friends of mine. And there are a number of almost physical—almost living, breathing—words that characterize these last days for me, and I think for each of us. Excitement, Sorrow, Relief, Anticipation, Pride, Eschatological (spelled with an "H"), Melancholy. And perhaps they can all be summed up in the one word—Ambivalence—mixed emotions, which have been likened to the feeling you might have when you see your mother-in-law go hurtling off over a cliff in your spanking new car. There are so many surging and battling emotions—mixed emotions—in each of us these days. We can't wait for the whole series of "last times" to be over and done with, but why do they have to go so fast? We yearn for the end with half of ourselves while the other half is staving it off. I believe this sense of ambivalence is common to all of us.

You who are parents of the graduates surely feel it today. You feel a sense of pride and satisfaction in your young man or young lady, and you look forward to a new sense of their and your independence. But there are tinges of regret and wanting to hold on for just a little longer. Every day of the child's life, one has to become a little less of a parent and that is a source both of joy and of pain. You lose a daughter, you gain a bathroom. And so we cry at commencements for the same reason we cry at weddings, as a reflection of the conflict between rejoicing in giving up, and yet wanting to hold on.

I have stood several times where you stand, applauded my children's accomplishments, and then wished that they were freshmen again. My youngest is now older than I was when I left home, got married, and started teaching school. He flies an airplane and has a responsible job, lives 2,000 miles from us, is financially independent of us, and all that thrills me. And then on some lonely nights I hear myself say—sometimes cry—"Oh, Kurt, why did you have to grow up so soon?"

So, parents feel ambivalent. And you who are undergraduates here today surely feel some of this sense of ambivalence. For some of you, it has been a very difficult year. The freedom that the Center offers often looks beautiful and seductive from a distance but is terribly scary when seen up close. You may rejoice in being able to sleep late come Thursday morning, but wish there were time left to demonstrate some greater accomplishments than you have. To come face to face with yourself in the mirror of your own evaluations and synthesis, and evaluations by others who know you, can be a traumatic event that can take the edge off the upcoming holiday. "We have met the enemy, and he is us." "I can't wait for next year," you say, "when I'll be a senior, but I wish I could have a piece of this year back again."

> The moving finger writes,
> And having writ, moves on.
> Nor all your wit nor piety,
> Can lure it back to cancel half a line,
> Nor all your tears wash out a word of it.
> So undergraduates feel the ambiguity of these days.

I think I speak for the entire staff when I say we have deeply mixed— terribly mixed—emotions as we go into these last days. We are weary to the bone. We are emotionally and physically and intellectually drained, and feel we have little more to give to anyone. I personally yearn for Friday, and for next week in Wisconsin, and for privacy, and for a tension-free environment without any syntheses or North Central reports, and for a quiet road to jog on, for my sauna to sit in at 200° and contemplate life, to pick a few blueberries, and to hear a laughing loon on the lake at sunset—and yet I wish it were only February or March!

There was so much I was going to accomplish! There were ideas I wanted to communicate but never did, and now there is no more time. There were bridges I had hoped to help build between people, people (including myself) who still stand and view each other wistfully across some chasm. There were programs I had promised myself I'd initiate, poems I would write, students I would eat lunch with, people—lonely people—I would try again to reach out to, parents I would contact. So many things seem unfinished about my life just now.

> The woods are lovely, dark and deep
> But I have promises to keep,
> And miles to go before I sleep.
> And miles to go before I sleep.

If only it were April! Oh, how I wish it were next Friday! Maybe if it were even May, I could yet do some of those things. So I urge on the calendar with the whip in my right hand and pull back hard on the reins in my left hand. And the irony is that I know I will feel this way again next year. For the thirtieth year, the dreams of inadequacy will begin about the middle of this coming August—I come into a room of 300 students who only speak Chinese, or I'm introduced to give a lecture on microbiology, about which I know absolutely nothing, or I realize halfway through the class that I have no pants on—but September will come and I'll know I'm where I belong, and June will come and I will wish I could hold back the clock, but please, please, please, hurry up the year!

But I think that none of us here today feel the ambiguity—the mixed emotions—in quite the way the graduates do. This is a day that you have, at least subconsciously, had on your agenda for years. Our society has made of it a puberty rite of the first magnitude, an entrance into another life. And now you're here! And it's marvelous! And you're through! And you can leave! And you have arrived! But I hear you saying "Just one more day." I spoke to one of you just a few days ago and you were talking about next fall, and a different life in college. "I'll be glad to finally be away from my bratty younger brother," you said, and not three sentences further on, you almost whispered, "I'll miss my brother so much." You look ahead with anticipation to your new life, whatever that may be, but you wonder if you will be adequate to it, and there is a strong temptation to stay in the warm and comfortable womb with its protection and familiarity. Birth is painful, at the same time that it is filled with views of excitement.

My synthesis is done, and it is filed, I've gotten my yearbook, my obligations to this place are over, my library fine is paid, I don't have to go back to 101 ever again but how about just one more card game? One for the road! I'll check my mail can one last time. Let's get out of here. I don't want to leave. Let me make one more free phone call. Some of you even feel so ambivalent about leaving that you will try artificially to preserve something that is really over. It is always a strange sensation for graduates to come back to school at, say, the Thanksgiving break. You will have read a little Schopenhauer and John Stuart Mill by then, maybe know a little calculus and perhaps have waded through *Paradise Lost* or tasted of a job, maybe known love and decision-making in a new way, and you will say "How this place has changed" My, how my home and family and parents have changed! Everything is so different." When in fact, it will be you who will have changed, and will be so different.

You really never can come back home again after a year in Africa. So, we are all in this together. And I find a sense of strength and satisfaction in that. We all feel a little strange these days. Robert Maynard Hutchins, who has had a deep influence on a number of us, tells of a bubbling psychology student, somewhat over-impressed by her own erudition and research, who confidently announced that on the basis of her data, 99% of the American population was abnormal! Well, 100% of us are abnormal these days, precisely because of our normalcy. And there is strength and satisfaction in knowing that the leaving is healthy and natural, no matter what feelings it engenders. I know of few things more pathetic than to see a 35-year-old still living dependently with his or her parents. It is good that you are leaving us. We're glad to see you go, even as we all hurt a little at your going. So goodbye! Don't ask for advice, and when we give it anyway, ignore most of it. Go live! Come back home again, even if you never can come back home again. Laugh a little this week, but take some time to cry a little too. This is the beginning, this is the end. It is alpha and it is omega. It is creation, it is Armageddon It is a time to dance; it is a time to weep. They were the worst of days; they were the best of days. It happened! It was good! Don't look back!

APPENDICES

In March 1973, Illinois Governor Daniel Walker signed a law giving local school boards the right to create "Self-Directed" alternative high schools. Eight Center students, facilitated by State Representative Harold Katz (a Center parent) and Center faculty member Arline Paul, researched contemporary education theory and practice, the Illinois School Code, and the school codes of all other states before writing the law. With Katz's guidance and legislative sponsorship, the eight worked their draft through the House education committee and debates and votes by the House and the Senate. With support by the State Superintendent of Education, they eventually witnessed the bill's signing by the Governor for its placement in the Illinois school code. For this project, each team member "passed" the required study of the Illinois Constitution.

"The students:" C. Michael Kendall, chairman; Philip Franz-Seitz, Susan Ringel, Christopher Robling, Elizabeth Baer, Sylvia Fuerstenberg, Brennan Crowley, and Mary O'Rourke Rosinski.

The Law:

> With the prior approval of the State Board of Education and subject to review by the State Board of Education every three years, any school board may, by resolution of its board and in agreement with affected exclusive collective bargaining agents, establish experimental educational programs, including but not limited to programs for self-directed learning or outside of formal class periods, which programs when so approved

shall be considered to comply with the requirements of this Section as respects numbers of days of actual pupil attendance and with the other requirements of this Act as respects courses of instruction. 105 ILCS 5/10-19

The *synthesis* was the final document each semester that synthesized the student's course assessments for that time. First, the student wrote a self-evaluation of each "experience" (e.g. small group course, internship, parent school class, project, etc.) for that semester. Students obtained written evaluations from each experience's facilitator and then wrote the final synthesis in the format laid out by the Center faculty.

No grades were given anywhere in this process other than in parent-school courses. (Even those courses required the faculty evaluation along with the grade.) The syntheses were saved and became part of the student's permanent record and college application portfolio. In the final semester, the graduation committee (the facilitator, a parent, a course facilitator and peers) reviewed the total submission against the Center's criteria for "self-directed learning" in order to qualify for graduation.

```
                              SYNTHESIS I

The Center for Self-Directed Learning              Douglas Gregory
New Trier East High School                         Sept.-Dec. 1976
Winnetka, Illinois                                 Dec. 15, 1976
```

CALCULUS: Although I could not put as much effort into this class as I would have liked, I
was pleased and satisfied with what I learned. Work was done independently by each class
member, and we met once weekly to iron out difficulties and set goals for the coming week.
We reviewed analytic geometry and algebra, covered limits, and were working with derivatives
at semester's end. I found the work difficult and challenging, but also enjoyable and rewarding, and I hope to work more extensively in the class next semester. "The concepts
presented in this class require an open mind to be utilized. Doug had difficulty with the
'newness' at times, yet was able to persevere in his effort to learn the material. I'm sure
he learned the basics about derivatives and limits and functions in general to apply himself
further in the field of calculus." K. Everingham

SOVIET LITERATURE: I accomplished my goal in this class of continuing to read and examine
literature, in this case Solzhenitsyn's The First Circle. At weekly class meetings we discussed the book and later decided that each of us would write a paper on a certain part of it.
I enjoyed immensely the opportunity to examine the work in detail, and I was very satisfied
with my paper on the main character. "Doug has shown a deep interest in Soviet Literature.
He has certainly been the most intent and dedicated student in the group. Doug's great
enthusiasm was completely evident in a paper he wrote after reading The First Circle. It was
a most thorough and profound study of the main character. Furthermore, Doug participated
actively in the coordination of class affairs, and took a major role in planning and plotting
the future course of the group." J. Levin

TRANSISTOR ELECTRONICS: This class suffered continually from organizational difficulties, for
after a time our initial teacher became unreliable, and two of us split from the group to
study with a newly-purchased text. This situation made learning somewhat difficult, but I did
work with Resistance, and was introduced to Capacitance and Inductance. My goal of becoming
familiar with basic electronic theories was thus partially accomplished. If I have time to
continue next semester, our new text should allow us to study much more effectively. "Doug
worked intently. He was expecially upset when the class almost fell by the wayside. His
initiative, though, kept it going. He was instrumental in its reformation, and showed great
interest in totally consuming all of the topics which were brought up. Doug very much wants
to gain a broad background in basic electronic theory. I am quite confident that he shall
eventually accomplish this." J. Levin

OPERATION: SAPPHIRE: I had intended to put much more effort into this project than I did, for
this independent work—the writing of my book—was one of the prime motivations for entering
the Center. I was able to define a clear theme and direction for the book, edit and revise the
introductions to two main characters, and write an introduction to the third. I am pleased
with that I have written so far. I am learning how difficult it is to weave a plot that is
cohesive and interesting, and to create and demonstrate believeably complex and human characters. More about this project later. "...I would make the following observations about part
one of the novel as it now stands: (1) It shows a definite grace and facility in handling the
language, along with careful attention to small nuances of style and mechanical ability. (2) It
indicates an ability to create life-like and credible characters. (3) It shows a concern for
logical and expanding plot development. (weaknesses): (1) Some of the dialogue seems forced,
or, in some other way does not quite ring true. (2) The opening incident/situation is somewhat difficult to follow. On the whole I would class this as an ambitious and impressive
effort." J. Johnson

ASTRONOMY: Eliot Neel organized this introductory course, and I enjoyed it very much. I
learned about the makeup and motion of the objects in the heavens, and the many techniques used
by astronomers to investigate them. I thus achieved my goals and found astronomy to be an
intriguing subject. No tangible work was done in this class, but the knowledge I gained is
certainly useful, interesting, and may serve as an aid/supplement to my study of astronomy in
Physics class. "For me, the class was a rehearsal for a second semester course. For you, it

to be a science interest introductory course. I will not write individual opinional evaluations for this semester, because no concrete, prominent individual work was done. However, I planned it this way. I will say that all of you expressed an interest in the course, regardless of how much you knew previously." E. Neel

CONSUMER AWARENESS: I entered this class in order to fulfill a graduation requirement. We achieved our goal of creating and holding a crafts bazaar, and I liked organizing and preparing for it. I learned about the special problems of financing, pricing, and advertising involved in a sale of this sort. Our success generated over $100 donated to the Center fund. "(Doug) has been most reliable, cooperative, and hard working in each stage of the endeavor.... He was efficient, careful, and quiet. He certainly has learned the importance of advertising—and what happens when others don't follow through on their commitments. He has experienced the problems of pricing goods and is aware of the considerations involved: costs, labor, quality, competition, and fairness to the consumer." A. Paul

ROOTS: I found Roots to be a most captivating and enjoyable book, and I read two thirds of it before the group reading it temporarily disbanded. This occured, I am told, because attendance at class meetings was irregular (I myself could attend only one of two weekly), and class discussions were not meaningful. We hope to continue when the TV series debuts in January.

PHYSICS: This parent school class is continuing smoothly, and I am satisfied with my progress. I like the work and am learning a great deal. We have covered basic kinematics, acceleration, gravitation, force, projectile motion, and are now studying astronomy. I chose not to evaluate this class or my other two parent school classes.

BOYS' ENSEMBLE and CHORUS-OPERA: I am continuing four years of singing at New Trier with these classes. They are teaching me more about performing and singing all the time, and both are enjoyable and stimulating. Because of my experience in Lagniappe this October, I am especially looking forward to performing in the opera "Kismet" next semester. In addition, my voice lessons this year have made singing even more satisfying for me. I hope to continue to use in college the skills that I have gained here.

I had two main purposes in entering the Center for Self-Directed Learning. First, I wanted to learn in a more free, unpressured, and flexible atmosphere than was available to me in the parent school. My senior year, the last year before probable entry into the Air Force Academy and its strict regimentation, was to be a time during which I could relax a bit and gather my strength for the future. I would have the time and the freedom to try activities which I had been too busy to try before, and I could also be free to learn at my own pace. My second goal was to write my novel, Operation: Sapphire. I had been trying to write this, first as a short story and later as a book, for three years. Schoolwork, however, left me no time to concentrate on it for very long. In the Center I could do nothing but write if I wished, and I thus awaited the start of the year anxious to begin.

The main lesson that I learned this semester was that these two goals do not mix. When school began, I felt so free to involve myself in learning groups that I became involved in too many. I was unable to go in depth into any one of them, and I barely had time to complete the assignments.. I did complete them, and was satisfied with most of my learning experiences, but I was disappointed when I realized that virtually no work had been done on my book. My graduation committee helped me to see that, if I was to complete this project, I would have to make it both a priority and an integral part of my schedule. I do wish to finish the book, and it will be my main goal for the second semester.

Aside from that disappointment, I enjoyed my first semester in the Center very much. I was especially thrilled about my participation in Lagniappe. "Made to Order" reminded me of how much I love performing on stage, and consequently I am looking forward to "Kismet" later in the year. In addition, feeling unpressured by school is absolutely fantastic! I am pleased that learning in a relaxed atmosphere can be such a pleasure and still produce concrete results. I hope that the next semester will produce more such results than the first one did, but that production in itself will be the most important result of this first semester.

_____   _____
Advisor's signature   Student's signature

Stuard Detmer and the Center: His Dad's Perspective

Mac Detmer, 2010

The Center served Stuard (Detmer) well for three years of challenging, healthy growth. The faculty was dedicated to the self-directed learning concept, intent on helping students make the most of the freedom to acquire life-long problem solving skills. The initial fall term's avoidance of school evolved over time to increasingly focused learning. One of the group study experiences he was a participant in focused on the Chicago Housing Authority. It took a lot of group planning, eventually leading to students making early winter near-sunrise visits to Cabrini-Green after perusing lots of news reportage on the problems and challenges of public housing, and ongoing discussion sessions among the group and with its faculty facilitator. Lastly these few (several?) students set up and gained an audience with the director of the CHA. That resulted in a satisfying give-and-take with the "chief." Most likely a report of this entire process resulted, backed up by faculty counsel. If so, it is a document I never saw.

From the beginning I was impressed with the Center's system for monitoring the students' progress within a designated support group. These included a faculty mentor; a couple of peers, and another unrelated adult or two of the student's choice. Their critiques of the student's selected programs of study for the term in which they named what they wished to learn and the following self-assessment of the degree to which those expectations were achieved aided Stuard in managing the continuing challenges of establishing realistic expectations of himself and a realistic awareness of his successes and failures. I looked forward to reading Stuard's self-assessments at the close of each term, finding them refreshingly revealing in a way that letter grades never were. No doubt, these assessments were even more valuable to his chosen college's admissions team. Traditional report cards never told as much about a student. (He applied to only one school, having been "brain washed" by his NU grad student tutor in calculus.) Before Thanksgiving of his senior year, Stuard had been accepted for admission at Vanderbilt.

The Center provided innumerable opportunities for him to develop skills in working with diverse personalities and how their perceptions of a situation could differ from his. All of this has to have had a healthy carry-over to his later undergraduate, graduate, and professional career experience. Stuard has long held fond memories of and gratitude for the Center faculty and fellow students. The Center concept has continuing relevance with a faculty willing to work and share in the risk. It was a definite godsend for a student who found the traditional model a bore.

A Mother's View

Elaine Madsen, 2010

My daughter, Virginia Madsen, was a student in the Center for Self-Directed Learning at New Trier High School. Her counselor in the main school came to my home concerned that Virginia wanted to transfer to the Center. She wanted me to understand that the Center was considered a haven for troubled misfits and she was certain it was a mistake for me to grant my daughter permission to leave the main school. Virginia was a vibrant outside-the-box personality and it seemed to me that the primary concern of the main school was to squeeze her brain and her personality in a way that I found alarming. The school seemed stuck in the educational pattern of the '50s.

Virginia's counselor was unaware that I had already been to the Center and seen for myself that it was designed to foster intellectual curiosity and individuality in a very positive way instead of forcing the students to conform to some pre-planned pattern. The teachers in the Center gave me such a feeling of competence so that I was certain Virginia would flourish there. Once in the Center, Virginia came home from school each day excited about what she was doing. The Center gave her artistic abilities free rein. For the first time she discovered the joy of making choices that actually had something to do with living in the world. She was encouraged to follow her own curiosity, to examine writers not in the standard curriculum. She found she could master math on her own. Most importantly, the Center permitted her the time to pursue her unique natural talents in the many facets of theater.

Considering the success of her professional life today—it is clear that the Center contributed greatly to the early development of that career. The best description of what the Center did for Virginia is that it freed her intellect and her spirit to soar. My prediction that she would flourish in this environment was validated many times over.

I was sorely dismayed and truly saddened when I heard that the Center for Self-Directed Learning had been eliminated by New Trier. We will never know how many other Virginias might have flourished if they had only had the chance she had. We can only hope a new generation of educators will take a look at what the Center brought to its students and give a new generation these opportunities once again.

MARCHING TO THEIR OWN DRUMMER

DAVID ABELL'S FATHER

When David told us he was interested in joining the Center, we agreed to let him join for a number of reasons.

First, I always thought my children should march to their own drummer. That is, I encouraged them to follow their own instincts, desires, and interests, not what the parents or other family members might have pursued—and all of them certainly did.

Secondly, our family had a strong belief in the value of education; going back several generations, the men and women in our family had college degrees and many had advanced degrees. We also firmly believed in the value of a liberal arts education and a well-rounded educational experience. For example, I created my own undergraduate major from five departments. Everyone read a lot.

Thirdly, David had a strong interest—and talent—in music, and wanted to pursue it in high school. I felt that the Center would provide him with the most flexibility to pursue this interest.

Lastly, we knew that David was a self-starter and would do well in a less structured environment.

David Abell is the father of David Charles Abell, Center class of 1976.

GLOSSARY

ADVISOR

In the parent school, each New Trier student is assigned to an advisory of thirty same sex students who met daily with the same faculty advisor for four years. In the Center, faculty advisors facilitated two mixed sex, mixed grade (10-12), advisories, called Community Groups, each with 12 students.

BRAINSTORMING

The basic creative thinking process used by the entire community at the beginning of each semester to generate ideas for different learning experiences and modes of learning. It was also used in Community Groups to generate ideas to solve problems, in learning groups to generate ideas for study, and by facilitators to generate ideas to assist students with individual problem solving.

BUMPY BACCALAUREATE

In addition to the formal New Trier graduation ceremony, Center graduates participated in a Center-only celebration at "Bumpy" Park, a municipal park with many berms a few blocks from New Trier. Center graduates were honored with music, poetry and speeches from their peers and facilitators before receiving the special Center diploma.

CENTER LAW

A revision to the Illinois School Code, conceived and written by a Center learning group whose facilitator was a member of the Illinois House representing a district within the New Trier school district. It passed the Illinois legislature and the governor signed it into law. Besides bringing the Center into compliance with state education standards, the learning group was an example of how Center students fulfilled a state-mandated requirement for a course on the Illinois Constitution. The law itself is in Appendix I; the process is described in Arline Paul's and Mike Kendall's memoirs.

COMMUNITY GROUPS

A group of 12 Center students, mixed-sex and from different graduating classes. The groups met with their faculty advisor once a week at a group-determined site, not necessarily at the Center. Each group planned its own agenda, focused on its members' support needs, and collaborated in helping each member attain self-directed learning goals. Community Groups also organized bonding activities, such as excursions and group lunches, to develop trust and collaboration among the members.

CONSENSUS

The decision making process used to make Center decisions in its various forums. The Center consensus was modeled after the classic Quaker process that required agreement of all present.

COORDINATOR

The faculty member whose duty included serving as liaison with the New Trier administration and as monitor of the annual Center budget, operations, and management.

EVALUATIONS

At the end of each semester and for each learning group, independent project, and internship, Center students reviewed their goals, listed their resources, described problems encountered (overcome or not) and evaluated themselves in terms of content mastered, skills developed, projects completed, and progress in becoming self-directed. The facilitator also provided a written and signed evaluation of the student's work, including completion of state course requirements. No grades or numbers were assigned.

FACILITATOR

There were two kinds of facilitators: (1) Center faculty who supervised Community Groups; each Center teacher facilitated two groups. (2) Every learning group, independent project, and internship had a facilitator, usually a Center teacher, but often an interested community member with knowledge of the topic, a college professor, business expert, working artist, or even, in some cases, another Center student with advanced knowledge of a subject.

Graduation Committee

A group formed before a student's final semester that included one of the student's facilitators and one to three others chosen by the student. This committee met with the student to review plans for the final semester and establish standards that would provide evidence that the student was self-directed and qualified to graduate. That endorsement was not automatic. Over the course of the Center's life, a few students had to return for another semester before receiving the committee's approval.

Internship

A mode of study undertaken outside the school walls under the guidance of an adult mentor considered an expert in a field such as sculpture, animal husbandry, music composition, etc. Internships were often practiced beyond a single semester.

Learning Group

Center students could form a learning group to pursue a topic together. Some examples of learning groups: a subject, such as Geometry, Biology, a specific historical period, or a group-determined reading list; mounting a theatrical production; or a project, such as the learning group that drafted and lobbied into law revisions of state laws to bring the Center into compliance. Every group had a learning facilitator who could be a Center advisor, New Trier faculty member, parent, business person, artist, student, etc.

Paddle

This carved canoe paddle was the symbol held by the speaker of the moment in a Town Hall.

Parent School

The common name given by Center students to New Trier High School. The Center was a small school within this high school, functioning as an alternative path to a high school diploma. Center students completed the prescribed graduation requirements of the regular program in different ways, but they received the same diploma as students in the parent school.

ROOM 101

This former study hall, equipped with moveable furniture, was the Center's home base, where faculty had their workstations and each student had a mailbox. It was the site for Town Hall meetings, some community groups, Center functions such as musical or dramatic performances and celebration lunches, and a place to just hang out. The Center also had a classroom for small group meetings. Many formal and informal learning experiences occurred outside Room 101 and outside the walls of the parent school.

SUPPORT GROUP

A group of three or four, not necessarily drawn from a student's Community Group but always including a facilitator, that provided counsel to that individual in advancing toward that student's goals. The student or any other member of the group could call a meeting of the group.

SYNTHESIS

A brief summary written by the Center student of all of the evaluations for a semester, including a fair quotation from each facilitator. The one or two-page synthesis served as the student's official transcript.

TOWN HALL

A two-hour, irregularly scheduled, morning assembly of all faculty and students convened by the Center coordinator, the faculty or the students. These brainstorming sessions debated important issues about Center policies, planned all-Center events and celebrated milestones. The Town Hall voted by consensus.

ACKNOWLEDGEMENTS, ACCOLADES, AND APPRECIATIONS

'Twas a long, long journey from Room 101 to the final edits of this book. We want to express thanks for all we can remember who had a hand in its creation and production. This includes those Center graduates who freely contributed their memoirs, those who showed short takes of their Center lives and those who helped *gratis* with the production's prep. Help came from many talents. Although time demands for professional editing and production made it impossible for a 100% Center-produced book as we had dreamed, 95% of the book's freely contributed preparation came from the hearts, minds, and creative talents of the Center family. How can we count these many ways of love contributed by so many? We would not even think of trying, but we do hope that the bottom line will produce more revenues than expenses. When this happens, we intend that all revenues in excess of the limited expenses will fund an on-going scholarship for future deserving students who seek to become the next generation of self-directed learners.

We apologize, Academy-Award style, for anyone we may have overlooked.

- For their leadership and support through the years of the Center, we thank the late Principal Ralph McGee (d.2005) and Assistant Superintendent Mary Ida McGuire. Without their special insight and the ability to blend two different worlds, the Center would not have begun, nor survived.

- We also thank those other faculty, both teachers and advisors, and those administrators at New Trier East who supported the Center during its decade of exploration and adventure. Many gave of their own time to guide individual student studies while others helped families decide about a student's entry into the Center.

- For their commitment and risk taking, we salute the New Trier faculty who collaborated with us in the Center, including Robert Applebaum, Marilyn Beskin, Irene Niebauer Cotter, Beverly Miller Kirk, Wendy Schreiber, Pamela Wood, and Julie Yost.

- For the parents of Center students who gave time and support in many different ways, we celebrate their foresight.

- To the members of the community—artists, business owners, teachers at other schools, government officials and university faculty who contributed time and minds to guide internships, small group studies and individual project—we say "thanks."

- To those members of the New Trier Board of Education whose vision and support provided the opportunity for families and students to benefit from risky, rigorous and relevant learning experiences well ahead of the times.

- For their help compiling the essays and early edits, we thank Centerites Ted Lowitz, Sue Ringel Segal, Doug Gregory and for her special valor, Linda Glass.

- For their contributions to the cover selection process, we thank Ted Lowitz and Guy Palm.

- For their two cents plain, we thank the steering committee for the Center reunions including Louise Berner Holmberg, Lynda Budwig Gaspar, Linda Glass, Debra Kaden, Russell Lane, Ted Lowitz, Bob Martin, Melissa Britt Perrin, Mary O'Rourke Rosinski, Michael Rosenzweig, and Sue Ringel Segal. Sue's persistent searches built the Center's e-mail list, without which this book would not exist. Bill Hughes deserves thanks for his early support and enthusiasm for the reunion idea.

- For the MS first proof, we thank the dedicated and contributed work of Center graduate Linda Glass.

- For his contributed and specialized legal work on this book and for Off Center Press, we thank pioneer Center lottery winner, Mike Kendall.

- Next, we hail the current members of the New Trier faculty who assisted our search for artifacts in the school's archives. Included among these are Lucia Dunn, Anne O'Malley. Peter Tragos, and Susan Holderread.

- We can't forget our spouses, Stanley Paul and Gerry Bellanca, whose lives we interrupted, but whose advice we were always glad to hear.

- For those who took the time to contribute their reviews of the proofs, give extensive written and verbal feedback, and many times over check the revisions.

- Likewise, we cannot forget to thank our professional compatriots who went beyond contracted publishing duties to provide insight and support for this book, which they too made a labor of love. Thanks to cover artist Jamie Keenan, photographer Kathy Richland, and multi-faceted editor George Verongos for their professional acumen and dedication in helping to bring this book to press.

This book indeed is the result of the Center's collaborative belief in which so many of its members gave of their time and effort to make the final product a reality. They indeed demonstrated that they walked the walk that the Center held so dear. They were the ones that made this book a reality. They are the ones who have earned the credit for this book's existence.

INDEX

About the Editors

James A. Bellanca

Jim is an educational consultant, executive director of the Illinois Consortium for 21st Century Schools and editor of the national blog for the Partnership for 21st Century Skills. He was recently named a Senior Fellow for the Partnership for 21st Century Skills. Jim's recent books include *The Focus Factor: 8 Essential 21st Century Thinking Skills, The Leader's Guide to The Common Core Standards,* and *Wad-Ja-Learn? Deeper Learning Assessments for the 21st Century Classroom.* He and his wife, Gerry, live in Glencoe, Illinois and tend to their award-winning garden (Chicago Tribune, Garden of the Year, 2007). Their children and grandchildren live in Winnetka, Illinois; Glenview, Illinois; Boulder, Colorado, and Sydney, Australia.

Arline Paul

Arline was the sole faculty person who taught in the Center from its alpha to its omega. After the Center closed in 1982, Arline Paul returned to New Trier's Social Studies Department until she retired. She then organized a self-directed reading group with former colleagues, joined an investment club, both of which have existed for 20 years and continued to travel the world. By volunteering at Wellesley College as the class fundraiser and serving as a Board member for the Illinois Consortium for 21st Century Schools, Arline has maintained interest in educational reform. During the past three years, she has facilitated organization of two Center reunions where the seeds for this book were planted. She collected the memoirs, and is bringing it to publication with pride and affection for all who dwelled in the Center for Self-Directed Learning.

273

MARK PAUL

Mark is an award-winning copywriter, filmmaker, advertising strategist, and journalist. There wasn't a Center for Self-Directed Learning while he was in high school, but he was among the first to take advantage of an opportunity at nearby Highland Park High School to create his own literature course, where he read Thomas Mann and Franz Kafka. In college, he leveraged his studies in philosophy, economics, and history into an appreciation of American music, taught himself bass, and co-founded a Western Swing revival band that delighted audiences in New England, Colorado, and Montana. He is enormously pleased to play a part in documenting the Center in this book, and hopes that its principles will be revived wherever students, parents, teachers, and administrators truly want to explore adolescent potential.

31327109R00170

Made in the USA
Lexington, KY
07 April 2014